Much More than
Stones and Bones

Much More than Stones and Bones

Australian Archaeology in the Late Twentieth Century

Hilary du Cros

MELBOURNE UNIVERSITY PRESS

MELBOURNE UNIVERSITY PRESS
PO Box 278, Carlton South, Victoria 3053, Australia
mup-info@.unimelb.edu.au
www.mup.com.au

First published 2002

Printed in Australia by McPhersons Print Group

National Library of Australia Cataloguing-in-Publication entry

Du Cros, Hilary.
  Much more than stones and bones: Australian archaeology in
  the late twentieth century.
  Bibliography.
  ISBN 0 522 85020 0.
  1. Archaeology—Australia. I. Title.
994

For Bob and Eve

Contents

Illustrations

Maps

Plates

Preface

HOW WOULD A BOOK like this one come about, a backstage or behind-the-scenes history of late-twentieth-century archaeology and concerned mainly with a group of case studies from the 1980s? As I was attaining professional status as an archaeologist in this period, other archaeologists were constantly saying things to me like 'we are living in Interesting Times' through gritted teeth. What was so special about this period in Australian archaeology? The answer is politics, and a realisation that archaeological authority is vulnerable in a rapidly changing world.

If the 1980s were an 'interesting time' for archaeologists, how interesting were they for others implicated in archaeological interpretations, such as indigenous groups, and those wishing to be more involved, such as archaeological volunteers? What did the community feel about archaeology then: value for money? For a long time, professional archaeologists saw these people as being on the outskirts of archaeological concerns. Thanks to a vigorous debate, this attitude is changing.

These questions spurred me to use a case study research approach as the best way to explore the questions. Mainly site-based case studies, associated with some kind of public controversy, were chosen. In order to understand the case studies presented here, it helps to go back to the last century and before to see how the history and development of archaeology has led to the debates associated with them. This is why I have included a potted history of Australian archaeology.

Maybe some older archaeologists would have chosen different case studies or would not have focused on popular notions about archaeology. However, in terms of how archaeologists operate politically and ethically *now*, the examples in this book were immensely significant. They provide important clues as to how and why archaeology has changed and will continue to change.

An understanding of how archaeological knowledge was constructed and presented in late-twentieth-century Australia should be of use to a wide range of archaeological data users as well as many budding archaeologists. This book is intended as a complementary text for those who are studying Australian archaeology and also as an entry point for those yet to discover that a rich body of work on archaeology exists. There is much more to stones, bones and the study of other archaeological remains than most people imagine!

For reading and offering advice on this book I would like to thank Peter Spearritt, Sarah St Vincent Welch, Bob McKercher, Brian King and Janette Bomford. Also, thanks must go to Rochelle Johnson for her excellent drafting work on the figures. I also owe a debt to Joe Glascott, Geraldine O'Brien, Bob Burton, Stephen Harris, Ian Jack, Yvonne Ivorr, Sandra Mullett, Chris Johnston, Marion Corry, Lori Richardson, Ken Atkinson, Celia Jones, Grace Karskens and Robert Bednarik for their valuable comments and criticisms about Australian archaeology and associated issues. They have helped me to hold up a mirror and to 'see ourselves as others see us'.

A number of archaeologists also contributed to this book by being both generous with their time and extremely helpful. Those people comprise: Richard Morrison (Australian Heritage Commission), Angela McGowan and Brett Noble (Department of Parks and Wildlife, Tasmania), Brian Egloff (University of Canberra), Sharon Sullivan (international heritage consultant), Anne Bickford (archaeological consultant), David Johnston (archaeological consultant), David Rhodes (archaeological consultant), Wayne Johnson (Sydney Cove Authority), Jane Lydon (La Trobe University), Peter Tonkin (Museum of Sydney), Robyne Bancroft (archaeological consultant), Isobel McBryde, (the late) Rhys Jones and Anne Clarke (Australian National University), Judy Birmingham and Robyn Stocks (University of Sydney), Stewart Simmons (Aboriginal Affairs Victoria), Ian Thomas (University of Melbourne), Marilyn Truscott (Environment Australia), Robin Aitken (New South Wales National Parks and Wildlife Service), Helen Temple (New South Wales Historic Houses Trust), Josephine McDonald (archaeological consultant), Richard Mackay (archaeological consultant), Garry Vines (archaeological consultant), Mike Pearson (archaeological consultant), Val Attenbrow (The Australian Museum), Richard Lange (Arizona State Museum), Jean Longpré (Fort Chambly Museum) and Keith Kintigh (University of Arizona).

A special thankyou to Denis Gojak, David Rhodes, Josephine McDonald, Sandra Mullett, (the late) Rhys Jones, and Angie McGowan for lending me material from their archives for analysis and use in this book.

For the courtesy of reproducing still images from film or using photographic material, I would like to thank: Robyne Bancroft, Denis Gojak,

Justin McCarthy, Lindy Kerr, David Rhodes, Andrea Murphy, Richard Mackay, Godden Mackay Logan Ltd, Artis Film Productions, Screensound Australia, the ABC, the Australian Museum and the Tasmanian Museum and Art Gallery.

Thanks also go to Australia ICOMOS for allowing me to reproduce the 1983 version of the Burra Charter in Appendix 1.

I was also very fortunate to have been the recipient of several research grants, which have assisted me to complete some of the early research. My gratitude goes to Monash University for their one-year scholarship and to the du Cros Trust in England for handing out a few last 'bickies' from their depleted travel fund.

Finally, for offering wisdom, love and support through various phases of elation, depression, fatigue, confidence, self-doubt and pregnancy, I thank my family Bob and Eve-Louise, Wendy, Dominique, Ian and Olivia, my friends David Rhodes, Denis Gojak, Angie McGowan, Sarah St. Vincent Welch, Jodie Andrews and the infamous *Beijing gau* Oskar, Lily, Poppy, Ben, Mei Mei and Chanel.

Abbreviations

AAA	Australian Archaeological Association Inc.
AAAS	Australian Association for the Advancement of Science (later ANZAAS)
ABC	Australian Broadcasting Corporation
AIAS	Australian Institute of Aboriginal Studies (later AIATSIS)
AIATSIS	Australian Institute of Aboriginal and Torres Strait Islander Studies
ANZAAS	Australian and New Zealand Association for the Advancement of Science
ATSIC	Aboriginal and Torres Strait Islanders Commission
DEP	Department of Environment and Planning NSW (now Urban Affairs and Planning)
DPW	Department of Parks and Wildlife (Tasmania)
GIS	Geographic Information Systems
HEAT	Hawkesbury Environmental Action Team
Hydro	Hydro-Electric Commission (Tasmania)
ICOMOS	International Council for Monuments and Sites (Australian chapter)
NSWNPWS	New South Wales National Parks and Wildlife Service
SAA	Society for American Archaeology
SBS	Special Broadcasting Service
TASNPWS	Tasmanian National Parks and Wildlife Service (now Tasmanian Parks and Wildlife Service)
UNESCO	United Nations Educational, Scientific and Cultural Organisation

1

What is Australian archaeology?

MUCH THAT IS written in the media about archaeology concerns new discoveries about the past. As an archaeologist, one of my most exciting discoveries occurred thanks to the keen eyes of Aboriginal field officer Caleb Pedder, who was working with me on a ground survey in Southwest Tasmania. We were driving up a logging track and he spotted a rockshelter peeping out of the forest, thanks to some recent logging near one of the lakes. We stopped immediately and raced up the slope to discover a pristine and undisturbed quartzite rockshelter that had been quarried in the past by Aboriginal people to make stone tools. More tools could lie within the soil deposit on its floor, which might date back to the last Ice Age. The dense forests of Tasmania do not often reveal such treasures so easily and we were pleased with our discovery. Excavation was not part of our brief, but the site was listed and protected, and archaeologists may yet excavate it to learn more about the way Tasmanian Aboriginal people lived.

What then is Australian archaeology? Is it just about discovering bones and stones, or is there much more going on as part of the construction of archaeological knowledge in this country? Archaeology is defined in this book as the study of past tangible evidence of human activity. Historical, social, cultural and political contexts as well as an environmental one have all shaped the nature of Australian archaeology.

Archaeology is often defined more by its practice than its ideology. At one end of the spectrum of views, it is perceived to be a romantic occupation with some special power to reveal information and artefacts by an almost mystical series of activities. It is seen as fun and similar to detective work. At the opposite end it is viewed as an obsessively neat and repetitive study undertaken in the driest and most technical way so as to be scientifically objective. Both these views fail to appreciate that archaeological research reflects the social and political context in which it is carried out.

1

It is important not to forget the popular or cultural context within which archaeology exists for many people. Some of them have been known to ask 'Are archaeologists Indiana Jones adventurists or all-seeing objective scientists?' Sorry to disappoint, but archaeologists are neither 'adventurists' nor 'all-seeing scientists' (much as some would like) and cannot be expected to completely reconstruct the past, either by magic or by technology, from often scant remains usually less than completely preserved. The truth about the occupation lies somewhere in between, as archaeologists strive with funding issues, community politics, environmental destruction, changing government heritage policies, rapid changes in technology and the pressures of trying to make a living. Most of us do try to have fun as well, but not at the expense of others (particularly indigenous people). Hence the concern with issues of authority and ownership of the past that underlie this book.

What is it that is special about archaeology, as against history or some other study of the past? The answer could be that archaeology investigates physical evidence in a certain way. As archaeologist Caroline Bird observes: 'Archaeologists cannot observe past behaviour directly but must interpret durable items of material culture, which constitute the residues of that behaviour, within their spatial and temporal context'.[1] This spatial and temporal context encountered in an excavation concerns the location that an artefact occupies; for example, the earliest artefacts are found in the bottom layer, the latest at the top. Unless disturbed by digging or development, archaeological sites conform to geological rules, with earliest buried layers of debris from a site at the bottom and the latest evidence of occupation at the top. This arrangement is known as the 'law of superposition'.[2] The association between an artefact or site and its context is central to all archaeological endeavours, whether survey, excavation, artefact analysis or general interpretation. Now archaeologists are beginning to realise that archaeology extends beyond this view of contextualisation, as ideas about the ethics and ideology of the discipline are examined and subjected to public scrutiny.

Some useful terms

In defining archaeological practice in Australia, my specific use of some common terms throughout this book needs to be clarified. The terms for the main sub-disciplines of archaeological practice here are 'pre-contact archaeology', 'historical archaeology' and 'maritime archaeology'. 'Pre-contact archaeology' replaces 'prehistory' in this book and 'historical archaeology' replaces 'post-contact archaeology'. The terms make for greater accuracy, given the state of current archaeological practice and methodology.

The problem with 'prehistory' as a term for 'pre-contact archaeology' is that it negates the presence of indigenous oral history, and its usefulness in archaeological interpretation. At the same time, written records and oral history can complement information collected by archaeologists for the 'frontier' period of contact and the following phases, for both indigenous and non-indigenous cultures. Ethnic distinctions between indigenous and European are also inaccurate: non-European people such as the Chinese and Macassans have a role in the post-contact Australian history along with Europeans. 'Post-contact' is not a useful term either, because it negates the presence of a lengthy contact period between all cultures. Unfortunately there is no current agreement as to how long the contact phase lasts, as archaeological and historical research into this phase is a recent development. Most of the research is being conducted by archaeologists who are trained in either pre-contact archaeology or historical archaeology but very rarely in both branches of the discipline. Hence, it is best to use 'historical archaeology' or 'contact archaeology' to cover all that is recent.

Maritime archaeology is the study of archaeological material occurring underwater such as shipwrecks, and it includes sites on water margins associated with shipping. It can also be undertaken in inland rivers and lakes and not just along the coast. No pre-contact sites, particularly waterlogged Pleistocene sites, have been excavated so far in Australia by maritime archaeologists, although there have been debates about the practicalities of doing so for some time. Otherwise, maritime archaeology employs many of the same skills as historical archaeology, such as historical research, site recording, excavation and artefact analysis.

Archaeological fieldwork in Australia tends to be based on particular sites rather than on cultural landscapes as such (although this is slowly changing). A site is generally defined as 'a locus of past human activity within boundaries distinguished by the presence of physical remains of that activity'. It can also have value and meaning beyond its interest for archaeologists. An archaeological site or group of sites can be part of a landscape valued by non-archaeologists for its cultural linkages and natural beauty, as in the case of Uluru and the Kakadu National Park. A spectrum of cultural values is attached to archaeological sites or landscapes by archaeologists, other heritage professionals and the community. More terms are defined in the Glossary.

The archaeological workplace

Many people think that excavating is the most common archaeological field activity. In fact, much of the data held in site registers by State site authorities and by the Australian Heritage Commission is the result of ground surveys to locate surface remains and not excavation.[3] The discovery of a rockshelter described at the beginning of this chapter took place during one such survey. Excavation is only a small part of the work associated with Australian archaeology, though not an insignificant part. Archaeological data can be gathered by surveys that take place underwater (maritime archaeology) or from the air. Other field activities include sub-surface testing and probing, measurement of structures, analysis of structural fabric and detailed recording.

In the workplace, Australian archaeologists conduct the same range of activities as their colleagues in other countries. The majority of archaeologists working in Australia are pre-contact archaeologists, and their disciplinary tradition is longer than that of historical or maritime archaeologists. There are also some archaeologists who, while employed by a university or museum in Australia, study the remains of cultures in other countries. These people are not the focus of this book.[4] Unlike the discipline in America, Australian archaeology has had only limited financial support for research in the Middle East and Europe, so most of the work is conducted in Southeast Asia and the Pacific or within Australia.

Archaeological consultant Andrea Murphy surveys a historic homestead ruin near Melbourne.

The last survey of archaeological employment in Australia found that 58 out of the 157 permanent positions are occupied by archaeologists in universities.[5] Together with consulting archaeologists and project officers on temporary contracts to State site authorities and Aboriginal communities, there are probably three times that number at present working full-time. The majority of archaeologists are employed in workplaces outside universities. These include:

- museum storage, conservation and interpretative display of artefacts
- archaeological heritage policy and site protection administration
- archaeological consulting as part of the environmental impact assessments and other heritage studies funded by developers and government authorities
- Aboriginal and non-Aboriginal archaeologists employed by Aboriginal communities.

Archaeologists working in these areas usually have a degree in archaeology, anthropology or even earth sciences, or the equivalent field experience. A Bachelor's degree in archaeology or anthropology (within which pre-contact archaeology has been taught in the past) is a minimum requirement for

An archaeological ranger, Robin Aitken of the NSW National Parks and Wildlife Service, interprets remains of the Davidson Whaling Station, Twofold Bay, to visitors as part of her daily archaeological work.

Consulting archaeologist Fiona Weaver and volunteers take measurements in a partially excavated section of Smeaton's Mill, Victoria, on a Victorian government excavation.

membership as part of the professional culture. Maritime archaeology and historical archaeology are sub-disciplines that are increasingly being taught as part of undergraduate archaeology degrees.[6] A range of postgraduate subdisciplinary options is also available at many universities.

Since the 1990s, Aboriginal students have graduated with degrees in anthropology from the Australian National University. Other Aboriginal and Torres Strait Islander students have been studying pre-contact archaeology and cultural heritage management as part of an Associate Diploma in Park Management through Charles Sturt University, Albury, or Bachelor College in the Northern Territory.[7] Many of these graduates subsequently gain employment as national park rangers, if they are not already employed as such while studying externally.[8] In addition, Aboriginal site officers have been trained or employed in the applied aspects of archaeology and cultural heritage management by the State heritage agencies.

Cultural heritage management is still perceived by archaeologists as having lower status and research opportunities than formal research jobs in universities. Archaeologist Anne Clarke also believes that much of the time spent in archaeological practice goes towards 'the delivery of archaeology to non-archaeologists'.[9] Table 1 is based on Clarke's analysis of claims of the 'archaeology without'—that which is not dealt with inside the discipline by such measures as publications and networking.

Table 1 Groups who may use archaeological information

Claims	User groups
Economic	Private sector, for example, developers
	Public sector, for example, land management authorities, government agencies and utilities
Heritage	Aboriginal communities
	Other ethnic or culturally defined groups
Social interest	Local history and archaeology groups
	Tourists
	Teachers and education groups
	Recreation and leisure groups

Source: Clarke, 'Cultural Resource Management as Archaeological Housework', p. 191.

In this book, Clarke's terms 'archaeology within' and 'archaeology without' will also be used in places to distinguish between the archaeological professionals and society at large. Over the years in Australia professional archaeologists have become the keepers of archaeological knowledge. Those who want to use or are affected by that knowledge may be considered to constitute the 'archaeology without'. It is hoped that this book will aid both sides in appreciating each other's viewpoints so that this artificial distinction starts to disappear.

Popular notions and myths

Romantic ruins, hidden secrets and excavating with paintbrushes are the stuff of popular notions and myths. The public's image of Australian archaeology is a combination of popular attitudes and shared notions and may occasionally be influenced by direct experience. After studying at university, or experiencing archaeological work on sites or excavations as volunteers, people often reject these popular notions for a real appreciation of archaeology.

A random sample of twenty-four callers to an archaeological firm in 1993 revealed something of the public's understanding of archaeology in Australia.[10] Most of the callers were between fifteen and forty years old, with a slight concentration of people under thirty years old. Slightly more males than females rang, and they included three children (under fifteen years of age). This study revealed that nearly half of the people interviewed did not see archaeology as 'the study of the human past'. Of these, eight confused it with biology or palaeontology by ignoring the 'human' part, mentioning dinosaurs a lot, and most of the others had no idea of its primary function. Thirteen of those interviewed were interested in Australian archaeology or an associated study in Australia such as palaeontology. This level of understanding was better than expected because media coverage of Australian archaeology, as opposed to overseas archaeology, was patchy at the time and ruled either by discoveries or by scandal.[11]

Requests for information by this random sample included: a child wanting to go on a dig for dinosaurs, a woman wanting to send her husband on a dig for Christmas, people wanting information on Egypt, and a New Age mother wanting her five-year-old daughter to attend a dig because 'it's in her stars!'[12] There was a call from a nervous-sounding man with a fragment of Classical sculpture from Rhodes wanting a valuation. It is possible he might have been selling artefacts on the blackmarket as he was reluctant to take the piece to a museum when this was suggested to him. It was the firm's policy not to have anything to do with valuations, so he was out of luck. A young couple visited the office when the archaeologists were out to deliver a sample of 'fossilised things' for classification, again as if it were a museum. Unfortunately for them, the news was disappointing: the prized remains were horse teeth.

The public's understanding of what constitutes an archaeological site is also associated with popular notions of archaeology. The general public has a spectrum of views concerning what defines an archaeological site. For instance, to bottle collectors one historic goldfields dump may appear much the same as the next—only its artefacts are of interest. The archaeological research value of these sites is often ignored. Accordingly, despite publicity over the last thirty years about the World Heritage archaeological sites at Lake Mungo and the Kakadu art sites, archaeologists interviewed for this book were still asked by the public:

- Have you found any treasure?
- Are there things old enough to be archaeological here?
- Do you work overseas?

Sadly, these questions are not uncommon outside Australia as well. Archaeologists in Hong Kong tell me they are still asked much the same thing. The first question is usually asked in the context of an excavation that is partially accessible to the public (passers-by lean over the fence and ask those digging) and is usually meant to be humorous. Three Australian archaeologists interviewed stated that well-educated people at social events had asked them the second question in the past. They thought that it was not being asked as frequently now because some knowledge of the significance of archaeological finds in Australia had been absorbed by this section of society, possibly due to the greater availability of information on pre-contact archaeology.

A more common question now in a similar social context is 'Can you make a living from it?' This question reflects economic times rather than a lack of perceived archaeological potential in Australian sites. The answer is probably the same as that for most professions: 'Yes, if you persist, and have a wide range of complementary skills as well as the requisite university degree'. Most successful archaeologists—those who are satisfied with their work and remuneration—I know have either come to the discipline later in their careers (after other work or study) or have built on other complementary skills or studies.

The third question about working overseas is more about stereotypes than misconceptions. People realise that archaeology is being conducted in Australia, but still hark after the glamour of excavating ancient ruins in the Middle East. Overall the questions that the interviewees said that the public asked indicated that the image of archaeology as 'glamorous and exciting' and male-dominated is still current, despite the lack of new Indiana Jones movies. There have, however, been a 'tomb raider' and two new 'Mummy' movies in the last few years.

The Indiana Jones phenomenon has fascinated archaeologists as well as the public. Robert Weissensteiner at the Australian National University has studied the portrayal of romantic action figures such as archaeologists from the 1920s onwards in films.[13] He found that, although archaeologists are generally shown as heroes (few heroines), their behaviour in removing artefacts from sites actually put them in the same category as ordinary looters. The lack of archaeological ethics displayed in the first two Indiana Jones movies attracted the ire of the Society for American Archaeology, which was then given the script of the third film, *Indiana Jones and the Last Crusade* (1989), to review.[14]

The fictional characters of old, wise, crusty or eccentric male archaeologists have also caused popular misconceptions to become part of a stereotype. This use of stereotypes occurred in films and books as early as the 1920s and later manifestations are in the films *Robbers of the Sacred Mountain* (1982) and *King Solomon's Mines* (1985).[15] The old academic archaeologist in *Robbers of the Sacred Mountain* is portrayed as reclusive and sometimes hostile to enquiries from outside.[16] A group of thirty new archaeology students whom I taught recently cited these stereotypes in the first lecture, even though they had seen a different and later set of movies. They were particularly insistent that archaeologists be male, crusty and old, even though I was standing there being female, stylish and middle-aged.

The reality of archaeology—safety gear is never glamorous. The author preparing to work on an industrial archaeological site near Melbourne.

In many celluloid archaeological adventures, emphasis is placed on the artefacts as a means to obtain power and wealth. Plots use the inflated value of the artefacts as a device to ensure the villains will seek to kill for them. It is difficult to imagine even nineteenth-century Australian gold coins being rare and valuable enough to encourage murder. Consequently no movies of this kind have been set in Australia.

Some of the common questions asked of archaeologists also indicate confusion about the nature of Australian archaeology itself, which probably has not been helped by the lack of visibility of Australian archaeologists in the media. There are some notable exceptions to this: Rhys Jones, John Mulvaney, Judy Birmingham, Alan Thorne and Anne Bickford either have made documentaries or have made themselves accessible to journalists. Hopefully, younger archaeologists will also learn to cultivate the media in a positive way.

The interest of the audio-visual media in Australian archaeology can be tracked back as far as Frederic Wood Jones's ABC 3AR radio lecture on Tasmanian Aborigines in 1935.[17] Since then there have been a number of radio and film documentaries, lectures and other features.[18] The *Science Show* produced by ABC Radio's Science Unit has regularly invited archaeologists on air to discuss discoveries and current debates within the discipline.[19] Karina Kelly, who presented the ABC TV programme *Quantum* in the 1990s, had studied archaeology at university and made sure archae-

ological issues were included frequently in the show.[20] Many of the archaeologists interviewed for this book found these two latter programmes excellent in their coverage of archaeological issues.

However, the mass media rarely discusses the development and structure of the discipline. This absence is partly what prompts people to think
archaeologists dig all the time (and dig up anything, including dinosaurs).
Archaeology has developed with a multidisciplinary base which has
borrowed from many other academic traditions—anthropology, history,
landscape geography, geology—to synthesise a way of studying the human
past. As one archaeologist noted, 'archaeologists wear many hats'.[21] This
multidisciplinary, multi-hatted aspect of archaeology can be particularly
confusing for users of archaeological data and the general public, who have
neither the time nor the inclination to study the history or development of
archaeology.

Another problem that restricts information in the mass media is that
many archaeologists complain that their ordinary workloads are too heavy
to allow them time to publicise their results. Admittedly archaeology can be
a demanding area of endeavour if you include publicity as an integral part,
as demonstrated in Graham Clark's description of the perfect archaeologist,

> The complete archaeologist, if such a being existed, would need to have a genius
> for travel, exploration, and reconnaissance; to be adept at business administra-
> tion, skilled in raising funds and obtaining all manner of permits from author-
> ities and owners, *few of whom can hope to gain by his (or her) activities,* and capable
> of administering and directing excavations which may well turn out to be
> large-scale enterprises; to be a competent surveyor, draughtsman, and photo-
> grapher, so that what he finds can be adequately recorded; to combine a *gift for
> exact description and analysis with a power of synthesis and a flair for journalism* [my
> emphasis].[22]

To deal with those who use archaeological data—the media, indigenous
or local communities and the general public—an archaeologist usually
needs a comprehensive understanding of the social and political workings
of society and how archaeological data may be used outside the discipline.[23]
A flair for journalism and public relations combined with the descriptive
and analytical skills listed above would assist in successfully communicating
the message.

Dealing with local myths

Archaeologists sometimes come into conflict with communities when
conducting archaeological research that impinges on local myths. This situation has reduced community support for archaeology in some cases. The

disdain of professional archaeologists for local myths investigated by non-professionals has parallels in other countries, particularly North America. American archaeologist Joan Gero notes that local residents in New England, USA, began to study the archaeological sites before the professionals.[24] In this case, the interest shown by professionals in the sites in the 1960s was not warmly welcomed. Non-indigenous residents of the New England area had surveyed and excavated a number of beehive stone structures, which they interpreted as being the result of settlement by pre-Columbian Celtic groups. The local residents themselves were of Celtic ancestry and were inclined to believe that these structures closely resembled stone megalithic structures in Europe. Professional archaeologists began studying the structures in the 1960s and were highly critical of this view and no less motivated by an independent set of social-political values. Gero observed the two groups could be characterised in opposite ways as the 'popularisers' and 'professionalisers' of the archaeological past:

> The former group, the popularisers, are amateurs who drag the archaeological past *through* the popular media and into the public eye. In contrast, the professionalisers are those who drag the archaeological past *away* from the popular media and circulation, guarding it as the territory of initiated specialists.[25]

This view of the professional archaeologists' reaction to community myth-making is only partly true for Australia, where some archaeologists have tried to popularise the archaeological view of the past to compete with other views. One example of this was the book *The Past Is Human* by the Sydney academic Peter White.[26] It was published to combat 'the rash of archaeological fantasies popularised by the von Daniken school' about visitation by aliens.[27] The book never outsold von Daniken's work. On the whole, local community myths are usually ignored by Australian archaeologists with only a few exceptions. Gero's beehive case study does have implications for archaeologists as experts coping with the views of other special interest groups. It is possible that, the more archaeologists strive to assert themselves as the 'expert' or prime authority on a subject, the more they risk alienating these groups.

Can archaeology be flexible in meeting the needs of a community trying to prove a local pre-modern myth? One community myth that has become a research issue, a tourist attraction and simultaneously a part of community identity is the search for the Mahogany Ship near Warrnambool on Victoria's south-west coast. Archaeology has only taken a glancing interest in this issue, allowing the locals to continue their fantasy or to be sanguine about it like Kevin in the ABC TV series *SeaChange*. On finding a Portuguese dagger by the beach, in an episode with a loose theme of heritage, Kevin observed that the dagger was still sharp and likely to injure somebody so it should be thrown in the rubbish bin.

The most highly publicised search for the Mahogany Ship lasted for most of 1992, with government support provided by Steve Crabbe, Minister for Tourism. As part of a tourism campaign, the Department offered a reward of $250 000:

> for the DISCOVERY of an international invader that has eluded authorities for more than 400 years. Believed to be a PORTUGUESE CARAVEL, this traveller is thought to be hiding somewhere along the world's most scenic coastline . . . Positive sightings could rewrite the HISTORY OF AUSTRALIA.[28]

Mark Staniforth was the only maritime archaeologist interviewed by the media on the matter during the search. He had transferred to the Australian National Maritime Museum in Sydney and therefore was no longer part of the Maritime Archaeology Unit in Victoria. Saying he thought there was a wreck there somewhere, he stated 'what the shipwreck is or was is an entirely different matter . . . pure speculation'.[29] It is possible that a wrecked ship, probably from the nineteenth century, could have been briefly revealed to observers by the shifting dunes. Many maritime archaeologists believe it is probable that such a wreck is not Portuguese, and they also think that accessible or registered wrecks should receive priority over the Mahogany Ship in their research. The search inspired by the Tourism Department ended in February 1993 after the Warrnambool coastline had undergone a range of remote sensing, diving and drilling with no success.[30] At the time of writing, no satisfactory evidence (such as Portuguese artefacts in Aboriginal sites or other forms of locational evidence) has been produced to prove or disprove the myth.

The possibility of an important discovery motivated many of the searchers in the saga of the Mahogany Ship, and it also pervades the popular notions that people have about archaeology. Discovery is usually seen as the most exciting feature of archaeology and is therefore the focus of popular fiction, films and the mass media.[31] Journalists find it hard to present issues in detail with limited time and space, and so they resort to stereotypes or otherwise simplify the issues. Visual stereotypes are particularly popular with photojournalists and advertisers. The misconceptions of popular writers, advertisers and journalists influence the stereotypes they use, which are in turn reflected in popular notions of the discipline that most people hold. Misconceptions are eliminated from stereotypes and popular notions only when the 'archaeology without' takes notice of direct information input by archaeologists.

The reality of Australian archaeology

The reality of archaeological work, as experienced by the 'archaeology within', is not as exciting and marketable as, for instance, people killing each other in an exotic location for treasure or discovering mythical wrecks of Portuguese traders. To a lesser extent, echoes of these films and myths occur in the minds of people dealing directly with archaeology (see Table 2). On the other hand, archaeological work is much more than counting and scrutinising 'stones and bones'.

Table 2 The misconceptions that unfortunately influence stereotypes that later become popular notions

Misconceptions	Stereotypes/Popular Notions
Archaeology is about digging up treasure, fossils or dinosaurs	Archaeology is about digging
There is not much Australian archaeology to do; archaeologists work overseas	Archaeologists in Australia only work on Aboriginal sites or overseas
Archaeologists are all male, bearded, academic, harmless and eccentric	Same
Archaeology is about digging and nothing else	Archaeologists only dig
Digging is always fun	Archaeology is a discretionary and slightly self-indulgent activity
Archaeologists dig slowly with brushes and trowels	Archaeology is time-consuming and expensive
Archaeological sites and material do not require conservation or protection as they are mostly ruins and garbage	Same
Archaeological sites belong to everyone equally	Same
Archaeology is rarely important in political situations	Archaeology avoids contention and has no politics unless an important site is threatened
Archaeology is an objective science with no links to present social attitudes and biases	Same (even some archaeologists believe this)
Archaeology has little relevance to Australian society	Same (except for providing dates of Australian occupation, which are useful for land rights claims)

I have observed that certain misconceptions can result in erroneous stereotypes, which can impact on heritage management issues to a greater or lesser extent. For instance, there is the misconception that archaeology is rarely important in political situations and has little relevance to society. Contention about the conservation of archaeological heritage can occur if these notions unconsciously influence individuals, such as property developers or bureaucrats. For example, some small property developers still view archaeological assessment prior to development as a discretionary activity. As a result, they can become hostile when told by a site protection agency, Aboriginal community or archaeological consultant that they will not receive a development approval without such assessment.

Another part of this spectrum of views concerns indigenous people's views of the authority of the 'archaeology within'. Unlike other archaeologists, pre-contact archaeologists have been challenged directly about the ethics of studying the heritage of another ethnic group. Aboriginal and Torres Strait Islander people do not always see the point of the work of pre-contact archaeologists as they have their own ideas about what happened in the past, or their Dreamtime as they define it.[32] They have come, however, to respect and criticise the power of systematically gathered archaeological information in certain political and cultural contexts. The most used piece of archaeological information in Aboriginal political struggles is the figure of '40 000 years'—the estimate of the length of Aboriginal occupation in Australia based mainly on the Lake Mungo dates. It has become such a well-recognised and exposed piece of information that it is now used in advertising. In these contexts archaeological interpretation can either aid or hinder Aboriginal calls for social justice and land rights.

In this book, the three key themes comprise challenges to archaeological authority; ideas about research; and provision of information to and involvement of the wider community. The themes are discussed in a series of case studies, which have primarily been chosen because the debates they embody have shaped the practice and professionalism of archaeology. As a result of these debates, archaeology will hopefully make an increasingly important contribution to Australian socio-cultural life.

2

Australian developments and discoveries

G OVERNOR PHILLIP CARRIED out the first archaeological excavation in Australia on an Aboriginal burial mound in Sydney soon after his arrival.[1] It was not until later in the nineteenth century, however, that consistent interest was shown in Aboriginal sites. From the 1890s onwards, a number of amateurs and non-professional enthusiasts became interested in the most visible features of archaeological sites. These people had no prior training in archaeology. They usually came across archaeological remains while carrying out work such as geological surveying or railway and road construction or as local residents interested in particular areas. This interest was displayed at meetings of various scholarly societies.

Early scientific societies were established in the seventeenth and eighteenth centuries in Europe. In Europe, interest in antiquities grew at the same time as a systematic classification of natural phenomena was being developed. Scientific societies appeared in Italy as part of the Late Renaissance. In Britain, the Royal Society of London was founded in 1660–62 and the Linnaean Society in 1790.[2]

In the nineteenth century in Australia, the Royal Society of New South Wales and Victoria, the Royal Linnaean Society of New South Wales and the Australasian Association for the Advancement of Science (later ANZAAS) were founded. They tended to consider a range of issues regarding both natural and modified environments. Their members discussed and published papers on Aboriginal archaeological sites. They also debated whether Aboriginal occupation was of great antiquity in Australia.[3] The separation of living indigenous people from their archaeological heritage by archaeologists and anthropologists has its beginnings in the discussions held in such scholarly societies.

The 1896 excavation of Shea's Creek, near Newtown, Sydney, where remains of a dugong and some axeheads were found. J. W. Grimshaw (left) and Professor T. W. Edgeworth-David (centre).

The 1936 excavation of Lapstone Creek rockshelter. (From the right) Members of the Anthropology Society of NSW: C. C. Towle, Fred McCarthy, Towle's father and G. E. Bunyan (his cousin).

Historian Tom Griffiths has described in detail the activities of early Australian antiquarians and their contribution to current museum collections.[4] Graeme Davison has identified two local historians, James Forde and Charles Bertie, as early Australian antiquarians. Active at the turn of the century, they paid most attention to the Sydney Rocks. Besides local historians, Ure Smith and other artists tried to convey the 'charm' and 'romance' of older buildings in their work.[5] These people would probably have joined or formed an antiquarian society for recording and preserving remnants of Old Sydney if one devoted entirely to the pursuits of antiquarians had existed. As it was, the Royal Australian Historical Society had members who felt some interest in the remains of early Sydney; they erected a plaque on the site of First Government House, as we will see in Chapter 5.[6]

Anthropological societies, which included archaeology enthusiasts, sprang up in most Australian states early in the twentieth century. Many of these organisations contained the same members as the scientific societies, including naturalist associations and royal societies.[7] Anthropology departments were created at the University of Sydney and in several State museums during the period between the two world wars.

The major feature of anthropological societies in the inter-war period was that anthropologists, archaeologists and ethnologists rubbed shoulders with non-professionals and enthusiasts stimulated by new books, such as the work of Radcliffe-Brown and Margaret Mead, and the flood of archaeological information coming out of the Middle East. Some of the most active members were white middle-class men who had had the opportunity to travel during World War I. Women were also motivated to undertake fieldwork.[8] Many of these people visited and recorded sites, either singly or in groups.[9] This activity may be related to increased interest in travel and the will to explore the landscape among the middle-class generally with the growing availability and convenience of motor transport in Australia.

Interest focused on Aboriginal sites: firstly, as distinct or aesthetic features in the Australian landscape, such as rock art sites; and secondly, because they contained collectable stone artefacts. Most archaeological and anthropological experiences were discussed and illustrated by 'lantern' or photographic slides at society meetings. Slides of archaeological sites demonstrated the speaker's authenticity of experience. This simple device is still a feature of meetings held by such societies. Publications and correspondence between the societies indicates that non-professional members of the Victorian and New South Wales anthropology societies considered themselves authorities on their particular interests, such as stone tools.[10]

As a result of the increase in tourism and recreation in the first half of the twentieth century, some holiday areas—the Otways and the Upper

Yarra in Victoria, and the coast round Sydney—became collecting grounds for many of the stone artefacts in private collections and State museums.[11] Many members of the inter-war anthropological societies were also keen collectors of stone artefacts, and meetings often included extensive show-and-tell sessions. Artefacts became discussion pieces as members tried to understand or explain the mysteries of a past much removed from their own knowledge of industrialised Europe and Australia.

The professionals in the Anthropology Society of New South Wales, such as museum employees Fred McCarthy and Elsie Bramell, organised trips to record rock art sites in the 1930s. McCarthy excavated sites, with and without help from the society, in the 1930s.[12] Non-professional members, with very little experience of excavation, also excavated some rockshelters around Sydney, in particular, the Burrill Lake rockshelter near Ulladulla on the south coast of New South Wales. Their intention during this work was to answer specific questions that they had discussed at meetings and in the society's journal concerning cultural change and stone artefact sequences.[13]

Later archaeologists lauded the excavations carried out by Norman Tindale, curator of the South Australian Museum, at Devon Downs, in the Upper Murray Valley (over 150 kilometres northwest of Adelaide) South

Example of a typical Aboriginal stone artefact collection made earlier this century. This one was made around Bacchus Marsh near Melbourne, and has since been donated to the Wathaurung Aboriginal Co-operative in Geelong.

Elsie Bramell and Fred McCarthy in the Anthropology Department, the Australian Museum, late 1930s.

Australia, as being more systematic than other investigations of the time.[14] Nevertheless, the research designs differed not in scope but in excavation methodology for these two sites. Poorly applied methodology caused the society members to miss the deeper levels of the Burrill Lake site that contained the necessary evidence for their theories. Because it had failed their expectations, they did not undertake any further archaeological work.[15]

Aborigines, antiquity and colonialism

As part of the background to the intellectual concerns of the last century in Australian archaeology, it is vital to note that attitudes to living Aboriginal people played a major role in the type of research undertaken and the interpretation of Aboriginal sites.[16] As an example, Robert Pulleine's statement characterised the attitude of anthropologists and others concerning Aboriginal people in the early decades of the twentieth century. In an article he described them as 'an unchanging people, living in an unchanging environment'. This view was given much credence in Victoria at least, despite being poorly argued.[17] John Mulvaney considered it a major deterrent to prior investigation of variation and change in the Australian archaeological record.[18] Pulleine's view also filtered through to society at large, and the richness and diversity of the indigenous past is still today poorly appreciated.

Cultural evolutionism, with its roots in the narrower concept of Social Darwinism, was another influence on the way interest developed in Aboriginal people and their archaeological remains. In the third quarter of the nineteenth century in American and European archaeological traditions, some authorities, particularly John Lubbock, were inclined to offer a racial explanation for the difference in stages of 'development' towards civilised (European) ways that they had encountered in other cultures. Some peoples were even assigned rungs on an evolutionary ladder in Darwinian style, with European industrial society at the top.[19] Bruce Trigger describes this view as stemming from colonial orientation of archaeology:

> Native societies were assumed to be static and evidence of change in the archaeological record, when noted, was attributed to migrations rather than to internal dynamism. The racist views underlying specific interpretations were more often implicit than explicit. Either way colonial archaeology served to denigrate the native societies that European colonists were seeking to dominate or replace by offering evidence that in prehistoric times they had lacked initiative to develop their own. Such archaeology was closely aligned with ethnology, which documented the primitive condition of traditional native cultures and their inability to change. This primitiveness was widely believed to justify Europeans seizing control of the territories of such peoples.[20]

These early attitudes concerning Aboriginal people, however, did not entirely deter investigations in New South Wales and South Australia, where excavations occurred in the 1920s and 1930s. These investigations did address research questions, which were current in the publications of the discipline at the time, concerning technological change and the antiquity of human occupation in Australia.[21] Cultural evolutionism was all but dead by the time that Mulvaney published his historical overviews on Australian archaeology.[22]

Several other factors hindered the resolution of the antiquity question late in the nineteenth century. These included the visible and physical nature of sites in Australia. Aboriginal sites such as scarred trees, scatters of stone artefacts and shellfish middens seemed 'alien' to researchers in comparison with the familiar 'relics' and monuments in Europe and the Old World. Also, the geological methods of dating sites which were then in use, such as the relative dating of geological sedimentary layers in association with archaeological material, could not be used at many Australian sites. This is because Australian climatic conditions do not allow for even, regular deposition of sediments in quite the same way, as those in Northern Europe, which could be counted back to estimate the age of a site. Nevertheless, some early attempts were made at this type of relative dating.[23] Radiocarbon dating was a breakthrough for researchers tackling the antiquity questions. By 1961 archaeologists had access to a few radiocarbon dates for Australia with the oldest being around 18 000 years for the Keilor site, in the Maribyrnong Valley, Melbourne.[24] As Trigger observed, the colonially oriented view that Aboriginal culture was static and unchanging could not survive 'the collection of archaeological evidence which indicated that internal changes had taken place'.[25]

Archaeological boom in the 1960s

A boom in Australian archaeological research followed the arrival of Cambridge-trained archaeologists such as John Mulvaney, Vincent Megaw, Isobel McBryde, Judy Birmingham, Richard Wright and Rhys Jones.[26] Three universities made lecturing appointments in world and Australian pre-contact archaeology in the early 1960s: Sydney, New England and the Australian National University. Most of the new arrivals worked in anthropology departments rather than history or classical archaeology departments, and this positioning affected the development of the discipline.[27] A number of factors contributed to archaeology's growth during the 1960s: university expansion, the availability of new dating techniques, the establishment of the Australian Institute of Aboriginal Studies and the availability of archaeological professionals, mainly overseas-trained.

Australian Institute of Aboriginal Studies and archaeology

The establishment of the Institute and university courses has been described as a 'time of exciting discovery in Australian prehistory'.[28] Archaeologists of 1960s vintage also see 1961 as the 'Dreamtime year' for pre-contact archaeology, with the first appointments of the overseas archaeologists to university positions. It was mostly young overseas-trained professionals who left overcrowded university departments behind them to emigrate or return to Australia. Their enthusiasm about working on archaeological sites in the Australian environment verged on the macho-adventurous in some cases. Most excavations were carried out in remote areas where little work had been conducted previously. The Institute was instrumental in allowing academic pre-contact archaeology to prosper, it being one of the main sources of funding for fieldwork. It was founded in 1964 after a landmark conference in Aboriginal studies held at the Australian National University in 1961. The Institute was the first national research organisation to promote Aboriginal studies, publish or assist publication of such studies, encourage co-operation among other institutions, and assist other institutions by employing research workers or assisting people engaged in Aboriginal studies.

At first, the Institute's role was one of salvage, because its founders were concerned that it should collect and preserve information on Aboriginal heritage and culture. This undertaking might have had its roots in the colonialist idea that traditional culture was dying out, not transforming. The Institute nevertheless collected information on the transformation as well.

As the Interim Council laid the beginnings of the Institute between 1961 and 1964, a federal statute was drafted to provide for the appointment of a hundred people as foundation members and a council of twenty-two people to conduct its affairs. Fred McCarthy, whose work was gradually being marginalised by younger researchers, was appointed principal in 1964 and worked efficiently in this position until 1971.[29] He emphasised that the Institute was 'not only a source of funds for research, but a co-ordinating and advisory body, building up slowly a corpus of information available nowhere else about our Aborigines'.[30] The amount and quality of information held on Australian Aborigines and Torres Strait Islanders by the Institute is unique. A few years ago it was renamed the Australian Institute of Aboriginal and Torres Strait Islander Studies, and plans to make its resources more accessible to Aboriginal communities, particularly those in remote areas, have been added to its perceived role.[31]

By the end of the 1960s historical and maritime sites had received little attention, although this was about to change. The archaeology of the late 1960s was being practised with increasing attention to professionalism, to the exclusion of some earlier practitioners. New archaeological legislation would see the influence of non-university-trained archaeologists and anthropological societies diminish over the next ten years.

The rise of archaeological heritage management in Australia

The introduction of legislation for site protection from 1965 onwards altered the face of Australian archaeology for both researchers and dilettantes. The new legislation, together with the formation of government and non-government organisations, combined to create an immediate impact by increasing research output. Legislation now requires special site protection

authorities, which include archaeologists, to administer the statutes of
each State and to manage the cultural heritage of archaeological sites and
landscapes.

Most authorities that deal with archaeological heritage management
now prefer the term 'cultural heritage management' to 'cultural resource
management'.[32] The latter's use is just one of the many debts that heritage
management in this country owes to the US National Park Service. Many
principles and terms were borrowed in the early 1970s by archaeologists
concerned to establish a systematic structure of heritage management
in Australia.[33] The substitution of 'heritage' for 'resources' is in line with
common usage in society. Cultural heritage managers perceive that 'cultural resources' is a term which is neither readily understood nor current
among the public to whom they are ultimately responsible.[34]

'Resources' usually differ in nature from archaeological heritage, in
that the former is exploitable and sometimes renewable, while the latter is
a nonrenewable legacy. A legacy implies certain obligations and responsi-
bilities, which are not followed strongly in the case of many resource types
(e.g. gold mining, forestry, and tourist attractions). Government tourism
agencies and the tourism industry are increasingly recognising archaeological heritage as a commodity, while archaeologist managers view it as
nonrenewable and in need of careful management if it is to be sustainable.

Archaeological heritage management, as a part of what is termed
'public archaeology', has shaped the development of some branches of
archaeology. Historical archaeology, for instance, owes much of its database
to excavations carried out prior to its development.[35] The assessment of
environmental impacts in Australia, and the legislation that supports it, has
also generated opportunities for archaeological research prior to development even though some developers have privately sworn at it.

Damned laws and heritage police[36]

Of all archaeological heritage, it was historical archaeological sites and landscapes that became acknowledged more as Australia's national sentiment
developed towards the end of nineteenth century. Historian Gordon Greenwood maintains that a national sentiment fed on and in turn inspired the
establishment of a sense of Australian history.[37] The public viewed such history both negatively and positively. The 'convict taint' was still a problem
for New South Wales and Tasmania in particular, although the significance
of Port Arthur as a tourist destination modified such uneasiness to mild
ambivalence. Port Arthur was also one of the first heritage places to be
administered by a government authority, the Scenery Preservation Board,

on behalf of the public. The Board was one of the first land management organisations, established to deal with areas of high natural and historic value. Instituted under the *Scenery Preservation Act 1915* by the State government to administer all the national parks and historic site reserves in Tasmania, it also managed the reserved public land at Port Arthur, or Carnarvon as it was briefly known.[38]

In New South Wales, historical archaeologist Helen Temple suspects that the national sentiment which wished to erase the past for the purpose of 'civic improvement and beautification' played a role in forcing historians to mobilise against Sydney's emerging town planning movement.[39] The Royal Australian Historical Society, formed in 1901, actively promoted Australian history and hoped to change attitudes to town planning. It began by establishing a network of local historical societies, publishing a journal, and running regular excursions to places of historic interest. The society also encouraged the State Department of Education to introduce local history programmes in schools.

The *Sydney Morning Herald* was also active in developing a 'historical sense' among the general public. From the 1920s it expressed concern about the future of particular buildings and tried to generate an interest in Australian history and heritage through its editorials. Research by Helen Baker (later known as Proudfoot) into the preservation movement in Australia notes that its 'letters to the editor' column demonstrates a trend of growing concern towards environmental and urban conservation from 1945.[40] The National Trust (now National Trust of Australia) was also formed in 1945 to preserve historical buildings and places of beauty. After the war it took over from the Royal Australian Historical Society, becoming the main advocate of heritage conservation.[41] Historical archaeological sites, however, were not of great concern to the Trust at that time.

Fred McCarthy and Elsie Bramell, acting as anthropologist-archaeologists at the Australian Museum in the 1930s, were responsible for the first push to protect indigenous archaeological heritage in Australia. They tried unsuccessfully (through the museum and the Anthropology Society of New South Wales) to raise interest in establishing an official organisation to control fieldwork and research affecting archaeological material. Their inspiration came from McCarthy's discovery of government commissions for this purpose, current in Indonesia and South Africa in the 1930s. McCarthy and Bramell failed in their objective due to the lack of government and public interest and the upheaval associated with World War II.[42] McCarthy's involvement in founding the Australian Institute of Aboriginal Studies in the 1960s is an echo of this earlier concern.

After McCarthy's efforts during the 1930s, John Mulvaney was the next archaeologist to become actively concerned about the state of archaeological heritage. He was particularly worried about the vulnerability of sites to disturbance from non-professional enthusiasts and private collectors who demonstrated no understanding of archaeological methods. Their impact on pre-contact archaeological sites and landscapes was of most concern at a time when he was hoping to establish systematic research with an academic base in Australia in the 1960s.

Archaeologist Stephanie Moser describes Mulvaney's actions in combating the influence of non-professionals as a private crusade. It resulted in a series of public lectures and publications on the topic. She states that 'it was in this context that excavation came to be seen as the exclusive province of the professionally trained archaeologist'.[43] As legislation to protect sites was enacted by each State or Territory, the public also gradually relinquished the collection of stone artefacts as a recreational pastime as it disturbs archaeological remains. Professional archaeologists, such as Mulvaney, also became members of the existing scholarly societies and enjoined the non-professionals to adhere to the legislation.

South Australia enacted the first State legislation to offer blanket protection for archaeological heritage, the *Aboriginal and Historic Relics Act 1965*. In this respect it was not McCarthy nor Mulvaney but Norman Tindale, curator of the South Australian Museum, who initiated the breakthrough.[44] Norman Tindale had been just as energetic as McCarthy about recording and interpreting archaeological sites and landscapes (for instance, Devon Downs).[45] Legislation for the protection of historical and maritime sites either occurred as part of the same bill as that of Aboriginal or Torres Strait Islander sites or followed later in separate Acts in some States.[46] Tasmania was the last Australian State to pass legislation to fully protect and manage historical archaeological sites as part of its heritage bill. Its *Historic Cultural Heritage Act* finally came into effect on 1 January 1996.

The State Acts are still the basis of most administration associated with archaeological heritage. They incorporate regulations to protect sites, and in some cases 'relics' or 'places', and allow prosecutions and fines. The main problem with the early 'relics Acts' was that they were not well integrated with other legislation and in particular with State and local planning provisions such as State environmental impact assessment and town zoning. One example of this lack of flexibility is that they did not offer landowners any strategies for retaining sites, other than resumption for a reserve or fines for disturbing sites and archaeological material. The statutes enacted during the 1980s sometimes included 'Heritage Agreements' or 'Covenants' between the landowners and the relevant Heritage Council or site authority, allowing the authority to offer the landowner financial compensation or other incentives to ensure preservation of a disputed site.[47]

Heritage laws have affected the research investigations of non-professional enthusiasts by regulating archaeological excavation. Today one needs an appropriate university degree and research design to obtain a permit from a government authority staffed by professional archaeologists who process such applications to excavate on behalf of the relevant minister. All legislation requires that an excavation permit be obtained from the relevant administrative body or site authority before an archaeological excavation is undertaken. It is important to stress here that even a systematic excavation by an archaeologist of soil deposits at a site can destroy their context—it is an 'unrepeatable experiment'.[48] This is why permits are so regulated. Where possible, archaeologists leave sections of sites unexcavated so that they can be investigated in the future, when different questions may be asked and better techniques may be available.

In addition to, and sometimes overriding the State and Territory legislation, there are two Commonwealth Acts, in particular, that are important for protecting archaeological heritage: the *Historic Shipwrecks Act 1976*; and the *Aboriginal and Torres Strait Islander Heritage Protection Act 1984*. The former protects designated shipwrecks in Commonwealth coastal waters from disturbance by salvagers and recreational divers. A system of awards has been established and publicised among diving clubs to encourage divers to behave responsibly after they discover a historic wreck. A 1993 amendment was enacted to extend blanket protection to all wrecks older than seventy-five years in Australian waters.[49]

Maritime archaeologists have succeeded in converting many relic-hunters or shipwreck bashers to maritime archaeologists by enlisting their help in protecting wrecks.[50] A confessed 'wreck-basher', Terry Arnott, converted to a non-professional archaeologist and protection advocate in the 1970s. Arnott realised the impact that relic hunting was having after visiting a newly identified wreck that his wreck-bashing colleagues had already stripped of all loose fixtures. He realised that this was an 'important and rare resource' that needed to be protected or there would be no wrecks for his children to enjoy.[51]

The *Aboriginal and Torres Strait Islander Heritage Protection Act 1984* has had far-reaching implications both for indigenous people and for archaeology. This Act was the first to provide indigenous people in this country with a certain degree of self-determination in relation to their cultural heritage. In certain circumstances the Act can be used to override State and Territory provisions, or be enforced where the political will to prosecute or protect sites under other legislation is lacking. For instance, it carries heavier fines than its State version did in Victoria. Victoria's use of this federal Act in conjunction with a State site protection Act is unique in Australian cultural heritage management. The significant feature of both the Commonwealth and Victorian versions of the same Act is that it can be invoked directly by Aboriginal communities who want to protect a cultural place. These emergency declarations are reviewed by the Commonwealth

Minister or State Minister after thirty days and can be extended further where required. Hypothetically, a fine of $50 000 may be incurred in cases where an individual or corporation knowingly destroys an archaeological site that is under an emergency declaration order. Both Acts have relevance to the management of Victorian Aboriginal archaeological heritage, along with some aspects of the earlier *Archaeological and Aboriginal Relics Preservation Act 1972*.

Despite legislation many terrestrial historic sites have been damaged through the activities of relic-hunters and bottle-hunters wielding metal detectors. Lightweight metal detectors became available during the 1960s. Although they do not locate glass and ceramics, they do lead the operator to rubbish dumps or pits that contain artefacts such as bottles and containers for hair oil with attractive coloured scenes on the lid as well as metal artefacts such as mining tools, coins and jewellery. After conducting archaeological surveys of the central goldfields area of Victoria for the Department of Conservation and Natural Resources, David Bannear found that such activities 'are responsible for much of the recent disturbance to, and destruction of, historic habitation sites in the region'.[52]

Efforts have been made in Victoria to approach the local bottle-hunters and relic-hunters about the impact of their activities. Not much has been done by government archaeologists to prosecute offenders under the *Archaeological and Aboriginal Relics Preservation Act 1972*. Archaeologists in Victoria have spoken at meetings of bottle-collector societies concerning site protection issues. As far as I know, these efforts have not yielded much. It was significant, however, at the Australasian Society for Historical Archaeology annual conference in Adelaide in 1993 that an archaeologist gave a paper on working with a bottle-collector society.[53] This joint undertaking caused the archaeologist extra work; she saw it as far from an ideal situation and made no additional effort, as far as I know, to enlist the bottle-collectors in less destructive pursuits afterwards. Again, educational programmes and alternative activities, such as those put into practice by the sister discipline of maritime archaeology, may apply here as well.

The further exclusion of non-professional activities

In the 1970s and 1980s specialist associations formed which dealt exclusively with, for instance, rock art, historical archaeology and maritime archaeology. Most of these organisations operated out of university departments and were founded by academics, two factors which reduced their impact on encouraging the activities of non-professionals. The largest of these associations or societies are the Australian Archaeological Association, the Australian Rock Art Research Association, and the Australian Society for Historical Archaeology.[54]

The gradual exclusion of non-professional scholars from the mainstream of Australian archaeology has continued since Mulvaney and others began to establish a professional culture for the discipline in the 1960s. Archaeologists who deal extensively with pre-contact remains have been particularly keen to divorce their work from earlier archaeological traditions, which they consider less rigorous and scientific. At least one archaeologist was eager to see membership of the Australian Archaeological Association restricted to professionals only (it is currently semi-professional in nature). He complained that 'any old zealot with an axe to grind' could join. Academic archaeologists have also been keen to maintain archaeology's professional standing by dissociating themselves from any research endeavours that could be considered scientifically contentious, such as Creationism. Few non-professional enthusiasts, however, fall into this category.

Home-grown practitioners versus 'Cambridge in the Bush'

In her study of Australian archaeological disciplinary culture, archaeologist Stephanie Moser notes that there was a recognisable tension between old and new views in the early 1960s.[55] John Mulvaney was really the first of the 'carbon date era' of archaeologists to work in Australia. Trained as a historian and employed by the University of Melbourne to lecture in history in 1951, he developed an interest in Australian archaeological sites that led him to complete an undergraduate degree in archaeology at Cambridge University in the late 1950s. In 1965 he moved to Canberra as a senior fellow and later foundation professor of prehistory (1971–85) at the Australian National University. He established courses in archaeology, which included subjects on Australian archaeology, at Melbourne and Australian National Universities.[56]

Mulvaney was the first to apply the skills and knowledge of British archaeologists of the 1950s to an Australian context. He effectively discarded the notions of Norman Tindale and Fred McCarthy concerning cultural sequences. Although Mulvaney did not ignore all their contributions to archaeological knowledge, he was nevertheless 'clearing the ground' and 'demolishing formulations based on insufficient evidence'.[57] Moser believes his main aim was to establish a platform on which to found modern Australian archaeology.[58]

Despite the transposition of overseas professionalism in the 1960s, there are still a few uniquely Australian features in pre-contact archaeology. Differences from other countries include geological sequences that vary greatly from those in Europe in formation and make for a heavy reliance on methods of absolute dating. Also, the social context within which archaeologists work, whether they acknowledge it or not, affects the way archaeological knowledge is structured.[59] Some aspects of archaeology's social context, such as the nature of race relations and government regulation, are unique to Australia.[60]

Archaeology of the 1970s and 1980s

The academic concerns and archaeological discoveries of pre-contact, historical and maritime archaeology grew over these decades. Until then, not much work had been undertaken on historical and maritime archaeological remains. This situation abruptly changed for these sub-disciplines and pre-contact archaeology continued to expand.

Pre-contact archaeology

The 1970s and 1980s have been characterised as the empiricist, positivist and modernist phase of Australian pre-contact archaeology.[61] Because of this view, the adventurism or opportunist aspect of this period has never been fully analysed. The continuance of this mode of data gathering well into the 1980s, when most museums were full of material, has been criticised within the discipline. Some archaeologists were also concerned about a certain disregard for detailed post-excavation analysis.[62] At the same time both excavation and regional surveys produced many discoveries of international interest, enabling this branch of the discipline to cultivate itself as a profession.[63]

The major research concerns and debates of pre-contact studies include:

1   arrival of humans into the Australian landscape and the subsequent effects (Pleistocene environmental adaptations of the people), for instance on megafauna (e.g. *Diprotodons*) and other animal populations, and the effect on vegetation of firing the bush practised by humans

2   the timing, number and types of waves of human arrivals, how they adapted to and impacted upon the landscape, and what they brought with them

3   seasonality and use of various food resources, particularly in the Holocene (less than 8000 years ago) along the coast

4   intensification of the use of resources as a result of a possible rise in population numbers in the mid-Holocene
5   dating and accuracy of the radiocarbon method for dating the earliest sites
6   typology, classification and functional analysis of stone artefacts with reference to some of the other concerns listed above
7   site formation or taphonomy of Australian pre-contact sites
8   rock art dating and analysis.

Lake Mungo will be dealt with in Chapter 7, but there could almost be a regional tradition in itself devoted to archaeological research of the Murray–Darling River Basin where it occurs. Such work has been under way since 1968.[64] The early Pleistocene dates stemming from this work had tremendous impact on the Aboriginal land rights movement and Australian society generally.[65]

Pleistocene sites in Papua New Guinea have been investigated in tandem with Australian ones, as researchers recognised that the two islands were once one landmass, known to geologists as Sahul.[66] Many archaeologists based in Australia also work partly or entirely on more recent migrations in the Pacific including those marked by the distinctive Lapita pottery.[67] Other researchers discuss Pleistocene arrivals in Sahul, with Tasmania seen as the furthest point of this advance.[68] To provide evidence of early Pleistocene evidence of occupation in Tasmania has been another breakthrough almost equal to that of Lake Mungo. Kutikina Cave and more recent finds in Southwest Tasmania, discussed in Chapter 6, have also provided archaeological information of significance to archaeologists and to special interest groups, in this case, conservationists and the Aboriginal community.

Research into the Pleistocene megafauna extinctions and environmental adaptation was generally conducted through site-based analysis.[69] Ethnography was also considered important for providing analogies to interpret results under controlled conditions, and there is still some debate as to what conditions should apply.[70] Moser also criticises the concentration of some researchers on excavating Pleistocene rockshelters as producing a professional culture where 'regional survey was neglected and this effectively meant that sites were not really understood in terms of the wider context of the landscape in which they were situated'.[71]

'Intensification' is the term used to describe a change in the economy of hunter-gathering societies towards a system that will support a greater number of people than previously. World interest in this research issue developed in the 1980s and encouraged researchers to subject archaeological and anthropological sets of data to scrutiny for evidence of such change. Archaeologists Harry Lourandos and Anne Ross saw the Australian intensification debate as being influential and 'intertwined' with that on the international archaeological scene.[72] Holocene sites in Australia that were investigated for evidence of intensification were those in Western Victoria and parts of Tasmania.[73] However, the intensification archaeologists had their opponents. Caroline Bird and David Frankel provided the most detailed argument against evidence of intensification.[74] Peter Hiscock also challenged the proponents about the variability of stone tool discard rates.[75] It was not a research direction that survived far into the 1990s in Australia.

Lourandos and Ross saw the debate about intensification acting as a 'democratising force' by changing the focus from Pleistocene excavatable sites to a wider range of Holocene sites and landscapes which are not necessarily excavatable. They go further to say that it 'was largely an intellectual debate which took Australian archaeology away from the cowboy era of data collection, where theory played a minor role and linked the discipline with the contemporary discourses of anthropology'.[76] The debate did not, however, excite nearly as much public interest as discoveries associated with early human occupation. No major film documentaries or radio series or public lectures were produced solely about intensification. It was truly an internal disciplinary debate of pre-contact archaeology and one that was difficult to transmit to the 'archaeology without'.

Historical archaeology

The research concerns and archaeological interpretations of Australian historical archaeology might be characterised as moving away from the non-professional 'lace doily' or genteel concern for pioneers by developing a systematic empirical and descriptive theoretical base. Historical archaeology grew quickly in the 1970s and 1980s in response to the increasing interest in Australian history and the excavation of urban sites.[77] Historical archaeology was taught as an interdisciplinary subject in universities and not as a separate undergraduate degree during the 1970s and for most of the 1980s. It was a focus for postgraduate research at most Australian universities that taught archaeology in the 1980s.

The Cambridge-trained archaeologist Judy Birmingham, originally hired to be a classical archaeology lecturer at the University of Sydney, co-ordinated the first Australian fieldwork and courses in historical archaeology. Since then she has been deeply involved in this area. Until the late 1980s, Sydney archaeologists trained by Birmingham dominated the field. This situation has affected the research directions taken in this branch of the discipline. Graham Connah also influenced academic research by including historical archaeology as an area of study at the University of New England as the founding editor of the journal of the Australian Society for Historical

Archaeology. Later La Trobe University, the University of Western Australia, Australian National University, the University of Canberra, the University of the Northern Territory and Flinders University all showed interest in this sub-disciplinary area. The Australian Heritage Commission and many State site management agencies, including the Victoria Archaeological Survey and the New South Wales National Parks and Wildlife Service, expanded over this period to employ historical archaeologists.

Brian Egloff, an archaeologist who was site director at Port Arthur Historic Site in the 1980s, is surprised that historical archaeology formed any type of sub-discipline, given that the two most active academics who fostered it, Birmingham and Connah, had not been initially employed to lecture in and research it.[78] He believes that its establishment was assisted, in Birmingham's case, by allies in other departments and interaction with archaeologists in cultural heritage management positions. One would also have to give credit to the assistance and free time given by interested members of the public through the Australian Society for Historical Archaeology who worked on sites and catalogued collections.

Historical archaeology's first two main research concerns were therefore to make inventories of historical sites and to establish a database while investigating the nature of the colonisation of Australia.[79] The first major theoretical framework for historical archaeology generated within Australia, 'The Swiss Family Robinson and the archaeology of colonisations', dealt with the latter.[80] The research framework with the odd name was published in the first volume of the society's journal and was supposed to give direction to what had been previously a multifarious and uncoordinated field of study. It was based on premises from overseas theory and was considered restrictive by its critics.[81] Anne Bickford was the first archaeologist who stepped outside such fixed preoccupations with European colonisation to analyse and interpret class and social circumstance within the society itself. She used the cramped servants' quarters at Elizabeth Farm at Parramatta as an example of how history and archaeology can offer different views. That the 'romantic fantasy of colonial grandeur' promoted by historians of the time would collapse, if these rooms were opened up with full interpretation for visitors.[82] Others have referred to her article on the 'patina of nostalgia' as an important reference for issues concerning history, archaeology, site interpretation and Australian society.[83]

Historical archaeology grew out of theoretical frameworks and methodologies borrowed from North American historical archaeology and from British industrial archaeology.[84] The dominant interest in all aspects of colonisation is not surprising in historical archaeology and its overseas counterparts, as they cover the period of European world expansion prior to the twentieth century. Migration, adaptation, diffusion and colonisation have long been research concerns in European archaeological traditions.[85] Significantly, industrial archaeology has always been a strong specialisation within historical archaeology, with much effort spent on regional surveys and excavations to record evidence of technological processes. Books on these processes have also been produced for the public.[86] The industrial sites investigated include mining complexes, mills, ironworks, lime kilns, salt-processing plants and explosive manufacturing works.

Much more than pre-contact archaeology, historical archaeological research has been influenced by cultural heritage management.[87] Excavations in urban areas associated with redevelopment have yielded information and a wide collection of artefacts from the nineteenth and early twentieth centuries. Important sites in this process during this time include Hyde Park Barracks, The Rocks and First Government House in Sydney, and Queen Street and the Little Lon' excavation in Melbourne.

The Port Arthur Conservation Project (1979–86) involved a team of archaeologists and was the first large multidisciplinary conservation project of its type in Australia. In collecting information to assist conservation works, archaeologists also excavated large quantities of artefacts that still require more detailed analysis.[88] A new management direction for the site in the late 1990s may inspire more of this work, which is important for its on-going conservation and interpretation.

Maritime archaeology

Like pre-contact archaeology, the boom in the study of Australian maritime sites in the 1970s and 1980s has been assisted by the development of technology. The first diving on wrecks occurred as early as 1836, but it was not undertaken extensively until the mid-1950s. By then scuba sets and manuals were being sold in some sports shops. Interest in wrecks included the thrill of discovery, accompanied by passive viewing or the removal of 'treasure and booty'. The public did not see shipwrecks as archaeological sites worthy of saving until legislation was put in place to protect them in the 1970s.[89]

Even more than pre-contact archaeology, early professional maritime archaeology was closely associated with museum research and is still largely museum-based with the exception of that which is carried out in heritage agencies around Australia. The Western Australian Museum has been an important centre for maritime archaeology since the late 1960s. In Western Australia interested divers and relic-hunters had identified many Dutch shipwrecks in the 1960s. The arrival in 1969 of Jeremy Green, a physicist with experience in remote sensing and diving, spurred more systematic work on the wrecks through the museum. The *Batavia*, wrecked in 1629 within sight of the Western Australian coast, was examined first in 1971, revealing one of the most significant collections of pre-1770 European arte-facts. The museum spent four seasons excavating the wreck between 1973 and 1976.[90] Examination and excavation of another five wrecks followed.[91] The sub-discipline received a boost in the public arena by the glamorous nature of these early finds.

Hence funding was made available and planning began for the Maritime Museum at Fremantle, now one of the best in the world.[92] Between 1976 and 1984 the other States began to develop maritime archaeology programmes. New South Wales was one of the last States to gain a maritime archaeology unit, which is part of the Heritage Office. It has three or more maritime archaeologists frantically making up for lost time.

In the 1970s Jeremy Green began teaching an evening course on maritime archaeology and later developed a diploma in the subject at the West Australian Institute of Technology. It stressed field techniques, rather than archaeological theory and management practices for cultural heritage. Most archaeologists were looking to overseas developments for theoretical frameworks though these have been sparse.[93] Keith Muckelroy's theoretical framework explores the scope of the discipline where gaps and opportunities exist for further research.[94] It was the most promising work of its kind in this period.

Self-analysis in the 1990s as archaeology meets post-modernism

Archaeology in Australia in the 1990s is likely to be remembered by many as a time of reflection or self-analysis.[95] After the major discoveries and public debates associated with discipline-building in the 1970s and 1980s, many archaeologists were left to scrutinise all aspects of archaeological practice, theory and methodology to gain self-knowledge and implement improvements. Gaps and problems were analysed and addressed in ways that began to rapidly transform the way archaeology is conducted in this country.

Some of the major problems became obvious from general practice and from the case studies to be explored later in this book. Australian archaeology's image and relevance to contemporary Australian society was being affected by problems, including difficulty communicating findings to the 'archaeology without' and involving non-professionals such as Aboriginal communities directly in research; gender and cultural bias in research; isolation from other disciplines (or areas of archaeology); lack of well-accepted theoretical frameworks for research; and over-emphasis on excavation as the main data-gathering activity.

One of the greatest problems for pre-contact archaeology at the time was its relationship with the custodians of Aboriginal cultural heritage. Nineteenth-century concerns about the nature and antiquity of Australian Aboriginal culture and its place in world prehistory generally denigrated the living culture. In order to come to terms with Aboriginal claims for custody of archaeological remains and data, many professional archaeologists have had to overcome this history of previous complicity with the cultural evolutionists. Until the 1980s archaeologists rarely had to consider the socio-political effects of their conclusions. Most new Cambridge-trained arrivals conducted themselves with little self-criticism until forced to by the growing national social conscience (and legislation in some cases). This conscience was stimulated by the increasing political activity of Aboriginal people. Archaeologists were first introduced to Aboriginal concerns about archaeology's role in their oppression during the late 1970s and have had regular reminders over the years since then.[96]

Finally, it is unfortunate for the morale of some pre-contact archaeologists that the end of the decade brought another major blow to their authority. New early dates for Aboriginal antiquity were initially hailed by the media as a momentous discovery. The debate over the use of thermoluminescence dating at Jinmium, a rockshelter in the Kimberley region, highlighted some of the difficulties of the dating and debating process in Australian pre-contact archaeology. Dates were initially produced for some of the remains that went back over 100 000 years, far in excess of any other archaeological evidence.[97] Subsequent analyses of the same sediments by other authorities, using different methods, came up with dates of less than 10 000 years.[98]

The authorities who produced the older dates had already released them to the media and an intense debate ensued. Other authorities questioned the dates in the public arena: the profession had not had an opportunity to examine the dates in the usual way on the conference circuit or rebut them in journals. Early dates are commonly scrutinised closely in pre-contact archaeology (to the exclusion often of more interesting matters at conferences). Such scrutiny in this case would have allowed the researchers to recheck their results before announcing them to the media. Discoveries that go awry can end up having the same impact as hoaxes, such as the so-called Piltdown hominid,[99] on the public image of archaeology and its authority.

Other pressures for greater reflexivity in the discipline have been internal. Several waves of graduates have been produced since the establishment of courses in Australian universities. Many of them have wished to engage in research beyond the concerns of Cambridge arrivals and their first students. Later researchers were also more concerned to identify the links between archaeology and contemporary society. Early radicals, such as Anne Bickford and Jeannette Hope, have found greater acceptance and a more productive place within this milieu. In both pre-contact and historical archaeology, the uncovering of evidence of gender in the archaeological record and in the construction of archaeological knowledge is becoming a new research area in this country.[1] That gender bias can be all-pervasive: Alison Wylie notes 'feminist critiques of science, broadly defined, have exposed a wide range of ways in which "taken-for-granteds" about status and activities of women, and about gender relations more generally, have shaped, and often compromised, even the most conscientious and well established of research programmes'.[2] This work has not only started to examine gender bias in Australian archaeology, but it has also opened the way to self-criticism of other biases and analyses of archaeology's place in the Australian socio-political context.[3] It has also allowed some further re-examination of the role of women in the management of archaeological heritage.[4]

In the early 1990s archaeological heritage management was being taught as an academic subject at some universities and began to have an impact on academic discourse. Researchers explored its usefulness to academic archaeological theoretical concerns, such as post-processualism.[5] Archaeologists tend to use this term instead of post-modernism or post-structuralism. One post-processual dilemma is the ranking of different aspects of cultural significance. The cultural significance of a heritage place is usually assessed by looking at aesthetic, historical, scientific and social criteria.[6] This problem was particularly difficult to resolve in the Swan Brewery case in Western Australia, where Aboriginal concerns over 'sacredness' or social value clashed with historic value.[7] The Swan Brewery, a historically significant building, was built on an Aboriginal sacred site. Local Aboriginal people lobbied the State government to stop the restoration of the brewery. Since their politicisation of the 1970s they became more confident about expressing their views about heritage sites to the government. The Australian Heritage Commission eventually became involved and learnt a valuable lesson in dealing with dissonant views over heritage. Other reviews of cultural heritage management have investigated standards of practice. These reviews include analyses of how archaeologists conduct Aboriginal consultation, conservation planning, artefact analysis, site management and interpretation to the public.[8]

Maritime archaeology and historical archaeology still require more rigorous attention to building theory, according to some authorities within.[9] They have also recognised a need for these sub-disciplines to work more closely together. It became clear at a conference held in Hobart in October 1995 that better links and increasing communication were required between them. It is surprising that such fundamentally similar areas of research have been allowed to run on parallel lines for so long!

Interdisciplinary projects, with both historians and historical archaeologists working closely together, have caused some tensions in the past, particularly in New South Wales. Some historians have accused archaeologists of indifference to historical context, of the exploitation of 'the scant and ambiguous historical evidence' in their interpretation of archaeological sites. Archaeologists have replied that social history is rarely written in a way that assists this interpretation and that some research questions historians ask are difficult to apply in an archaeological context.[10]

Potential tensions, however, were neatly overcome in the excellent excavation of the Cumberland–Gloucester Street Site at The Rocks in Sydney. There had been some debate at the beginning whether the initial

The Cumberland–Gloucester Street excavation in The Rocks, Sydney, was widely publicised. Television, radio and print media took the opportunity to visit and record the findings.

Groups of school children both visited and participated in the Cumberland–Gloucester Street site excavations. The media is filming one group of students.

Northeast view across the Cumberland–Gloucester Street site with archaeologists and volunteers in action.

questions about the convict inhabitants' quality of life asked by Grace Karskens, a historian who has also studied historical archaeology, would contribute much to the analysis of the archaeology of the site.[11] In the end, these questions not only contributed a great deal to the archaeology, but also allowed information from both sides to be well integrated in an interpretation of the site that added to the quality of the final outputs. Such outputs have included a book, articles and an education kit that clearly highlight the material culture and social context of that part of the Rocks in Sydney.[12] This fascinating site and how it was excavated and publicised is described in the next chapter on the culture of excavation.

3

The dig, diggers and
the community

ARCHAEOLOGICAL EXCAVATION has always seemed to me to be a strange
mixture of scientific method and art performance. This view may
be due to my first professional experience on a site excavation, where the
workers included several unemployed artists funded by the Community
Employment Programme. These women stretched my ideas about excavation and site preservation by setting up art happenings and events. They
greeted the felling of trees by a developer during an archaeological site
excavation with an art performance. The artists and some others stood on
the remaining stumps of the trees. It was intended as a political demonstration against alterations to the site's setting. Archaeologists and others
working on the site also carried a banner through the streets as part of an
anti-nuclear demonstration, bearing the slogan 'Archaeologists Against the
Bomb—don't roast our footings!' We even had our own balloons. After years
of lectures on processual archaeology, we needed to put the fun back in
archaeology.[1] For some archaeologists that has meant working harder to
understand the socio-political setting of their work. Writing a book such as
this one is another way.

One view of excavation is that it involves archaeologists, sometimes
assisted by volunteers, striving towards the scientific recovery of data and
artefacts from a site. An English post-processual archaeologist, Chris Tilley,
argues that archaeologists who attempt to excavate while 'striving towards
total objectivity untainted by human purpose' are living in an empiricist's
dreamworld.[2] Such archaeologists, in his opinion, are therefore creating
something close to a theatrical performance by this pretence (this aspect and
others of archaeological theatre will be explored further in the chapter).
Tilley reached his conclusions about the interpretive nature of excavation
when considering how seldom excavations in England result in archaeologists' portraying their experience of the site successfully in their final

Spontaneous art performance by site workers after the removal of trees from First Government House site by the Sydney City Council, 1984.

'Don't Roast our Footings' (foundations). Site workers at First Government House marching in the annual anti-nuclear protest in Sydney.

reports. He argues that much excavation is interpretation in action and as such is not easily committed to paper and understood by any audience, even of other archaeologists. The plurality of interpretations (and attendant speculations) that was made during the excavation process is curtailed by the nature of the critical scientific analysis that followed in the laboratory and office.

Once an excavation is over, the fun has often gone out of it, and some archaeologists move on to the next one without adequately reporting on the first. Not only had the fun gone but also much of the funding. With the rising cost of excavation, a much smaller proportion of funding is being allocated to analysis and reporting. Often it has been difficult to attract sufficient money for archaeologists to finish a project properly and produce information for the public. In consequence, the latter is often sacrificed. Experimenting with the archaeological interpretation of an excavation is often far from an archaeologist's mind during a funding crisis. Another problem lies in the political nature of some excavations, where their clients have placed public archaeologists under certain restrictions. Nevertheless, some archaeological information about urban sites does reach the public.[3]

The dig or excavation. What is it?

Archaeologists in Australia carry out a wide range of field or outdoor activities which are not excavation. These include:

- ground surveys to locate and identify sites
- detailed recording or photogrammetry (using stereoscopic cameras) of archaeological features
- detailed recordings of rock art by tracing or photogrammetry
- sub-surface testing by auger, probe, shovel or backhoe
- resistivity planning or remote scanning.

Excavation projects may only take up a small part of an archaeologist's fieldwork time, unless it is his or her special field of expertise to the exclusion of most others (for instance, urban excavations of historical sites). As the guidelines of the New South Wales Department of Planning's for historical archaeology excavation state, 'archaeological sites are a non-renewable resource' and so the decision to excavate is not made lightly.[4]

Ideally, archaeologists should not allow the excavation phase to dominate the project. Excavations generally need five main ingredients: a source of money; logistics (food, housing and transport); training and supervision of personnel; the designing and carrying out of research; and interpretation and communication of this to the public. Excavation directors spend about

Ground survey to locate and identify sites is by far the most common archaeological activity in Australia. David Rhodes examines an Aboriginal scarred tree in the Upper Maribyrnong Valley, Melbourne, 1989.

half to three-quarters of their time in administration and writing progress reports, while others handle personnel training, laboratory analysis, archival research and actual excavation.

In salvage excavations, where the private developer is also the project's backer, another difficult situation can arise. The developers are sometimes pleased to see the excavations occur, hoping to receive good publicity while digging is in progress. They are often not so enthusiastic about funding the less glamorous or well-publicised activities such as detailed post-excavation analysis.

Chris Tilley has also queried the justification many archaeologists use for large-scale excavation in his criticism of 1980s practices in Britain.[5] Chapter 2 showed that excavation can destroy a site's context as surely as the looting of individual items. To undertake a large-scale project presupposes a certain confidence that the methodology is sufficient to the task and the results are likely to be worthwhile. Whether the excavation is for academic research conducted over several seasons with a view to providing conservation information, or last-minute salvage, it will have to satisfy site protection authorities and other peers that it is adding to archaeological knowledge, and inevitably, to history. It is also necessary to outline research designs in case it could be argued that the same information could have been located more efficiently using historical research.

These concerns have, to some extent, shaped the present Department of Planning guidelines for historical excavation in New South Wales. A section titled 'when are excavations appropriate?' gives three prerequisites to justify a historical excavation:

- when evidence is about to be lost through unavoidable action
- when it is necessary to provide information for conservation work on a site's fabric
- when preliminary research has indicated that the site is likely to add to knowledge about the past through excavation, and excavation is an appropriate activity within the site.[6]

The first prerequisite is usually the reason for carrying out salvage excavations, not academic or conservation research. A salvage excavation occurs when plans for redevelopment or refurbishment cannot avoid disturbing the site. The second prerequisite was the main argument for most of the excavation at Port Arthur Historic Site during the conservation and development project (1979–86), while the excavations at Sydney's Hyde Park Barracks (1979–81) were for a combination of the first two reasons. The last prerequisite is commonly cited as a reason for excavating all sites by both academic and non-academic archaeologists.

Excavation methods can differ according to the phase in the history of archaeology, the country, level of professional expertise, the type of site, and even the individual archaeologist's preferences. Port Arthur has a manual devoted entirely to the recording and excavation techniques that have been used there, for the information of future workers on site and for use on other historical sites to make comparative study easier.[7] Unfortunately such comparative work has proved difficult, since historical archaeologists use many different systems of post-excavation cataloguing and analysis. There appears to be no prospect of them agreeing on one single system.[8] Several other manuals have been produced for Australia,[9] prior to which archaeologists relied on those produced overseas.

A popular misconception (and I have even caught my family saying it) is that archaeologists always excavate carefully and slowly with trowels and toothbrushes. While this is sometimes the case, a much greater range of tools and excavation techniques are available. What is used depends on the integrity of the layers being excavated and their nature. Historical archaeologists in urban contexts are granted permission to remove, with care, recent demolition fill using a backhoe, once the stratigraphy is known.[10] This strategy saves time when excavating demolition layers of mixed recent and earlier material as these layers have been disturbed by the demolition activity. In other cases, extremely hard deposit is excavated using geo-picks, picks, spades and even pneumatic drills. Another misconception is that all archaeologists dig trenches. Different sampling techniques are available, including open excavation of an area larger or squarer than a trench, which is becoming popular in both pre-contact and historical archaeology when excavating material near the surface.

The experience of excavation

The experience of excavation extends beyond the practice of the associated scientific methodology, particularly for non-archaeologists. There is the notion of discovery, possibly a feeling of bonding with the past and involvement in an activity which can feel almost ritualistic. Archaeologists need to recognise such perceptions and not be afraid to use them in the way that they choose to explain sites to the public. Non-archaeologists, whether volunteers or paid labourers, are not privy to a great deal of information about the process they are involved in, without undertaking intensive study of archaeology. A lot of what is being done may seem irrelevant to the task at hand.

Non-archaeologists have only their own experiences and popular notions as a context in which to understand the excavation process. An artist might see the activity on an excavation as art performance complete with installation, especially considering the aesthetics of the string-gridded squares on some sites.[11] Others may see the recording of data and the repetition of certain actions as either ritualistic or obsessive. For many volunteers the act of finding an unexpected item can have several stages. The first is the uncovering of the tip of the item, then the suspense of fully exposing it, and finally the classification of it, using their own experience or that of their trench supervisor. Some volunteers are pleased to be photographed with their finds, as they would be with a large fish they had caught. It is possible that many archaeologists are no different in this respect. Rarely do archaeologists arrange for someone else, perhaps the local Aboriginal community responsible for a site, to announce a major discovery to the media.

We need to explore further Tilley's view of archaeology as theatre.[12] Archaeological excavation is an experience very similar to that of putting on a play. When the activity associated with removing soil is deconstructed, a number of questions arise. What exactly is the activity that is occurring in an excavation; why is it viewed by those who undertake it as scientific rather than artistic or ritualistic; and why are its results not seen as more socially determined? Part of the answer to this is the distancing from the present that professional archaeologists experience while interpreting the past in its most tangible form during excavation. It is almost as if the constant practice of staring at a pit while trying to interpret the stratigraphy and other inform-ation can cut archaeologists off from their current social context like an actor performing in a play. Even so, the thrill of discovery is there for archaeologists as well as for volunteers. It is exciting to make a discovery that narrows the gap between the past and the present by affirming our present behaviour. One might discover that 'they were just like us because they used a toothbrush—I just found part of one'. Or in turn it could chal-lenge our beliefs about society and change—'they never brushed, but there's no sign of caries on these teeth, why?' Despite some overlap of interest in the past, research questions devised by archaeologists may not serve to answer the queries of non-archaeologists. Most archaeologists can only serve one view when interpreting the past, and that is often the one current in the discipline. Although multiple interpretations of excavation data are called for, and possibly justified in a post-modernist, post-processual world, archaeologists find it difficult to produce them with current research designs and methodologies.[13] It would be like writing many different versions of the same play, only one of which can ever reach the stage.

Why is there a perception in Australian archaeology, as in many places overseas, that only 'real archaeologists' dig, and why must we always dig? If Tilley is right about archaeology being theatre, are we natural exhibitionists? Certainly much of the archaeological excavation of Pleistocene sites has attracted something like the glamour of the stage since the early dates associ-ated with the Lake Mungo discoveries in 1968 appeared in the mass media. Archaeologists Stephanie Moser and Joan Gero suspect that high status is attached to conducting excavation and fieldwork in archaeology because in many countries it is a male-dominated activity.[14] For instance for most of the twentieth century, it was common practice in North America, for male archaeologists to go out on a dig and bring back artefacts for the female archaeologists to analyse in laboratories. It was a situation that uncomfort-ably parallels assumptions about gender roles in Western society. Also, the total number of field component archaeological projects in America supervised by women has been lower than the total of those run by men.[15] Because fewer women are involved in American fieldwork, a male culture has been built up around it, which is often termed 'cowboy archaeology'. Australian archaeologist Wendy Beck describes the situation in Australia for pre-contact archaeology as being almost the same in the late twentieth century:

> I think that the hard-drinking 'cowboy' image does persist amongst Australian practitioners as Joan Gero [has] illustrated for United States archaeology. Having said that, however, there may be less of a division of labour into 'field-work' and 'other' amongst archaeologists in Australia because we are still very much involved in the data collection phase of research and nearly all research and management projects involve general fieldwork and analysis.[16]

Despite the greater involvement of female archaeologists in fieldwork, there is still some discrimination in Australia concerning women and excavation. I have encountered it only once myself when working as a consultant, when the archaeological heritage manager at our local site authority removed all female consultants' names from a list requested by a client. After hearing from a male consultant that the job was available, I contacted the client. Apparently the list had been abbreviated because the site authority archaeologist did not believe that female consultants were capable of working in remote locations like the one proposed for the excavation work. I found this ironic, considering I had just returned from working in the wilderness of Southwest Tasmania. After some trouble with the then female-dominated consultants' association, the Australian Association of Consulting Archaeologists Inc., the site authority archaeologist has not repeated his action.

Gender discrimination has occurred in the recruitment of students for fieldwork. Anne Bickford believes that mature-age female students suffer the most from discrimination when trying to get experience in pre-contact excavations. She noted that 'older women or women with kids can't make the breaks to go out in the field, and male archaeologists never thought of them'.[17] As a result of this belief, Bickford has included some affirmative action on her urban historical archaeology excavations and also allowed women to bring their children, if they needed to, for their student digging experience.

Is there archaeology in your community?

If excavation has a theatrical element, it also has an audience. Such an audience may also want to participate in certain situations. The involvement of the community in excavations, particularly large digs, raises public interest in preserving heritage as well as allowing the recovery of data for

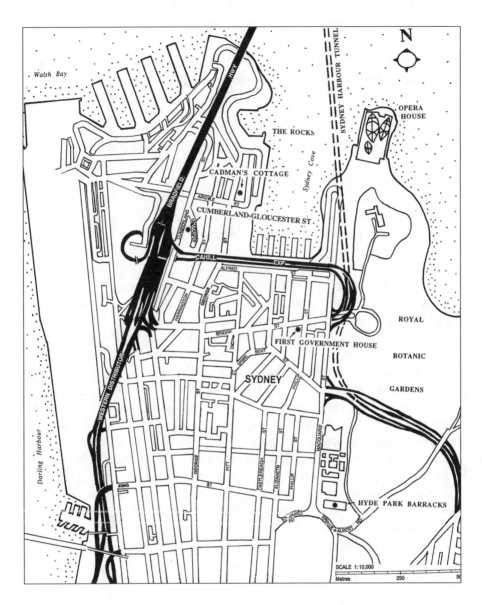

Excavations mentioned in the text that occurred in the centre of Sydney, 1970s to 1990s. Adapted from **UBD** Directory, *Sydney, 30th edn, 1994, pp. 1–2.*

Wonderworld (a children's programme) and the ABC's *Behind the News* and *Quantum*.

The Historic Houses Trust of New South Wales used the site in conjunction with its museum at Susannah Place (also in The Rocks) in a school interactive programme. Students received a hands-on experience of archaeology in addition to the interpretation provided through Susannah Place over a twelve-week period.[32] At least a thousand schoolchildren visited the excavation and 'walked along old paths, peered down cesspits, touched and handled artefacts'.[33] Except for Tasmania's Port Arthur (during the conservation project in the early 1980s), Sydney's Cadmans Cottage, and the Little Lon' site in Melbourne, few large excavations of that period allowed tours by school groups. Unless specially funded to undertake programmes, most excavations do not have the extra resources to deal with schools. The view of the developer or public funding source tends to determine whether archaeologists should service such groups. Anne Bickford observed a few years ago that the New South Wales Heritage Council encourages school visits to excavations but does not have the policy or the capacity to provide funding to ensure that it happens.[34] Other archaeologists have noted that there are some potential problems with insurance liability if school groups have access to some sites.

Another approach that should be considered in Australia is that of holding archaeological activities in conjunction with youth organisations. The US National Park Service encourages special camps for instruction about archaeology. Florida has run a successful programme of summer camps for children through its museum on pre-contact, historical and maritime archaeology. Activities have included flint knapping (manufacturing stone tools out of flint), surveying and some mock excavation. For instance, archaeologists employed a special 'box dig' to impart the principles of excavation.[35] Canada's Fort Chambly site museum, south of Montreal, has an intriguing box with a set of drawers to show children the formation processes of sites and how superposition works. In demonstrating the box, the curator puts on gloves at the beginning of the talk to emphasise the 'care needed and the scientific aspect of excavation'.[36]

Little Lon' and the Melbourne community

The 1989 salvage excavation of the Commonwealth Centre and Telecom site, known as Little Lon', is seen by many as demonstrating how the community can be informed about and involved in archaeological work. The interaction with the mass media over the site was extensive and sometimes unusual. The excavation took up part of a city block near Chinatown in the centre of Melbourne.

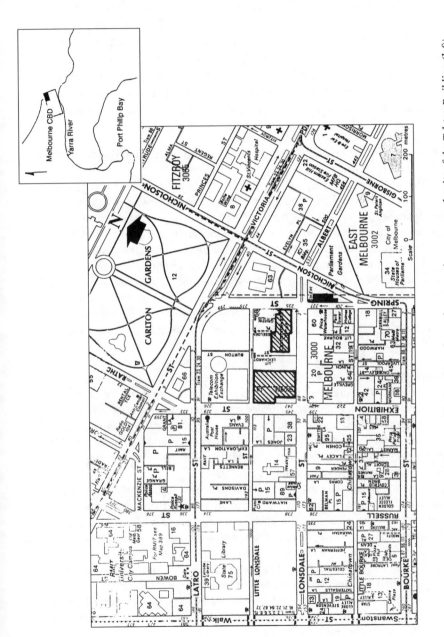

The 1989 Little Lon' excavation, Melbourne. The hatching shows the excavation areas on the site of the Telstra Building (left) and the Commonwealth Centre. Adapted from Melways Street Directory, Melbourne, 22nd edn, 1993, Maps 1A, 1B; H. du Cros and D. Rhodes, 'Commonwealth/Telecom Sites', p. 17.

I worked on this excavation as one of the laboratory archaeologists supervising cataloguing of artefacts by volunteers, analysing and conducting first aid conservation work on the excavated artefacts as they appeared each day. The actual digging was conducted over six months, but with the historical research, artefact analysis and writing up, the project took over twelve months to complete. During the excavation three press releases were made through the Victoria Archaeological Survey,[37] the first of which generated considerable interest in all sections of the media. Although it was long, it put the site into its social-historical context in an interesting way:

ARCHAEOLOGISTS EXCAVATE OLD CHINATOWN

Archaeologists are investigating a city block that was once a notorious red-light district and part of old Chinatown.

The site is bounded by Spring, Exhibition, Lonsdale and Little Lonsdale Streets, is owned by the Commonwealth Government who is funding the excavation prior to redevelopment. The project is supported by the Victoria Archaeological Survey, part of the Ministry for Planning and Environment.

Archaeologist Mr. Justin McCarthy says the project is the largest urban excavation ever undertaken in Australia. He says: 'It is also unusual for Australian Archaeologists to focus upon the lives of the poor. Little Lon'—the name Australian writer C. J. Dennis used for the area—was once alive with the sound of voices, merchants, the slum dwellers, the workers, miners, prostitutes, missionaries and hawkers—people of all races who lived and worked together in these narrow lanes'.

First sub-divided in 1847, the area was soon built up with workshops, stables, small shops, hotels and numerous tiny cottages, many only 20 feet by 20 feet.

In the 1870's Chinatown expanded northwards to include the site area.

Cheap lodging houses were crowded with Chinese labourers returning from Victoria's Goldfields and awaiting passage home. Others stayed to start small businesses such as furniture manufacturing, food halls and fruit and vegetable marketing. Gambling halls, opium dens and brothels provided meeting places, entertainment and refuge for the lonely.

Several brothels catered for wealthier clients. Scandalous stories were common. The most famous of these began on 9 October 1891, when the Mace from Parliament House went missing. Parliament had sat late the previous night and, though there was an attempt to hush up the affair, it was soon rumoured that the Mace had been taken to Annie Wilson's Brothel.

As people left, the character of Little Lon changed . . . Justin McCarthy says: 'the fact that the area has remained virtually untouched offers us an ideal opportunity to discover the structures and materials people left behind. For a short time a community of people filled these lanes with energy. For the most part their stories are never recorded . . .'

Mr McCarthy is looking for volunteers. You don't need previous experience. In return for labour he promises a free lunch and chance to join a unique archaeological adventure.[38]

There followed contact details and more snippets of history from the site.

The press release tried to engage the enthusiasm of both journalists and the general public about the history of the site and exploited current popular mythology about archaeology to attract volunteers; one colourful phrase was the 'chance to join a unique archaeological adventure'. The press release provided ready-made quotes and a wide range of 'historical facts' to entice busy journalists to ask for interviews or to write up the story quickly and (if necessary) with a minimum of contact. It was successful in all of its aims, and afterwards volunteers poured onto the site. The headlines read: 'Secrets from Brothel-site Bedrock' (*Weekend Australian*) and 'Digging up our Seamy Past in Quest for Mace' (*Age*).[39] In these articles, the journalists focused on the red-light district more than on old Chinatown and the site became known from then on as the 'Brothel Site Excavation' or 'Little Lon'. This case was a classic example of sex and scandal selling newspapers and the site to the public, even when it was old sex and scandal. The press release was issued at a quiet time of the year (after Christmas) with no wars, disasters or political intrigue, and no other excavations occurring to compete with Little Lon' for media coverage. The electronic media showed an intense interest in the project.

In the next stage of the publicity the most interesting finds appeared in newspapers and on television, as the media was kept notified about the progress of the work. Stories included: 'Stump Goes Back to City's Roots' (*Age*), about a massive red gum stump found underneath the foundations of an old cottage, and 'New Light on Old Chinatown' (*Herald*), which mixed photos of bottles found on the site with historical photos of opium dens and brothels.[40]

The site archaeologists gave interviews describing the finds to television and radio journalists. Members of the public and journalists then started to ask why it was necessary to destroy the site in the first place. This uproar caused the local State parliamentary member to ask 'why archaeologists had not realised the site had rich potential years ago instead of waiting until shortly before demolition had begun'.[41] Unfortunately, prior to the decision to destroy the site, there had been no incentive for the developers to pay for an excavation as an exploratory measure or as an earlier part of the planning approval process.

A feature writer at the *Age* was kept regularly informed of happenings on the site on an informal basis, so there was a certain amount of coverage besides that generated by the press releases. The *Age* journalist also visited the site regularly as a volunteer who enthusiastically excavated some of the largest cesspits for bottles and other finds. Working on this site excavation changed the way he spent his holidays. He became so keen on archaeology

An enthusiastic volunteer at the Little Lon' excavation, Melbourne.

Typical artefacts deposited by townsfolk of Little Lon' in their rubbish pits (some of which were disused cesspits) during the second half of the nineteenth century in Melbourne.

that he has spent most of his holidays working on further urban excavations in Adelaide as a volunteer. Another case of excavation changing someone's life occurred when a volunteer and an archaeologist fell in love with each other and moved in together. They now live in Castlemaine and the volunteer has since produced a child, as well as a book on the history of Melbourne.[42]

Schoolteachers heard about the excavation and asked to visit it with school groups. No real contingency was made for this in the budget or in the project schedule and tours by the site supervisors. The tours slowed down work on the site until Heritage Week when the running of them was handed over to volunteers, who had time to devote to discussing details. This arrangement enabled the site supervisors to keep working and concentrate on the excavation. People who did not have the chance to work on the excavation could see it first hand instead of through the fence. The Victoria Archaeological Survey also put together a small educational package of some photocopied handouts, with a map showing areas of interest, for a self-conducting perimeter tour of the site. Archaeologists in the Southwest of the United States have found that special open days are more productive and less disruptive than continual tours within the working area of excavations.[43]

The Victoria Archaeological Survey was able to use the publicity and goodwill gained from this excavation as a positive example to encourage other developers to conduct similar operations, which would occur much earlier in the planning and design of a development. Little Lon' influenced the coverage of the 1989 excavation of the City Link Development Site at Footscray and assisted in the negotiations between the Victoria Archaeological Survey, the local council and the developer.

Heritage Victoria ran an excavation at Viewbank in the Melbourne suburbs over three seasons (1996, 1997 and 1999) with limited public participation.[44] Publicity was more circumspect than that at Little Lon' because the site is vulnerable to looting. Melbourne archaeologists consider Little Lon' has had the greatest impact on community awareness of any urban excavation in that city.

Finally, such excavations can elicit interesting reactions from the community. The publicity and presence of site excavations often draws informants with important historical information who would not be identified though other channels. An architect who had worked on an early-twentieth-century building constructed over the site of Sydney's First Government House heard about the 1983 excavation and visited it with useful information because of the publicity the site had received. The community can provide more than an audience for many archaeological productions.

Publicity attracts one of the architects who when younger worked in the Government Architects Building that was built over the top of First Government House foundations in Sydney. He is shown here describing the building he worked in to excavation director Anne Bickford, 1983.

The community, archaeology and developers

Not all digs are open and accessible to the public. Developers are not always as welcoming of publicity as the Sydney Cove Authority at The Rocks or the Commonwealth and Telecom at Little Lon', and they often place restrictions on what can be passed on to the rest of the community. Aboriginal people have special concerns about the security of some site excavations, fearing that such sites could become the targets of local racists or looters if their location is publicised. Excavations of Aboriginal sites do not always occur close to cities or towns, and special tours are not usually encouraged. In the 1970s and early 1980s, the Victoria Archaeological Survey used to run summer schools for students and interested members of the public, which included site recording and excavation of Aboriginal sites in remote parts of Victoria. The field schools were discontinued with the politicisation of Aboriginal heritage.

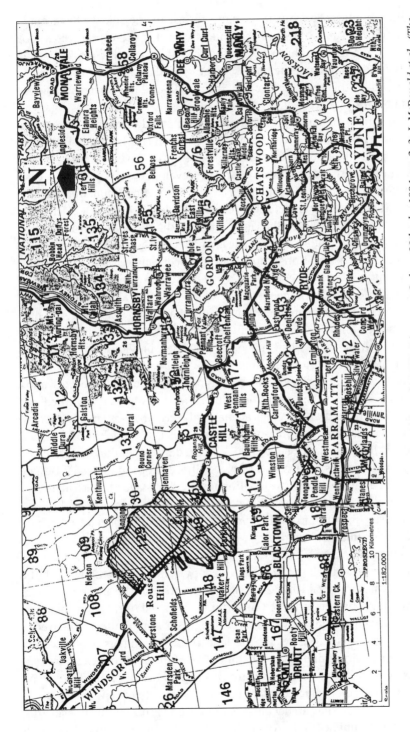

The Rouse Hill study area (hatched), Sydney, 1993. Adapted from the UBD Directory, Sydney, 30th edn, 1994, pp. 2–3; J. McDonald et al., 'The Rouse Hill Infrastructure Project', p. 260.

Such politicisation can take many forms. In the mid-1990s a major programme of sub-surface testing and salvage for pre-contact sites took place in the Sydney suburb of Rouse Hill. Although this work was not heavily funded, much of the money went towards hiring excavators in the first season, as there were no volunteers sought and the developer allowed little publicity.

Consulting archaeologists Brayshaw McDonald Pty Limited were first contacted by the Rouse Hill Consortium Pty Ltd in late 1992 to salvage sites originally recorded by another archaeologist in the development area. The Consortium consisted of a group of private developers working with several government developers—a popular cocktail for development with the Liberal State government.[45] After reading the brief, Josephine McDonald and Helen Brayshaw asked the client whether the rest of the area had been surveyed for archaeological sites. The area affected by development was not fully surveyed, as the Consortium had not been advised to do a comprehensive survey for archaeological sites because of a glitch in the planning process, caused by the changing nature of the project and political pressures to fast-track such developments.[46] Not only that, but 37 kilometres of proposed sewage lines crossed areas of the Cumberland Plain in the Rouse Hill area through parts that had not been disturbed previously by European settlement except for stock grazing.

In May 1993, the consultant archaeologists started a salvage excavation programme to assess the scientific value of the sites already recorded and determine whether archaeological material existed in other likely areas. The latter were generally areas where site prediction models for the region indicated that sites might be located, obscured by vegetation or recent soil formation processes, which had received little European impact.[47] Despite the lack of archaeological investigation for the first stage of construction, to begin within a few weeks, planning approval had been granted to the Consortium. This pressure from the construction schedule obliged the archaeological consultants to work fast, with two archaeological teams testing a site each week.

The unskilled labour was provided by paid representatives of the Daruk Local Aboriginal Land Council, which cared for the area's Aboriginal heritage. Over five months the Consortium employed twenty-five members of the land council and thirty-five archaeologists.[48] A minimum of one week's work on the project was set for the land council members, who received on-the-spot training due to the schedule. Two of the land council's representatives were sufficiently inspired by the experience to enrol later in an external archaeology degree offered by the University of New England.

Tilley's claim that archaeologists are all-powerful and responsible for distancing the public from excavation and active interpretation of sites falls apart in this case. Josephine McDonald, lead archaeological consultant for the project, believes that the Consortium did not want adverse publicity and this was probably the main motivation for getting the work completed although the planning approvals had already been granted.[49] Its concern arose partly as a result of protests that the development had already attracted from a resident action group in the area, Hawkesbury Environmental Action Team (HEAT). This group watched every move and put the 'heat' on the consortium, while making some inaccurate claims about the area's significance. For instance, they asserted that bulldozer scrapes in a sandstone rock platform represented a male initiation site and that burial sites abounded in the development area.[50] The Daruk Local Aboriginal Land Council allowed themselves to be involved in the protest up to the point where they were satisfied that their requirements for compensation by the Consortium were being met in the short and long term. The land council was not easily influenced by HEAT, having been involved previously in a number of controversial projects where its Aboriginality had been exploited.

To handle HEAT's allegations, the Consortium hired a publicity troubleshooter, Denise Eisenhuth, who had worked previously on the Sydney Harbour Tunnel's publicity. She was accustomed to acting as an intermediary between developers and the community. The archaeologists were bemused by her mode of operation, and amused when she made the initial mistake of inspecting the test excavations in her best Gucci shoes. After that Eisenhuth always wore her special 'ladies' steel-capped boots. The archaeologists could speak to the media only through Eisenhuth,[51] and the only other archaeological results to reach the community appeared in her public newsletter *Rouse Hill Infrastructure News,* funded by the Consortium. At least two of these newsletters discussed the archaeological work, but in superficial terms.[52] The newsletters were intended to reassure the public that the Consortium was doing its best to be environmentally and culturally responsible.

A second stage of the Rouse Hill project was carried out a few years later, during which six sites were salvaged and over 50 000 artefacts recovered. This time the work occurred in perfect synchronicity with planning requirements, again with the Aboriginal community fully involved. It was also notable for its lack of controversy, and no publicity agent was required.[53]

Just diggers? Archaeologists and volunteers

In Australia there are few if any archaeologists who go it alone on excavations. Most have adopted the field school approach, or use volunteers. A small number recruit volunteers through organisations such as Earthwatch, the international conservation action organisation, expecting the volunteers to pay for their amenities and instruction. The rest, particularly academics, use archaeology students. The latter are not regarded as volunteers because they are moving towards being professionals within the archaeological system. Non-professional enthusiasts—or as Richard Lange calls them, 'avocationalists'—can also be counted as volunteers in cases where they are not paid or are not actually directing the project.[54] Sometimes these people go on to study archaeology and adopt it as a professional occupation, like actors who get their start in local amateur theatricals. The role of volunteers on excavations provides a ready-made case study for examining the relationship and relevance of archaeology to wider society.

Who are the brave souls who become volunteers? On one excavation run by the NSW National Parks and Wildlife Service of Cadmans Cottage in The Rocks in 1988 (see Map 1), all volunteers working on the site were asked to fill in an information sheet. The survey was carried out so that the archaeologists could better understand the nature of the volunteer workforce. The Department of Planning has tried to encourage archaeologists to collect this information at every excavation using volunteers, but no results have been forthcoming since 1993.

A total of 228 people worked as volunteers at Cadmans Cottage during the excavation between June and September 1988. Denis Gojak (director of the excavation) noted that there was a broad age range from nine to seventy-eight years of age.[55] Excavation rules for the site had allowed children only when accompanied by an adult; the minimum age for teenagers participating through school-facilitated work experience programmes was fifteen. The largest age group was twenty-one to thirty years. Perhaps this group saw archaeological excavation as a constructive outdoor activity with potential as a hobby, a talking-point or even a career.

The publicity campaign for the site stressed that no previous experience was necessary. Despite this absence of preconditions, forty-seven volunteers (20.6 per cent of the total) had worked on other projects. Gojak tried to collect some responses concerning the expectations and understanding of the work by the volunteers. There seemed to be a widespread adherence to the popular stereotype that careful digging would be needed to recover fragile objects. Many volunteers were surprised that hard labour was also required. He found that most volunteers appeared to have a general interest in archaeology, but confused it with related pastimes, including bottle-collecting (which has been known to destroy archaeological sites). Gojak believes archaeologists need to be more active in communicating the nature of Australian archaeology to the general public.

Gojak also discovered that the retention rate of volunteers was related to their expectations of working as a digger. People were warned in advance that work would sometimes be hard and tedious and would include the sorting of artefacts. When faced with the reality, half of them left before the minimum of three days.[56] Archaeology Abroad (based in London) must have found the same problem with their rural excavations. On some digs they ask volunteers to pay a sum that covers instruction and provides for better amenities and food, hoping that this will prevent people from leaving early.[57]

Additional research and analysis, which are carried out before or after the excavation phase, are often not acknowledged by the public, who tend to see the main work as just the digging. People realise that some activity of the sort must go on, but do not consider it as significant as excavation until they have experience of it first hand as volunteers or non-professional enthusiasts. When Richard Lange rated the effectiveness of using volunteers in American excavations, the question arose about the importance of special research and analysis which volunteers are not equipped to carry out.[58] The post-excavation analysis is completed by students for their undergraduate and postgraduate research projects or is undertaken by both archaeological and non-archaeological specialists.

Despite tough deadlines requiring fast work, volunteers are given a warmer welcome on historic site excavations funded by developers than on any other kind of site. In the 1990s, however, the Australian Heritage Commission and the Australian Museum staff have linked up with Earthwatch, and taken paying volunteers on rock art recording programmes and excavations. The volunteers are expecting to broaden their horizons and help out in a way that will aid conservation and management of archaeological sites. The archaeologists are expecting to get volunteers who will stay around and work as asked. Unfortunately, these two sets of expectations are not necessarily complementary. Archaeologists find themselves acting like tour operators for paying volunteers who naturally expect good amenities, food, entertainment and instruction for their money. They will also leave if the work itself is dull, hard and tedious.

People wishing to work on excavations are often at a loss as to who to contact unless the excavations are publicised. There are no Australian volunteers' newsletters through which prospective diggers can find digs, such as those published by the Archaeology Abroad group through the British Institute of Archaeology in England. The first step for any dig director hoping to attract volunteers and public interest is publicity. Most archaeologists realise that publicising a site in the right way is vital to the recruitment of sufficient volunteers. Whether aided by their client or by the State site protection authority, they need to consider a number of factors in attracting the interest of potential volunteers.

After attracting volunteers through publicity, the next step is to educate them about the aims of the project and train them in the types of tasks required. Volunteers are usually asked to make a minimum time commitment to assisting at the site, for three days or one week. Of course no one is expected to stay if they do not like the work or find it too heavy. Site supervisors, other paid professional archaeologists or experienced volunteers (who are probably also non-professional enthusiasts) help to show new volunteers what is expected of them. Sometimes volunteers are given a lecture introducing the history and archaeology of the site, with some handouts from various archaeology manuals to read. They then receive on-the-job training from the site supervisors.

Most archaeologists interviewed for this book believe that offering a greater range of tasks to volunteers on a site is important for sustaining interest. Richard Mackay has identified a learning curve among Sydney archaeologists regarding the use of volunteers. Since the 1970s, volunteers have received more information during excavations and are not treated as drones or robots. Archaeologists have been careful to add a social dimension to each dig and become more aware of dangerous or unpleasant conditions with which volunteers should not be expected to cope.[59] As Australian historical archaeologists have to rely increasingly on volunteer labour in urban excavations because of tight funds, they are trying various strategies to retain experienced volunteers.

A special hat party livens up the excavation of Little Lon', Melbourne, 1989.

Special events are important for dig morale. A 1984 ceremony launched a time capsule that is now preserved below the pavement with most of the reburied and conserved remains of First Government House, Sydney. Site supervisor Denis Gojak does the honours.

One strategy is to build a 'dig culture', with parties and other social occasions. Anne Bickford sees this as important for urban excavations, which do not necessarily build the strong social ties that excavations do in remote places.[60] At her excavation of First Government House in Sydney, activities included an art competition that was judged by Australian painter Stanilaus Rapotec, as well as numerous birthday celebrations.

Other types of social occasions include fancy dress parties, weekly dinners and slide nights. Some excavations have tearooms decorated with funny photographs, newspaper clippings about the dig, cartoons and other items on the walls. Not only does this build a characteristic atmosphere for each long-term excavation, but it also gives the place where workers congregate a backstage feel.

Other archaeologists have offered reports and pamphlets as souvenirs after the dig. Richard Mackay observed that volunteers on sites that he has directed were more likely to become involved in assisting during the analysis period 'because of a rapport that they had built up with individual trench supervisor people'.[61] Many of the people participating in the analysis of artefacts are retirees. This age-group often has the longest retention rates for archaeological projects, but this is not necessarily because they have more time on their hands than younger people. Retirees who work as volunteers on sites are also involved in a wide range of socially useful pastimes.[62] It is more likely that a combination of the nature of the work and the congenial atmosphere persuades retirees to continue as volunteers throughout the analysis phase and to return for dig after dig.

Eureka! More champagne bottles and corks! Exciting finds from the brothels of the Little Lon' site made by long-term volunteers Robyn Annear and Vicki Brown in 1989.

Another strategy used by archaeologists to retain volunteers is to offer individual experienced volunteers a choice of archaeological features to excavate or of a task to undertake. At the Little Lon' excavation, cesspits and garbage pits were always awarded to the keenest and most experienced volunteers as they yielded the greatest range of finds in good condition. Some locations were even set aside specially until the part of the week when these individuals attended the site excavation. Other privileges included supervision of a square or trench, reassembling pottery sherds, drafting plans or any of the rarer tasks that require special training. Unlike Britain, Australia has no volunteer accreditation scheme, so the training of experienced volunteers is usually carried out on an ad hoc basis or as an incentive to stay.

Several other factors have prevented greater public participation in Australian archaeological investigations. Heightened awareness of safety standards on sites and the need for on-site liability insurance has caused some archaeologists to prefer paid assistance instead of voluntary help. Even so, there are still a number of opportunities for public participation in Australia, particularly on government-run excavations.

Community support and pressure for archaeological work

Europe and Australia are very different in their support bases for archaeology and for the retention of archaeological heritage. Europe has a wide base from which it draws volunteers, including local volunteer-run archaeology societies. General awareness and acceptance of the value of archaeological sites in Europe is usually high. Although it is not as high in Australia, there are a reasonable number of government and non-government organisations that try to supervise and encourage field archaeology.

Even so, the European societies do not contribute as much as they could towards pressuring governments to protect archaeological heritage. Riemer Knoop, a Dutch archaeologist, notes that the Green movement has been more successful in reaching its objectives through its local branches and Greenpeace-like tactics than have supporters of archaeological heritage. She observes that 'we are standing at the threshold of a new era in European cultural management'.[63] Knoop predicts that government moves to make the private sector responsible for funding and initiating archaeological heritage projects will end in disaster without a vigilant community. As globalisation disempowers grassroots and indigenous groups in relation to heritage preservation, people are now looking to non-government organisations such as the International Council of Monuments and Sites (ICOMOS) to take an advocacy role. Recently, Australia ICOMOS alongside other non-government organisations lobbied the federal government about issues such as proposed changes to heritage and environment legislation and the construction of the Jabiluka uranium mine in Kakadu National Park. An increasing level of advocacy for conservation of cultural heritage, including archaeological heritage, is proposed in its business plan for the next three years.[64]

In the last twenty years, salvage of sites in urban areas was viewed as preferable to stopping a development or redesigning it to leave a site intact. City property frequently commands high prices, and such economic concerns usually cancel out other claims, especially in Southeast Asia. While some of these societies still operate, they are quite unlike the volunteer- or advocationalist-run archaeology associations that Knoop describes, which can lobby for the conservation of archaeological heritage. It is often left to professional archaeologists (within Australia ICOMOS) and public intellectuals such as John Mulvaney to perform this role. Where are the amateurs waiting in the wings? In returning to Tilley's analogy about archaeology and theatre, it is fair to say that, although the community enjoys being part of the play, they need to be more concerned about the upkeep of the playhouse.

4

Romancing the stones

LEAVING THE STAGE for the screen, romance has never been far away from archaeology even in television documentaries. Tom Haydon was one of the most skilled and creative documentary filmmakers to take a major interest in Australian archaeology. His life and work demonstrate how non-archaeological attitudes have shaped the presentation of archaeological information to the public in film and television documentaries. It also shows that there is a legacy to be traced from his work, not just in the interpretation of recent discoveries, but also in the handling of other issues, such as the controversy over the accuracy of dates for the site of Jinmium, which was discussed in Chapter 2. Haydon covered archaeological topics during a period (1966–83) when many exciting discoveries were being made in Australia, strongly influencing socio-political beliefs.

In particular, Haydon's film *The Last Tasmanian*, released in 1978, was considered controversial in the 1970s for its treatment of Aboriginal identity. Its view of Tasmanian pre-contact technology and isolation was considered less contentious. Archaeologist and co-writer Rhys Jones was not solely responsible for the view of *The Last Tasmanian*. Tom Haydon provided much of the philosophy behind the film. These views of Aboriginal cultural continuity from the past to the present became crucial to understanding the role of archaeological authority in this debate. This documentary raised issues that were to shape the way archaeology was practised and presented in following years.

Tom Haydon's films and Australian archaeology

Tom Haydon, the main instigator of the film, was born on 22 January 1938. He grew up in a middle-class environment in post-war Manly, in Sydney.

Haydon attended Manly Boys' High, which had just been established as a selective, segregated State school. It had higher academic standards than most State schools of its time and produced numerous students who later became attracted to studying history or archaeology. While at high school, Haydon met fellow student Jim Allen and also developed a special attraction to the classics. Haydon's deep interest in Latin and classical literature later had an impact on his style of documentary analysis.

Haydon graduated from the University of Sydney with a Bachelor of Arts (Hons) in 1960. Haydon had majored in Australian history at a time when it was not well regarded. Rhys Jones observed that Haydon 'felt deeply about the problems of a British-derived history which still imposed upon an indigenous and independent Australian identity'.[1] This attitude was probably inspired by a certain disgust at the nature of Australian history that was taught at the University of Sydney in the late 1950s, which portrayed British imperial expansion as a triumphant move from convict settlement to pastoral riches.

Haydon then joined the Australian Broadcasting Commission as a 'specialist trainee'. He soon began making television documentaries after joining the Science Unit as producer. His style of 'ironic juxtaposition'[2] first became apparent in his documentary on Lang Hancock, *Dig a Million, Make a Million*.[3] In this documentary, humour and savage comment appeared side by side as Haydon examined Hancock's mining interests in Western Australia. This characteristic of Haydon's work is also evident in parts of *The Last Tasmanian*.[4] In 1969 Haydon moved to Britain and joined the BBC, where he made several films for the *Horizon* television documentary series. He became an independent producer in the mid-1970s and established Artis Film Productions, which he controlled until his death in 1991 from lymphatic cancer.[5]

Tom Haydon's interest in portraying Australian archaeological research began with his involvement in an ABC TV broadcast of one of Professor N. W. G. Macintosh's lectures.[6] Titled *Fossil Man in Australia*,[7] the lecture was given at the 39th ANZAAS Congress in Melbourne on 16 January 1967. This experience inspired Haydon to make a full documentary film on Macintosh's 21-year search for the Darling Downs find spot of the Talgai Skull, where it had been first discovered by non-archaeologists in 1886 and later purchased by the University of Sydney. The minimum age for the piece is between 14 000 and 16 000 years.[8] *The Talgai Skull* was televised nationally and won Haydon the first of his Logie awards.[9]

Haydon's next foray into Australian archaeology also dealt with skeletal remains. *The Long Long Walkabout* was a BBC–ABC co-production as part of the *Horizon* series.[10] It was made at a time of intellectual upheaval in Australian archaeology: new finds were inspiring a wide range of theories concerning human arrival on this continent. This film also contained one of Haydon's first efforts at staged or symbolic dramatic reconstruction—a strategy he also used in *The Last Tasmanian*. In the former film, Haydon wanted to show how Macintosh (representing University of Sydney) and his theories were being challenged by younger researchers at the Australian National University. The two sides re-enacted their meeting near Lake Mungo. Filming in the bar of the tiny Hatfield Hotel, Haydon staged a grand entrance by Macintosh and his research assistants. Whether intended or not, some humour is generated in a visual reference to the shoot-out in *High Noon*.

Rhys Jones met Haydon in a Melbourne pub and they became friends. Jones and his archaeologist wife, Betty Meehan, were living in Melbourne at the time. Late they all shared a flat together before Haydon went to England. Jones also appeared in *The Long Long Walkabout* and part of the hotel scene when he was at the Australian National University. He reconstructed a bark canoe for the film that, unfortunately, sank off Rocky Cape when they were filming in Tasmania. Part of the footage of the canoe before it sank was recycled for *The Last Tasmanian*.

Haydon did not tell Jones until much later what had initially inspired him to make a documentary feature about Tasmanian Aborigines. A few days before Haydon died, Jones drove him to a radio interview and they started talking about the film. Haydon mentioned that he thought of the idea in a pub in Sydney when someone said, 'Tell me Tom, what *did* happen to the Tasmanian Aborigines?' and he thought, 'There's a film in there somehow'.

The Last Tasmanian—the movie

Tom Haydon and Rhys Jones planned *The Last Tasmanian* in a Welsh farm-house in 1976 when Jones had sabbatical leave to study in Wales. The title was Haydon's idea. The intention was to allude to various nineteenth-century 'projections of melancology' such as Fennimore Cooper's *The Last of the Mohicans*. Jones notes that 'it is unfortunate that these subtleties became lost in an issue which eventually turned out to be so controversial and even offensive to some Aboriginal people seeking to re-affirm an identity with their past'.[11] That the filmmakers were more interested in these subtleties than in their audience both makes and mars this documentary feature. While it allowed Haydon and Jones to be extremely focused about how they portrayed the central theme of genocide, it prevented them from seeing that this approach would impact on the aspirations of rapidly politicising Tasmanian Aboriginal people by denying them their Aboriginality.

The documentary is more clearly structured than most of Haydon's previous films. It has three distinct sections: Before 1803—Ancestors; After 1876—Descendants; and 1803–76—Extinction. The last concerns the main statement that Haydon wanted to make in the film about genocide and ties in with the opening scenes of the repatriation, cremation and scattering of Truganini's ashes.[12] The concept of the Tasmanians' extinction by colonial sponsored genocide is what inspired Haydon in the first place.

In the film, Rhys Jones and Jim Allen demonstrate the artefact assemblage outside a hut that they reconstructed from illustrations of Aboriginal people made during the historic expedition to Tasmania (1800–03) led by zoologist François Péron. The point they are trying to make with the scene is that research conducted by Jones indicates that the Tasmanian Aboriginal people's pre-contact culture was the simplest known. The assemblage comprised twenty-two types of artefact—held to be far less than that known for the mainland Aboriginal peoples. There is also the assertion that they could not even make fire and had to carry it with them, although this notion has since been discredited.

Archaeologists Jim Allen and Rhys Jones demonstrate shellfish-eating skills in The Last Tasmanian, *1978.*

Rhys Jones warms up to talk about the Tasmanian Aboriginal toolkit in The Last Tasmanian, *1978.*

In the film, Jones enthusiastically discusses the apparent isolation that the culture suffered after sea levels cut Tasmania off from the rest of Australia 12 000 years ago. The film presents an unusual archaeological theory: the likelihood that the Tasmanian Aboriginal people faced extinction through isolation if no interference had occurred. This theory did not have any currency elsewhere in archaeology at the time, and even Jones later described it as speculative.[13] Debate about it occurred after the film was released, but it became lost in the furore about Aboriginal identity. The isolation theory resembles in some ways the justifying arguments used by British colonising society in the section of the film 'Extinction', and as such warranted closer scrutiny and debate. Are Jones and Haydon also guilty of nineteenth-century cultural evolutionism or Social Darwinism by implying that the demise of the Aborigines would have happened anyway? Archaeologists debated this issue, but it was largely ignored by the mass media in the debate that followed the release of the documentary.

Jones later argued that his view on the inevitability of extinction was misinterpreted by archaeologists such as Anne Bickford, who questioned the evidence for his view.[14] He believes that the problem may be partly caused by his use of the word 'doom' in the narration: 'Tasmanian history

... ends in catastrophe but that catastrophe began 12 000 years ago [when the sea level rose and cut off Tasmania] ... in a sense their doom was sealed by that event'.[15] Jones falls back on artistic licence, using the word to depict something akin to destiny in classical Greek tragedy.[16] This concept was obviously too subtle for the audience, who quite naturally wished to take it literally, like the implications behind the name of the film. So the communication of the idea failed. The authors of the script were distracted by a dimension of the story that was too complex for anyone except other documentary makers and some archaeologists. When presenting any archaeological and historical interpretations of the archaeological record, clarity is as important as style, as some archaeologists have found along with filmmakers. The audience's needs are the main concern when moving from the small 'stage production' of an archaeological report or book, which reaches a limited audience, to a larger screen production, such as a documentary, that may attract a mass audience.

In the documentary, Haydon also tries to present what he believed at the time was a hidden history. Information from historian Lyndall Ryan's doctoral thesis on Tasmanian Aborigines[17] was used as well as other historical material gathered by the authors. Later, historian Henry Reynolds published *Fate of a Free People*, which claims to be a radical re-examination of the Tasmanian Black Wars.[18] As *The Last Tasmanian* was produced before much of the debate which has occurred about treaties and indigenous self-determination, the narration concerning the Black Wars and European attitudes differs from Reynolds' later analysis. Reynolds' statement about Aboriginal political continuity, which is not an idea considered anywhere in Haydon and Jones' film, holds that the contemporary land rights movement in Tasmania 'is merely the latest manifestation of a political tradition stretching back to the Black War and the settlement at Wybalenna'.[19] If Jones and Haydon had had access to the historical documents that support this idea, maybe they would have made a very different film.

It is true that there is a certain amount of theatrical passion and even some romanticism in *The Last Tasmanian*, but it does not develop into sensationalism as might so easily happen with such a topic. This is one of the main strengths of the film. In avoiding sensationalism and a number of clichés, the documentary was remarkable for its time; it holds up well today considering the treatment of the past in later documentaries, such as *The Resurrection of the 'Batavia'*,[20] which also used historical and archaeological information. Unlike *The Last Tasmanian*, it relies heavily on clichéd and overly dramatic reconstructions of violence, including abundant and explicit scenes of hangings, rapes, and skulls of murdered people. In *The Last Tasmanian*, such passion is portrayed in the relentless retelling of historic events

Annette Mansell plucking mutton birds in **The Last Tasmanian,** *1978.*

against their settings in the Tasmanian landscape. Some dramatisation occurs but without period costume. One of the most memorable scenes is of Jones and Allen sitting in Montague, a settler's house, reading a letter discussing strategies for the Black War in the very room where it was written.[21] Another scene which is dramatic for a different reason occurs in the 'Descendants' section. In an ironic juxtaposition Annette Mansell is shown denying the continuity of Aboriginal political tradition while plucking mutton birds. It is possible that the film would have been less controversial if it had been made with the scene set in Ms Mansell's modern home with her reaffirming this concept.

The release and the reaction

The Last Tasmanian was released in three languages—English, French and Welsh. The English version of the film first opened on 22 May 1978 at the Collegiate Theatre, London. Some Australian papers followed its progress overseas and proudly reported its success at the Cannes Film Festival and elsewhere.[22] Some overseas critics described it as 'a brilliant document on genocide ... dramatic and fascinating'; 'a horrifying chronicle of greed, cruelty and ignorance'; and 'A cautionary tale of our times . . . a vivid slice of history'.[23] The only overseas critic and filmmaker who did not laud the film, Dennis Potter, described it as 'a long and sickening film . . . which demonstrated that when taboo and anxiety and any other of the difficult restraints we needs must place upon ourselves are too easily disregarded, then real horror lies waiting in its old, slithery coils'.[24] The length of the documentary was something that did concern television networks and later it was cut to run for a much shorter time than the 109 minutes original. The effect of this on the continuity of the historical account is difficult to imagine. The uncut version is available for viewing through the Australian National Library in Canberra.

The film's portrayal of Tasmanian history was not always interpreted by critics as sickening or gruesome. Some commented on the film's style and sensitivity. Geraldine Pascal observed that 'the genocide is by no means explained away' and that Haydon 'doesn't hammer it sensationally'.[25] Douglas Aiton noted that 'it has all the recognisable Haydon touches of light-handedness, subtlety, tact and delicacy'.[26]

The filmmakers held the Australian premiere at the Melbourne Film Festival in June. Significantly, this occurred a few days before its premiere in Hobart on 20 June 1978. Whether they expected trouble or not, Haydon and Jones had heard objections about the film from the Tasmanian Aboriginal community. The statement 'Tasmania was empty of Aborigines—the most complete case of genocide on record' is made near the film's beginning. This was the statement which drew the most fire from the Aboriginal community. The film's historical narrative ignored the fact that they had suffered discrimination for many years for being black or Aboriginal and concentrated on denying their identity to suit the film's preoccupation with genocide. Historian Bain Attwood describes this approach to Aboriginal identity as yet another type of dispossession. He is also critical of historians and others who defined the nature and extent of Aboriginal people's identity for them in a similar way.[27]

Journalist Robert Milliken reported that Aboriginal activists demonstrated outside the Hobart opening of the film.[28] Local analysts Kay Daniels and Mary Murnane castigated him, observing that if he had been in Hobart, he would have known there was not a demonstration and that he was publicising Haydon's version of events.[29] They went on to point out that no one at that stage had allowed Aboriginal people who had objections to the film to speak for themselves. A few days later Daniels and Murnane published an article titled 'The last Tasmanians are alive and well'.[30] It was reprinted in a student union publication on Tasmanian racism, which also contained articles by Michael and Clyde Mansell and Heather Sculthorpe.[31]

The publication also questions 'Jones' apocalyptic vision of a race locked in a closed society by the rising waters of Bass Strait, a race doomed by their simple technology'. This issue was lost in the ensuing debate on the *Monday Conference* television programme.[32] Bob Moore, the presenter, invited Michael Mansell and Tom Haydon to speak about the film and then answer questions from the Hobart audience. Moore wanted to discuss the identity issue and stated in the introduction that the film was 'under attack from a surprising direction, at least at first—there are now living in Tasmania 2000 to 4000 people who regard themselves as Aboriginal here and now'. The problem was identified in the programme as 'a political and social stumbling block of the worst kind' because *The Last Tasmanian* implicitly denied Aboriginal identity and thus its portrayal of Aboriginal history dealt a blow to the land rights aspirations of Tasmanian Aboriginal people.

Lyndall Ryan was present in the audience for the televised debate and her comments from the floor showed some insight into how the film inspired the controversy. She believed that 'by denying the cultural continuity of Bass Strait Aboriginals, [Haydon] was . . . making them a lost tribe in an archaeological sense'.[33] By this, she means that Haydon and Jones believed that cultural continuity had broken irrevocably with Truganini's death. The descendants would then have lost authority by which to define themselves as Tasmanian Aborigines. Unless they used archaeological and historical methods to assemble a case to oppose the film's premises or were sufficiently dark-skinned to satisfy the more racist members of Tasmanian white society, their identity would not be seen as authentic.

In hindsight

This lack of understanding concerning cultural continuity is curious in a documentary that was unusually well-produced for its time. Its faults may have their basis in Haydon's decision to allow the film to be dominated by Jones's positivist or processual archaeology rather than by history. But then the 'history' conducted in the 1990s (by Henry Reynolds, Bain Attwood and Cassandra Pybus) would have been too revisionist for Haydon to have envisaged in the 1970s while making this film. Archaeology in Australia at the time still held itself as being apart from society; consideration of the political and ethical issues associated with defining another group's identity for them and the likely repercussions were beyond its understanding.

Jones has observed that in hindsight it is easy see where the film ran into problems.[34] While this is true, his complaint about the use of the film by the Tasmanian Aboriginal land rights movement for national publicity of its cause is unjustified. Documentaries by their nature should inspire interest and debate.[35] Haydon and Jones should have seen that critical acclaim of the film's style and bravura would not be the only mark of its success. By engendering such debate and allowing these issues to feature nationally, the film had an impact beyond that of many art-house documentaries. Bob Moore's introductory comment on *Monday Conference*, 'it had its heart in the right place, but its head decidedly isn't', put the dilemma well.

In the years that followed, Haydon continued his interest in archaeology and Tasmania.[36] He produced an education kit to supplement the film in the early 1990s, shortly before his death.[37] The kit is intended for secondary schools teaching Aboriginal and Australian studies. It contains a synopsis, information on the makers, excerpts from critics' notices and a summary of the controversy. The kit encourages senior students to discuss the film and the debate. The attitudes contained in the film have continued to haunt other archaeologists in more recent encounters with Tasmanian Aboriginal people.

Later efforts

The racial politics uncovered by *The Last Tasmanian* was a strong influence on the making of later documentaries. It was not particularly evident in the earlier documentaries, such as those that presented the origins of Australian Aborigines as interpreted by archaeologists and physical anthropologists.[38] Some of these films were well regarded by critics at the time.[39] Haydon's highly praised film *The Long Long Walkabout* would not receive the same recommendations today. It included no Aboriginal views and showed Professor Macintosh, from the University of Sydney's Department of Anatomy, patting a row of skulls on the cranium while describing his theories.[40] This scene is bizarrely paternalistic and would be considered offensive by most Aboriginal people. Nonetheless, the film itself is of anthropological and cultural interest.

The programmes made by Alan Thorne and Robert Raymond for the ABC TV series *Man on the Rim* offered a broader approach to questions about human origins and colonisation in the Pacific region.[41] They gave space to Aboriginal people to voice their opinions about the significance and treatment of Aboriginal remains. No indigenous people, however, were involved in the writing or production of the series. Aboriginal filmmaker Ricki Shields complained about this type of documentary as cultural appropriation: 'whites are endlessly making documentaries about us but they won't give us a role. It can be like body snatching all over again.'[42]

Far more specific than *Man on the Rim* was the excellent radio series *From Mungo to Makaratta,* produced by Kirsten Garrett for the ABC Science Unit. Compiled and broadcast in 1983, it dealt with issues concerning human remains and Aboriginal self-determination much better than almost any piece before or since. Garrett followed the progress of a project concerning the examination and reburial of skeletal remains at Robinvale on the Murray River by Sandra Bowdler. Bowdler was a consultant to the Victoria Archaeological Survey and was involved only at the request of the Robinvale Aboriginal community. The radio documentary features interviews with Aboriginal people as well as archaeologists. It sets the progress of the project against a discussion of the history of Australian archaeology and of continuing race politics. The series proceeds from the discoveries at Lake Mungo in 1969 to the 1983 push by Aboriginal people for land rights—the proposed treaty or Makaratta (as it was then known). Concerning the debate about skeletal remains, she notes that 'these are the rocks over which the storm-tossed ship "archaeology" must find a way'.[43]

More rocky shoals have loomed ahead as the skeletal remains debate was replaced by a dating controversy. The Jinmium site with its initial dates of around 120 000 BP excited not only archaeologists but the media, as we saw in Chapter 2. The media were allowed to run away with the story before the results had been fully checked.

The BBC *Horizon* series, which is still running thirty years after Haydon worked for it, followed up the issue. In 1998, it covered the Jinmium debate in a Haydonesque style. There was even a wailing harmonica as the background music to scenes around Lake Mungo, reminiscent of *The Long Long Walkabout*! Haydon's legacy can also be seen in some of the cheekier narration, such as 'it seems Java Man (*Homo erectus*) had played the field and had been very intimate with our (*Homo sapiens*) earliest ancestors'.[44] The documentary does present a wide range of archaeological dating techniques and theories in a logical and accessible way for the layperson. It is probably more technical in its approach than Haydon's work had been, but then archaeology has become more reliant on dating techniques and their rigorous application than in the 1970s.

It is hoped that further documentaries will continue raising controversial issues and continue 'romancing the stones' and bones in order to both entertain and inform audiences about Australian archaeology. There is no doubt that Tom Haydon's work has played a major role in bringing archaeological discoveries to the public and stimulating discussion about important issues. Future filmmakers with an interest in archaeology can learn a lot from both his successes and his failures.

5

Exposing First Government House

THE FATE OF the First Government House archaeological site has made it one of the most contentious archaeological sites in Australia. Situated in the centre of the largest of Australia's cities, the site had been subject to the pressures of redevelopment for many years. It was finally preserved from development in the mid-1980s. The community and the media were closely involved in the debate to save it. The site's archaeological excavation proved a convenient focus for debate, by preventing the issue from disappearing from the public eye. After the site's development was renegotiated, it was agreed that it should be presented to the public, either with a site museum or with low-key interpretation, such as signage on the site. First Government House archaeological site became the Museum of Sydney (on the site of First Government House) in November 1993, and the museum opened to the public 17 May 1995.

From residence to remains

First Government House was once a group of related buildings, which, having been completely demolished, became an archaeological site. The complex served as the residence and office of the first nine colonial governors. The building of First Government House commenced four months after the First Fleet arrived. From the beginning the building was viewed as integral to the establishment of colonial authority. Governor Phillip ceremoniously planted a foundation plaque between two dressed sandstone blocks on 15 May 1788, before the structure took shape. The first section of the house was designed and built by either James Bloodworth or Henry Brewer—historians are not certain which. As the Governor's residence in Sydney, it grew from being a relatively modest, two-storey house with a stairwell, to what public architect Mortimer Lewis described as 'an incongruous mass of buildings built in different periods'.[1]

In Governor Phillip's time, it was a place of contact between the newly arrived Europeans and the local Aboriginal people. Phillip returned to England in 1792 with two Sydney Aboriginal men, Bennelong and Yemmerrawannie, who had been visitors at First Government House. The house was also the site of the colony's first newspaper, the *Sydney Gazette*, which was printed in an outbuilding. After the first issue was produced 5 March 1803, and the paper continued to be printed on the premises for seven years. The printers used the typeface that was brought out by Phillip in 1788 at first and then it was replaced by a newer stock, which arrived in June 1804.

Governor Bligh was seized within the house on January 1808, during a much mythologised search by the New South Wales Corps. Later the house witnessed the relative peace and prosperity of Macquarie's governorship, and the first meeting of an appointed Legislative Council under Governor Brisbane in 1824.[2]

A brick drain constructed during Governor Macquarie's occupation of First Government House, Sydney, which was uncovered in 1983 and reburied in 1984.

Each governor made some extension or alteration to First Government House. But it was Mortimer Lewis, government architect, whose dislike of the building became the motivating force behind the Government House Committee Report, which recommended its removal so as to extend Macquarie and Phillip Streets. In 1845, Lewis drew up a final plan of the ground floor of the house just before it was demolished.[3] This plan has emerged as a significant historical document and was used in the later excavations and interpretation of the site. Lewis saw the house as unfashionable and unsuitable for the expanding colony. It was also inconveniently located and an obstacle to the new street plan being developed to give better access to Circular Quay. Few in the government or among the local community had qualms about getting rid of it.[4] Following the building's demolition, the site was occupied for a variety of purposes, which gave it the longest continuous historical archaeological sequence of any non-indigenous site in Australia.[5] The structures built over the original house site did not have deep foundations, so potential existed for the discovery of First Government House's structural remains lying intact underneath the twentieth-century car park, and sections of Bridge, Young and Phillip Streets.

To dig or not to dig

Archaeologists were not the first to find indications of the subterranean survival of First Government House. In 1899, workmen laying telephone lines in Bridge Street located foundation stones, the remains of some walls and the foundation copper plaque laid by Governor Phillip (now held by the Mitchell Library). Founding member of the Royal Australian Historical Society, James Houison, lived around the corner from the site in Phillip Street. He may have had some role in the society's decision to erect a small ceramic plaque on a sandstone plinth in 1917 to commemorate the site. This second plaque was the first public recognition of the historical significance of the site, and the monument marked its location up until the 1980s.[6]

Historical archaeological sites and remains received little acknowledgement in urban planning during the early 1980s. Australia had made advances towards preservation of its cultural heritage as a result of the creation of the Australian Heritage Commission, the Register of the National Estate and the endorsement by government authorities of the Burra Charter (see Appendix 1). The Hope Royal Commission into the National Estate, however, flagged historical archaeological sites as a category of cultural heritage requiring conservation action because they had not received much attention previously.[7] Helen Temple was at that time the archaeologist with

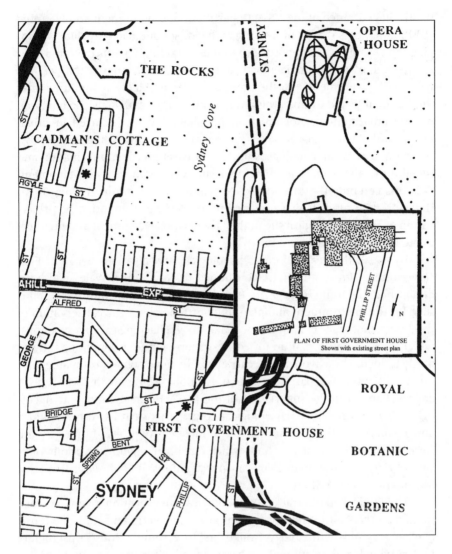

First Government House, Sydney. The inset shows an overlay of the house plan on the existing site. Adapted from Helen Proudfoot et al., Australia's First Government House, *p. 5.*

the Heritage Branch of the NSW Department of Environment and Planning (DEP). She notes that in promoting archaeology one had to be like 'a dripping tap [using] every opportunity to make the same points over and over again . . . don't forget archaeology . . . at every public seminar that we had with local government'.[8] At the time, however, much of the funding under the National Estate Grants Programme still went to managing the built and natural environment. Not much archaeological work occurred in urban areas until the *Heritage Act* was passed in 1977.[9] Accordingly, the most common brief for archaeologists until then was to recover information and remains by salvage excavation before a site was destroyed by development. This was certainly the case in the excavation of part of the Sydney Town Hall Burial Ground, which occurred in 1974.[10] Most importantly, preservation of an archaeological site in the face of city development and high real estate prices was almost unknown.

By 1982, the year before archaeological investigations began at First Government House, the Heritage Council of New South Wales had been established under the *Heritage Act*. It provided advice to the Minister responsible for the environment and planning portfolio about the conservation of the State's heritage. It had directed that six archaeological investigations, which produced information for conservation planning, should be fully or partly funded. These works were carried out by development companies and other government departments, such as Public Works, with the council's approval and with the supervision of the DEP's Heritage Branch archaeologist, Helen Temple.[11] Archaeological consultants such as Anne Bickford and Justin McCarthy did the work. The most costly project funded by the Heritage Council in that year (and which had been ongoing in various ways since 1979) was the archaeological investigations at Hyde Park Barracks, Macquarie Street, Sydney.

The Hyde Park Barracks archaeological investigation might be considered a precursor to the excavations at First Government House in terms of objectives and methodology. Unlike First Government House, the building had survived and continued to be occupied after changes in function. Between 1887 and 1980 it was used as an administrative centre for legal and other State government departments. The decision to retain Hyde Park Barracks was based on the ideas 'solicited from learned societies and community groups'.[12] Although this consultation was undertaken and the building was handed over to the Museum of Applied Arts and Sciences, demolition work commenced before a management plan for a museum had been developed. Site management or conservation plans are now considered essential for directing the type of heritage and conservation management appropriate for heritage places of high significance or any complexity. They were rare in the 1970s. Belatedly, a plan was developed for restoration of the barracks by a multidisciplinary team of archaeologists, historians, architects and museum curators.

In 1981, the National Trust had unsuccessfully challenged the building of a new hotel on the site of the Old Treasury Building, opposite First Government House. The latter was nothing more than a car park bounded on two sides by the Phillip and Bridge Street terrace houses, which until that stage had escaped multi-storey development. The State government called for development proposals for the site, announcing the winning tender in September 1982. This tender was a proposal for a multi-storey hotel by a consortium of the Hong Kong Land Corporation and the NSW State Superannuation Board.[13]

The DEP notified its Heritage Branch architects that the site was scheduled for development before the announcement of the successful tender. One of the architects sent Helen Temple a memo saying, 'This site is going to be developed, I understand there is a plaque on the corner. Do you believe the site has any significance?'[14] At this time, no archaeological priority plan existed for the central business district which could be used to predict the possibility of potential sub-surface remains. If it had not been for the Royal Australian Historical Society plaque, the memo from the Heritage Branch architect and Temple's persistence, no investigations would have been mounted prior to development.

An Archaeological Advisory Panel had been established in 1978 to guide the Heritage Council in managing historical archaeological sites. At the time, only half a dozen historical archaeologists worked in New South Wales, and the DEP employed only one archaeologist. The Panel provided additional advice to the Heritage Council as it still does today.[15] In 1982–83, the panel comprised Anne Bickford (consultant); Judy Birmingham (Department of Archaeology; University of Sydney); Mike Pearson; Helen Temple; John Wade (Museum of Applied Arts and Sciences), Peter White (Department of Anthropology, University of Sydney) and the chair was Sharon Sullivan (Aboriginal and Historic Relics Unit, National Parks and Wildlife Service).[16] As with the early days in any area of expertise when the number of professionals is small, people end up wearing more than one hat. These names would appear in several instances in the investigation and assessment of the site, besides their role on the Panel. Anne Bickford, for instance, directed the excavation.

The National Trust was not involved in consultations before the beginning of works on the site. During the consultations regarding the development of the Old Treasury Building into the Inter-Continental Hotel, it suggested to the State government that the hotel developers be given the site of First Government House as an alternative. The Trust did not show concern in 1982 that foundations and other cultural material might still remain intact beneath the car park there. However, in fairness to the Trust, there were doubts about the integrity of the site:

- There was reason to believe that the buildings might not be located square on the car park area (as it turned out, part of them lies under Phillip and Bridge Streets). It was known from historical records that the remains had obstructed the construction and continuation of Phillip and Bridge Streets.
- This implied that most of site could have already been destroyed by street construction.
- There was also a tradition going back some time that the 'First' Government House was actually an old cottage in George Street, The Rocks (despite the discovery of the foundation plaque in 1899).[17]

Expectations embodied in the objectives of the archaeological investigation created a dilemma for interpreting the archaeology of the site, which was to pursue the consultant archaeologists during the next eight years. The objective of all investigations on the site was for the archaeologists to 'detect the presence or absence of the buildings and they were not to excavate entire living areas'.[18] Not once during the digging were archaeologists permitted by the Archaeological Advisory Panel or the DEP to excavate a whole room of the First Government House complex.[19] The information gained from excavating a room or a series of rooms would have been helpful for better archaeological interpretation of the site as a whole. The archaeologists were instructed to define the location of foundations of the 'great artefact that was First Government House and assess how much remained below the surface and in the way of the proposed development'.[20] The investigation was neither for research nor for salvage. It provided information for planning and negotiating the development, but limited the amount of information that could be extracted from the stratigraphic relationship of structural remains and artefacts.[21] Such information would have been important for telling the story of the site to the public later. It was, however, possible to gain some impression of the spatial layout of First Government House structural remains.[22] For this purpose the analyst could use a combination of Lewis' plan and other historical documents in conjunction with the archaeological plans of remains. The disturbed nature of some of the site was also a problem for detailed artefact analysis, because much of the artefactual material from First Government House phase had been reduced to fragments by its demolition and other site formation factors.[23] For these reasons, whole sections of the site were left unexcavated and unavailable for analysis and interpretation. The fragmentary information derived from the excavation was enough to satisfy the Panel regarding the site's significance and integrity, but made it difficult for archaeologists to bring the site to life for the public after the excavation work was completed.

First Government House becomes a public issue

Several incidents and turning points in the development of the debate over the preservation and management of the site are important to acknowledge.[24] Between 1983 and 1984 archaeological discoveries made in the first three seasons included the foundations, the printing press in the outbuildings and the Australian Club plates, all of which were of interest to the mass media and the public.

Some key dates are:

- August 1983: Historians present a petition to State parliament.
- 10 August: Premier Neville Wran visits the site.
- 17 August: The Friends of First Government House is formed at a
- rally near the site.
- 5 October: Sydney City Council refuses planning permit to allow site development.
- 13 October: Private developers back out of the contract with the Government and Wran announces a competition for a design proposal to allow development and conserve remains.
- November: Australian Archaeological Association Statement of Significance released (see Appendix 2).
- February 1984: Government agrees to site backfilling, while a design is being found.
- 1987: Conservation plan is adopted by DEP and developers with the airspace idea/museum idea agreed.
- 1987–90: New developers employ project managers who create a few difficulties for site archaeologists—DEP can only offer advice.
- 20 November 1993: First Government House Site Museum is renamed 'Museum of Sydney (on the site of First Government House)'.

The first excavations commenced in February 1983 when the historical investigation was nearly complete. The dig was planned to run for several weeks, but after only five days sandstone foundations of the back wall of the 1788 house were discovered. The unearthing of these tangible remains of First Government House was crucial to the continuation of the archaeological investigations and the debate to preserve the site.[25] On the basis of this evidence a second season was initiated.

A call for volunteers to excavate was made in June 1983. It began that month and was only expected to take three months. A team of twenty-five excavators with six professional archaeologists as supervisors continued the work begun in the previous preliminary season.[26] Around them the debate raged concerning the site's future. As the season progressed, more evidence of First Government House was uncovered and public opinion increasingly supported its preservation. More finds of high note were made—including some print from the *Sydney Gazette* in the remains of one of the outbuildings.[27] Privies were also discovered which contained fragments of bones, ceramics and glass dumped while in use and after when they were filled in with rubbish.[28] These finds contributed to the understanding of the style and standard of living of the occupants. These discoveries increased the significance of the site's role in the history of early Sydney for the heritage community.

A petition organised by public historian Alan Atkinson and the 1838 Bicentennial History Collective may have had some impact on the Premier's Department and helped to promote the site in the debate. The petition had 200 or so signatures from all the university history departments in Australia.[29] Academics at this time had mobilised over environmental issues, as shown by the full-page advertisement put in the *Australian* during the campaign to oppose the dam on the Franklin River. Now they had mobilised over on an issue of urban heritage.

The site was in the limelight when Premier Neville Wran visited it in early August. The visit enabled the media to go to the excavation and talk to the archaeologists without having to go through the DEP. The debate was also taken further forward by community organisations. One of the main supporters of the site, the Bloodworth Association,[30] held a public rally in Macquarie Place near the site on 14 August 1983. From it sprang a new group, 'Friends of First Government House'. After the August rally, the Friends undertook major publicity and lobbied for the site's preservation.

Then the Sydney City Council refused the developer's planning development application for the site, allowing the site's supporters a brief respite. The City Council had tried deferring judgement on the application several times in the months leading up to the decision, and at least one alderman attacked the State government over the site.[31] The City Council inspected the site on 20 September. It finally rejected the development plan because the developers were unwilling to change the design. The design was at fault as extra floor space was evident at the expense of the Council's parking requirements. A spokesperson from the Friends observed to the press, 'historical significance of the site did not seem to have been a major consideration'.[32] Historical and social significance may not have been a major factor in the City Council's decision, but it probably had some covert influence. The City Council suffered several delays arriving at a decision through political factional disagreements.[33]

The City Council's rejection of the development application allowed the private developer, Hong Kong Land Corporation, to retire gracefully from its government contract. The company had been in financial difficulty overseas because of losses on deferred property payments.[34] Premier Wran released them from their obligations under the contract signed in 1982 with the government developer, the State Superannuation Board. This release allowed Wran to follow his political instincts and announce a compromise that he hoped would settle the site's future. On the same day the contract was broken, he announced a national competition for a development design 'to ensure the conservation and protection of the 1788 remains while still allowing development'.[35]

In November 1983, as the second season of excavation was nearing its end, a group of heritage professionals, including Anne Bickford the dig director, drafted a formal statement of cultural significance for the site, based on the Burra Charter (see Appendices). A formal statement like this had not appeared previously in the debate and they released it through the Australian Archaeological Association (AAA). The statement changed the character of the public debate with its structured argument concerning the site's significance and future. Many of those interviewed saw it as an

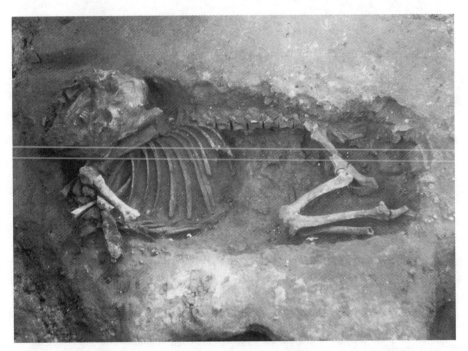

Goat skeleton discovered near the corner of Bridge and Phillips Streets, First Government House. A goat was kept on site at the turn of the century to keep the grass down.

excellent example of its type at a time when well-constructed statements of significance were still rare.[36] Essentially, it prevented the debate from being side-tracked by arguments about whether the site was significant or not. It made the point clearly, and from then on all parties had to deal with the high cultural significance of the site as a fact.

A third stage of excavation and works occurred on the site between March and June 1984. Further remains of outbuildings were identified, and the decision was made to carefully backfill the existing trenches before the end of the season. As the future management of the site was still unresolved and no conservation plan existed, the Premier's Department accepted the Heritage Council's advice that the foundations should be protected until the matter was settled.[37] Leaving the trenches open for an indefinite time without adequate conservation measures would have exposed them to damage from water seepage and other environmental factors.[38] The trenches were treated chemically and carefully packed with shade cloth and plastic under the direction of a conservator. The trenches were then bolstered with sandbags and buried in sand, and the main area of the site was retarred to resemble the car park it had been prior to excavation. Thus it remained

Conservator Janet Begg (left) and site supervisor Shanda Kelly at First Government House carry out conservation work during the third excavation season, 1984. A fungicide was sprayed to prevent the growth of mould on plastic sandbags used to line the pits before reburying them.

Many people who visit the Museum of Sydney are not aware of the elaborate array of sandbags, shade cloth and sand fill that lies below their feet, keeping the unexposed remains of First Government House from harm.

until the establishment of the museum allowed several of the trenches to be reopened for public display. The rest are still conserved beneath the pavement and museum courtyard in their wrappings, sandbags and sand. This operation was the first of its type in Australia.[39]

In January 1985, Premier Wran announced that the production of a conservation plan would precede the architectural design competition. He also proclaimed that a museum would be built on the site and that some of the foundations would be publicly displayed under glass. Helen Temple described the decision to preserve the site *in situ* as 'not only an historic one but a triumph for colonial archaeology, which had never achieved great respectability in Australia'.[40] Finally, a conservation plan was prepared during 1985 by architects Conybeare, Morrison and Partners, in conjunction with Anne Bickford and several specialists from the site. Its main findings in relation to future options for the site were that remains of First Government House should be conserved *in situ* and that a commemorative display and interpretative facility of high quality should be constructed without disturbing the remains.[41]

The new Minister for Environment and Planning, Bob Carr, was cautious regarding development on the site. Two proposals, one for allowing unrestricted development and one for retaining the foundations of First Government House within the development, had been made to the government. Carr stated that he felt that the situation was still delicate: 'no other country can point to stones and say these are the remains of the first permanent building on our soil. So it is our very genesis.'[42]

Whether or not being able to point to the first foundations of the first permanent building is important will be dealt with later. What is significant is that Carr was not eager to hurry the situation in order to make the site presentable in time for the Bicentennial celebrations. Instead, a further season of excavations was ordered for Macquarie Place in March 1987, across from the original site excavation. These test excavations located the wall of the south outbuildings of First Government House, and also a drain and a privy sump.[43]

The government finally found a developer and a strategy to fulfil its hopes for the site in August 1987. Sid Londish of Comrealty Pty Ltd bought into the site development.[44] He and the government developer, the State Superannuation Board, organised a deal with the DEP and the City Council to allow him to buy extra airspace over the building site furthest from the foundations of First Government House. The transfer of airspace rights has been used as an incentive for preserving heritage places in New York and some other cities around the world. By gaining permission to build a much taller, 64-storey tower, the developers were satisfied (and the State government made $25.2 million). This decision was positive: it allowed the site to survive and the majority of the funds from the sale could be put towards the establishment of a museum on part of the site where it would not disturb significant remains. The development became known as the Governor Phillip Tower.

The conservation plan suggested the Historic Houses Trust of New South Wales, a quasi-government authority established to restore and manage historic places, as a possible administrator of the site museum.[45] They were appointed managers later in 1989, despite the initial hesitation of the director, Peter Watt; he was not sure how managing the site would fit with the Trust's charter to conserve standing buildings.[46] The Trust manages a foundation fund that comprises government funds and donations from individual and corporate sponsors. The foundation was originally promised $15 million of the money from the Governor Phillip Tower to build the museum and a $5 million endowment from Sydney City Council and the State government.[47] The Trust also engaged the designers of the Governor Phillip Tower, Denton Corker Marshall, to create a design for the site museum. The final cost of the museum was $24 million, with construction comprising $20.8 million and a setting-up fee of $3.2 million to cover staff, interiors and displays. The Historic Houses Trust Foundation had publicly promoted an appeal for further private sponsorship to defray the cost of setting up the museum. The sponsors included Australian Glass Ltd, Heidelberg Press, *Vogue* and *Time Magazine*. News Limited also paid $500 000 to the museum over a five-year period for education programmes from 1995.[48]

A fifth and final season of archaeological work was commissioned as part of the Governor Phillip Tower development. In June 1990, the excavation team uncovered the original guardhouse for First Government House. This was an extremely stressful season; it was closely supervised by the developer's project manager, who was concerned that the work be completed as cheaply and quickly as possible. This attitude is not unusual, and similar examples are still to be found in construction and engineering firms with little interest in, or understanding of, archaeology. Another difficulty for the archaeologists involved was the pressure from the Archaeological Advisory Panel to complete a book on earlier work,[49] which would be published by the DEP.[50]

The denouement occurred when the Historic Houses Trust and the State government named the museum and announced its proposed direction. In August 1993 the Trust had received the results of a market research report. The Trust and the government agreed that the new museum needed to have broader appeal than that evoked by the archaeology of the site, despite its significance to the site's iconic status. Hence it became the Museum of Sydney (on the site of First Government House) with a focus on both historical and archaeological themes associated with the development of Sydney as a whole, rather than a specialist museum interpreting First Government House and its archaeological evidence. The Friends of First Government House objected to the Minister for the Arts, Peter Collins, but to no avail. The new name of the museum was announced by the Minister on 19 November 1993.[51]

Archaeology and the 'good fight'

Archaeological arguments to protect the site and interpret it had an indirect rather than direct impact on the nature of the site's future. Organisations such as the AAA, ICOMOS, and the Australian Association of Consulting Archaeologists Inc. all made statements at various times about the archaeological significance of the site. The main contribution to the debate by AAA was the statement of cultural significance produced by archaeologists and other heritage professionals concerned about the site's conservation.

ICOMOS did as much as it was able regarding the site, but did not speak to the media. Laila Haglund, the president of the consulting archaeologists' association, was interviewed once about the site, describing it as the 'most important historical and archaeological site in Australia'. She also noted the lack of a conservation order to protect it.[52] Two Canberra archaeologists, Professors John Mulvaney and Isabel McBryde, were able to play a larger part on their own and working through the Australian Heritage Commission.

Anne Bickford saw John Mulvaney's activism as significant in the debate and as having a big impact on the Premier's Department. She later observed that 'they couldn't dismiss him, and he was a very powerful academic'.[53] He wrote the department several well-argued letters, calling firstly for adequate time to study the site, and then for the government to preserve it and present it as part of the Bicentennial celebrations in 1988.[54]

The debate was most visible in the media after bureaucrats or politicians had visited the site or had made a major announcement concerning its future. Whether the sight of tangible remains made any difference to them is an intriguing question. Unlike many excavations overseas, which allowed for open excavation, First Government House was exposed in trenches, or sometimes squares, in accordance with the directives of the Archaeological Advisory Panel. A major section of the foundations (including much of the 1788 building) was not revealed in the investigation; it probably still lies under Bridge Street. The nature of the remains identified by the excavation also made it difficult as they could be linked to many different phases of expansion and only small parts of the whole complex were exposed by the excavation. It might be argued that it was not easy for a non-archaeologist to gain a quick impression of First Government House from these features. It is no wonder Bob Carr was talking about 'pointing to stones' in media interviews;[55] he could not point to the entire remains of walls, rooms or outbuildings of the first permanent building, as its spatial layout could only be glimpsed in fragments with much flashing of historical documents for explanation.

The role of the media in the debate was to give the site investigation public exposure. The discovery of the foundations was not revealed publicly to the media until June 1983, when Helen Temple and her supervisor, Lorraine Cairnes, were interviewed by Joseph Glascott, the environment writer for the *Sydney Morning Herald*.[56] This information was released nearly four months after the first evidence of the foundations had been found through excavation.[57] Other than letters to the editor from concerned citizens, there was little media attention prior to Glascott's article and certainly nothing like what was to come. The most extensive coverage and publicity coincided with the start of the second excavation season in June 1983, and continued through to Premier Wran's decision to conserve the remains and to allow development in October. Nearly one hundred articles, including magazine features and letters to the editor, were published during this time. Television coverage was also extensive.[58]

At the beginning of this period of mass media interest in July 1983, journalists thought that they were being excluded from reporting on the site because timber hoardings shielded it from view.[59] Helen Temple believes that the hoardings attracted the media instead: 'The site investigation was all supposed to be done in secret behind these high hoardings . . . the site got publicity it would probably not have had if the hoardings had not been there'.[60]

Several journalists ran stories claiming that the archaeologists were being 'gagged' by the Premier's Department,[61] which immediately issued a directive to the DEP and the site archaeologists banning all media contact. Anne Bickford remembers that a 'big truck from one of the television stations parked on the footpath and the cameraman stood on the roof and filmed over the wall'.[62] With one newspaper running the headline 'Big Dig is Veiled in Secrecy'[63] and television coverage, the DEP convinced the Premier's Department that the ban was counter-productive.

A new system was then instituted with the DEP as the initial media contact. Bickford could not discuss the site's past with the media until a request for an interview had been processed by the DEP. Andrew Andersons, one of the Heritage Branch's architects, was the only person authorised to discuss the 'present and future of the site'.[64] Bickford believes the new system was instituted because the government wanted to consider a range of options. Helen Temple has argued that it was done to standardise views about the management of the site.[65] Restrictions on media access to the archaeologists did not always work in practice. Joseph Glascott followed the story from the first announcement of the development until he left the *Sydney Morning Herald* in 1988. In that time he broke the story, as we have seen, and wrote nearly thirty articles on the site and its progress. Glascott always dealt directly with the archaeologists, although he imagined that the DEP would have preferred him to work through its spokesperson. He recalls that during 1983 'the archaeologists were under a great deal of pressure to do the work and make the site free for development'. He personally wanted to 'point out how important this area was and it wasn't a site that should be hurried and left half explored. It should, on the contrary, be given plenty or ample time to have a complete dig so that the importance of the site was given priority over any development.'[66] His view probably coincided with the personal views of many archaeologists of the time. The initial three months of the second season was extended beyond that to allow more assessment.

Protest groups and concerned individuals made better and more frequent use of the media than archaeological professionals or professional organisations did. A wide range of community groups protested against development on the site at various stages of the public debate. These groups ranged from the (self-interested) Phillip Street Terrace squatters[67] to the Australia Club (because the excavation uncovered remains of an early coffee service with the club's pot mark on it). Perhaps the club, as a Sydney establishment body, had influence with the government, as some believed, and all these things together had a lot of impact. Neither could the government ignore left-wingers such as Edna Ryan. Anne Bickford heard that 'Neville Wran responded to her (Ryan's) letters personally because she [had been] a comrade and supporter of the Labor Party for many years'.[68]

Judy Birmingham, who was a member of the Archaeological Advisory Panel at the time, believes that the most conscientious protesters were 'that very strong older guard of very dedicated women, particularly women who'd fought for the recognition of Australian history'.[69] They included Nell Sansom (a Bloodworth descendant), Mary Jane Lawrie, and heritage consultants Meredith Walker and Helen Proudfoot. They undertook months of unpaid work—distributing leaflets, writing to the media, lobbying the government, and organising rallies and fund-raising functions. When the Friends of First Government House formed in August 1983, all four women appeared on the Action Committee. Nell Sansom had the highest media profile; she was playfully dubbed 'Nell the Giant-Killer' by one journalist because of her determination to take on the government.[70] The costumed rallies in front of State Parliament and the site were particularly popular with the media because they offered good photo opportunities, as the Friends were well aware.

Another means of spreading information about the site outside the media was through the Friends' Foundation Day public lectures. The 196th anniversary of the day Governor Phillip laid the copper foundation plate, 15 May 1984, became the date of the first annual Foundation Day lecture. It was delivered by Professor John Mulvaney and published through the Australian Heritage Commission.[71] The Friends even sent a copy to the Queen. Her secretary replied on her behalf that 'Her Majesty was much interested and delighted to think that careful consideration had been given to the preservation of the site'.[72]

Whether Her Majesty read it or not is hard to know, although the State Governor showed interest in the site at the launching of the book *Australia's First Government House*.[73] The governor could not comment during the height of the debate for political reasons.[74] A lecture by Isabel McBryde on Aboriginal experiences at First Government House was published in an expanded form as a book by the Friends and the DEP.[75] The Foundation Day lectures still continue on an annual basis.

Joseph Glascott, who wrote many of the newspaper articles on First Government House, regards Anne Bickford as extremely skilled at communicating archaeological information about the site, recognising she was under pressure to be discreet.[76] The media was drawn to write stories about Bickford herself because they saw her as a dramatic departure from the archaeological stereotype discussed in Chapter 1. Two articles took a personal interest in her under the headlines 'Anne Digs her Job' (*Daily Mirror*) and 'Bottoms up and Mud in her Eye' (*Australian*).[77] The former is one of Bickford's favourite articles from that period.

> They took a photo of me trying to look sexy standing in this drain ... The women's [television] programmes, they were always interested in the fact that I seemed to be so young ... [and] that I was in a rockabilly band ... It seemed anomalous to them that I would be involved in popular culture, very involved in popular culture, and also that I would be an archaeologist.[78]

Significant in the debate was the lack of promotion of the pro-development arguments. The first private developer, Hong Kong Land Corporation, was based overseas and more or less left it to the State government to clear the way for the development.[79] The private developer's concerns regarding a loss of money from delays while investigations continued was reported only once in connection with its other financial difficulties.[80] The only public attack against preserving the site was made at this time in a letter to the *Sydney Morning Herald*. The correspondent, Kane Savage, stated that he was anti-convict, pro-development and pro-Aboriginal. He argued that 'the original inhabitants of this country were brown. Bricks and mortar cannot conjure up dreamings of the past.'[81] Helen Proudfoot answered the letter in strong terms and stated that she did not believe he was writing from an Aboriginal viewpoint, just a viewpoint of 'abysmal ignorance'.[82]

The impact of the First Government House debate on the later excavation of other sites in the Sydney central business district is hard to measure. Some have argued that it gave archaeology the image of being expensive, time-consuming, and ultimately non-productive. The project manager's attitude to archaeologists during the final season of work in 1990 indicates that this may have been her view as well.

The main change to urban redevelopment observable since 1983 is that the potential need for archaeological work is usually made known to developers by government agencies much earlier in the planning process. By allowing more lead-time in the early planning stages, developers are less likely to incur heavy costs or delays should precious archaeological remains be revealed. The general reaction at all levels, when such remains are revealed late in the planning process and a call is made for preservation, has not necessarily changed since First Government House. The discovery of a fragment of convict road underneath the grounds of the Sydney Conservatorium in 1998 is a case in point. Again, this was a development that the State government kept extremely quiet until the archaeology started making headlines.[83] Some have argued that the archaeology was used as a scapegoat for other problems that required some face-saving, but this is difficult to ascertain. Even so it is hoped that this incident would encourage heritage managers to refine existing predictive models for identifying areas of archaeological sensitivity where such remains may be expected. Also, that the funds for this important proactive research and testing prior to development will be made available by the government and developers much earlier in the process. This is the only way that such surprises can be minimised.

Whether salvage could have produced more information about First Government House is an interesting question. Some still feel that salvage or monitoring is not likely to produce much of use to anybody. Others feel that, as new projects are occurring that will deal extensively with analysing

Not all the structural features of an archaeological site are tangible remains. Here some soil has been excavated to reveal the negative impressions of post holes belonging to the stables in one corner of the First Government House site, 1984.

existing collections of excavated artefacts from The Rocks and the rest of Sydney, such work was worthwhile.[84] Results of this analysis in a more publicly accessible form, however, may be obtained by synthesising it all into a neighbourhood-type analysis like that published by Grace Karskens for the Cumberland–Gloucester Street site excavations in The Rocks.[85]

First Government House—symbolic and social significance

The symbolic significance of First Government House was obvious to those involved with the site from the beginning. Bickford argues that 'the primary importance of the site is its symbolic significance, rather than its value as a source of information for historians and archaeologists'.[86] She suggests that the physical remains are valuable because they are:

- still *in situ* (in place)
- evocative of the 'infant colony, of the government, of the power, in that very first year of settlement'
- made by convict labourers (newly arrived)
- able to trigger the public imagination
- able to help people 'move spiritually closer to the very foundations of our society'.[87]

These criteria were referred to when the site's proponents enlisted the ideals of the Burra Charter in the debate.[88] Relevant to the site's symbolic significance was the charter's basic principle: that the cultural significance of a place is embodied in its fabric. Alteration of this fabric would alter the nature of this significance. The discovery of the structural remains of First Government House still in place was important for supporting the argument that its symbolic significance was influenced by its authenticity. The focus on the original fabric in the definition of its symbolic significance also explains why the idea of building a replica on the site, as suggested by some members of the community, was never taken seriously by heritage professionals, particularly those who advised the government.

Symbolic significance was promoted and argued in government documents, reports, newspaper articles and even wall posters. In a seminar paper on First Government House, McBryde recalls an eye-catching poster affixed to the site hoardings by the Bloodworth Association, which stated 'Government Was Born Here'.[89] Aspects of early settlement history seemed to come alive for some members of the public and the remains acted as both a focus and a trigger for their imagination.[90] The site was seen also as a spiritual prop in the face of seemingly uncontrollable change. Proudfoot argued in response to pro-development sentiments at the height of the debate that 'we as a nation desperately need to keep the powerful symbol of our foundations that these first Government House footings represent ... these bricks and mortar can conjure up the dreamings'.[91] Later, Premier Wran maintained that the winning design for the site 'will provide a challenge to the skills of architects and engineers to produce a memorial to the past and a symbol of faith in the future'.[92] Wran apparently did not at the time see the footings as adequately speaking for themselves without extensive architectural assistance.

Other statements concerning the symbolism of the site have come from the Museum of Sydney. When some of the footings were uncovered for display in the museum plaza, Peter Tonkin, one of the archaeological curators, stated to the media: 'these are the first signs of human settlement in Australia [*sic*] ... the whole site is a symbol of 1788 of contact between two cultures, and the museum will be exploring all the meanings associated with that'.[93] In his enthusiasm to include Aboriginal social significance more neatly in the equation, he accidentally excluded Aboriginal pre-contact history. The museum, however, has always strongly emphasised Aboriginal history and its social significance for the Sydney area in its displays. It adds a perspective, which was first promoted by McBryde in her public lecture organised by the Friends and later in a book on the Aboriginal presence in Sydney and at First Government House.[94]

More recently, the Museum of Sydney web site describes the museum as being built 'not as an imperial mausoleum but as a meeting place ... [which] clears a post-colonial space where an array of Sydney voices, of past and present, may speak and converse.[95] None of this is directly relevant to the preservation or interpretation of First Government House; in fact, it is probably the antithesis of the symbolism identified earlier by the AAA's Statement of Cultural Significance.

For heritage professionals, the symbolism was closely related to its cultural significance. Sharon Sullivan, chair of the Archaeology Advisory Panel, stressed in 1984 that 'though the "method" of revealing the site's significance has been archaeological, its primary significance is historical and public. Clearly any plan for the future of the site must consider all aspects, including those, which will be revealed by further research.'[96] She pointed out that the site has always been particularly significant to descendants of those 'early settlers and convicts associated with its buildings and history'.[97] This aspect of the site's significance would become less important later to site managers when its significance was reassessed by the curatorial staff at the Museum of Sydney.

A government bureaucrat at the time of the debate over First Government House, John Whitehouse, noted that the government had finally accepted the significance of the site in 1984. Premier Wran had told State Parliament: 'The discoveries so far are of clear historic, cultural and national significance, representing in a tangible form the literal foundations of modern Sydney and modern Australia in a way that is probably unique in any city or nation in the world'.[98] But does First Government House have national or world significance, particularly in comparison with other early sites, such as Port Arthur as a colonial convict site? In the heat of the debate concerning its future, most proponents for its preservation considered that it did. The Franklin River was probably higher in the public consciousness at the time and had significantly more national coverage.[99] Can a site or place be of world symbolic or social significance if only a small percentage of the population or certain ethnic and community groups care about it? Fortunately or not, national and world significance is not judged on public interest. So to whom is First Government House of high symbolic significance? Possibly to the heritage professionals, urban planners, informed members of the public and such people who view themselves as custodians of Australian heritage for future generations. The Australian Heritage Commission defines cultural significance as 'its aesthetic, historic, scientific or social significance, or any other special value, for future generations as well as the present community'.[1] The mention of future generations in this definition recognises that researchers' and society's needs may change.[2]

It could be argued that these needs did change in the1990s. Recent debates about deaths in custody, native title, repatriation of human remains and the Stolen Generations have challenged and expanded many people's understanding of indigenous and non-indigenous race relations. While much is still being produced and consumed in the catch-up mode for non-indigenous Australians, many domestic and international visitors cannot be expected to know the historical background to colonial dispossession as thoroughly as indigenous people and certain heritage professionals. One further question that might be asked: Is it important for a post-colonial nation to be able to point to the foundations of its first permanent building? If it is accepted that Australia is moving on a continuum towards post-colonialism (many people already aspire to this and the formation of a republic), does this alter the symbolic significance of First Government House? Returning to Bickford's criteria[3] listed above, it might be argued that some ambivalence could be generated unless the evocation of the 'infant colony, of the government, of the power, in that very first year of settlement' is conducted along post-colonial lines. There may also be a problem with helping people 'move spiritually closer to the very foundations of our society'.[4] Indigenous people, post-colonialists and recent immigrants may not be moved spiritually in the sense that protesters were in 1983. It may eventuate that the symbolic significance of First Government

House is in the process of alteration as historical reinterpretation occurs, and this process will continue into the future.[5]

Small areas of the foundations of First Government House are visible beneath glass in the lobby of the Museum of Sydney and in the plaza outside. Some interpretation accompanies them, but visitors are expected to extract contextual information from the museum displays. These displays are hailed by the museum's management as important for helping the visitor enter 'the material, imaginary and remembered worlds of Sydney'.[6] An alternative view is that they do little to highlight First Government House or its remains and offer limited interpretation for those seeking more accessible narratives of the past.[7] I recommend that you visit the museum yourself, preferably with a cross-section of friends and family, and see whether its approach works. If you need to buy a handbook explaining its philosophy and displays from the bookshop downstairs, then maybe it has failed.

The Museum of Sydney in its current manifestation could not possibly have appeared in anyone's vision of the site's future back in the embattled days of 1983, even though John Mulvaney had raised the option of a site museum as early as that time, in the media and in letters to the Premier's Department.[8] The exact type of museum had not been pictured clearly by him or any of the other heritage professionals involved with the site at the time. The more conservative supporters of the site have been the most surprised by developments. Multiculturalism, republicanism and other late-twentieth-century socio-political perspectives pushed the museum project to take its current form.[9] Social change has caught up with museology and historical archaeology, as it has with pre-contact archaeology in Australia.

The museum, as a public asset, has the financial security of flexible, recurrent State funding assessed on a triennial basis, which may be reduced but will never be removed. It is also attracting a growing amount of private sponsorship administered through the Historic Houses Trust Foundation. The Museum of Sydney's annual budget for running costs is therefore not entirely reliant on gate fees or government grants for core funding, as is the case for many other heritage attractions. It is therefore free to innovate and try experiments on museum visitors as few other Australian museums can.

The input into the museum from the site's archaeological excavations has been disappointing so far, though this may soon change. No comprehensive technical report of them exists; even if one did, only archaeological interpretation created out of extremely recent (or even future) research questions or interpretative frameworks would suit the current post-modern curatorial policy of the Museum of Sydney. The lack of integration of archaeological information in the museum's display may be redressed, as further work is being conducted by archaeologists and others on Sydney's excavated artefact collections. Three major collections of artefacts excavated from the Sydney sites of Paddy's Market, Lilyvale and Cumberland–Gloucester Street will be examined along with First Government House as part of a jointly funded government and private sector project that will gradually provide information for museum displays and other media.[10]

The museum's significant budget and additional sponsorship will allow it to thrive, and like most museums it will no doubt evolve beyond the original vision of those who set it up—the Historic Houses Trust, the State government and the museum curators they appointed. While museums always experience some inertia in 'reinventing themselves' as Karskens maintains, there is hope that the potential of the archaeological collections they hold will be demonstrated and new insights found.[11] As for the remains of the First Government House archaeological site, after all the controversy and exposure, readers are advised to visit the Museum of Sydney and see for themselves whether these remains still evoke the past and 'trigger the imagination'.

6

The battle for Southwest Tasmania

THE FIGHT TO save the Franklin River and the archaeological sites in Tasmania's Southwest (1980–83) was the most controversial and widely publicised debate in which archaeology has had a stake in Australia. Not only did archaeological evidence receive national and international coverage, but it was crucial to the case put for World Heritage inscription and strongly influenced the final High Court decision. It is also significant that no professional archaeologists broke ranks and worked directly for the Tasmanian Hydro-Electric Commission during the assessment process or aided it in any way. The discipline was still at a size where such a position could easily be maintained and the importance of the finds for research overrode any other considerations.

In the late 1970s the Hydro-Electric Commission (known as the Hydro) proposed further developments in Tasmania. The dam planned for the Franklin and Lower Gordon River catchment area would destroy any archaeological sites in that area during construction and the subsequent flooding. Vandalism was also a risk, through increased visitor access for boating and fishing to remaining sites on the waterline.[1]

It was not compulsory for Tasmanian developers to conduct environmental impact assessments before major development in the early 1980s, but in this case one was undertaken. However, the research for it was minimal. Angela Lister[2] first raised concerns in May 1980 about the archaeological section of the Hydro's environmental impact statement on the proposed dam. She wrote in protest on behalf of the Tasmanian Archaeological Society, which is now unfortunately defunct. The letter was sent to the State government and to archaeologists Rhys Jones and John Mulvaney in Canberra.[3] Don Ranson, State archaeologist with the Tasmanian National Parks and Wildlife Service (TASNPWS), also contacted colleagues in Canberra.

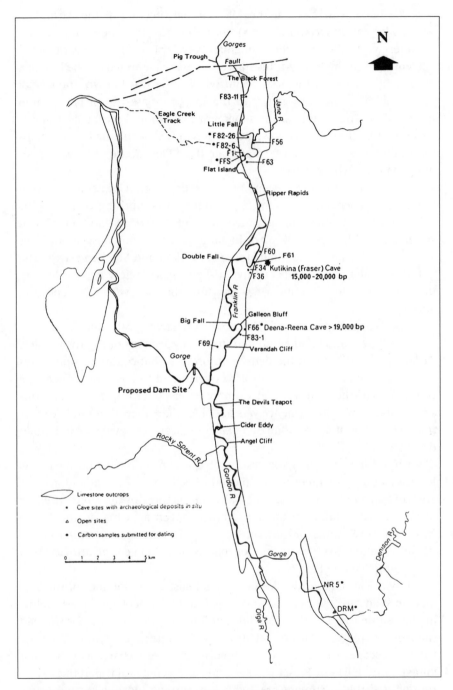

Proposed Franklin Dam Development showing archaeological sites. Adapted from R. Jones et al., 'The Australian National University–Tasmanian National Parks and Wildlife Service Archaeological Expedition to the Franklin River', 1983, p. 62.

The issue was raised at the May annual meeting of the Australian Archaeological Association (AAA) in Canberra. The president, Sandra Bowdler, wrote a letter to the Tasmanian Premier Doug Lowe regarding the inadequacies in the EIS.[4] At this stage, they were identified as: the lack of a ground site survey of the area, about which little was known; the lack of consideration of historic sites; and the inappropriate use of background information. The writers of the statement had ignored archaeological discoveries at Beginners Luck Cave in the previous year that had implications for finding sites of a similar type and age (Late Pleistocene or Late Ice Age) in the dam's catchment area.[5]

Over the next three years, four archaeological expeditions were mounted independently into the catchment area, comprising archaeologists from the Australian National University and TASNPWS, and Tasmanian speleologists. The first took place in January 1981 and consisted of Rhys Jones, Don Ranson, Greg Middleton, Brian Blain and Stephen Harris. The last three members had been involved in speleological expeditions up the river between 1974 and 1979 sponsored by the Sydney Speleological Society.

The Australian National University archaeological expedition used TASNPWS personnel and equipment to survey sections of the river valley. Despite poor visibility in the dense rainforest, a chance find of stone artefacts in soil clinging to the roots of an overturned tree was made near the confluence of the Denison and Gordon Rivers (see Map 5). It was considered likely that this evidence was not older than a few thousand years. A trial excavation of a limestone cave failed to locate any evidence of human occupation.[6]

Rhys Jones reported the results of the expedition to the media, as he was the only member not employed directly by a government agency. The coverage of the original find was avid: pictures of the stone artefacts were beamed around Australia and articles even appeared in the *Borneo News* and the *Sarawak Gazette*. During this time, the media 'reinterpreted' the information given by Jones. Journalists had changed the artefacts into an exciting 'Ice Age Find'.

Kevin Kiernan, academic geomorphologist and a founder of the Tasmanian Wilderness Society, had taken part in the speleological trips exploring limestone caves in the Franklin–Gordon limestone karst areas. He had some exposure to archaeological ideas and was interested in more than the karst landscape. Kiernan had recorded a cave with charcoal in it (then known as cave F34 or Fraser Cave) during a speleological trip in the 1970s. He revisited the catchment area with Bob Brown and Bob Burton, campaigners with the Tasmanian Wilderness Society, in February 1981. Kiernan wanted to return to check if the cave had evidence of human occupation.[7]

Kiernan and Brown organised a helicopter to take them to the area and then walked in to examine the cave. When they viewed it, they realised it had evidence of human occupation which should be verified by an archaeologist. Kiernan took a small sample of stone pieces from the cave to Don Ranson, TASNPWS archaeologist, who identified them as artefacts. Kiernan released news of the find to the media, although the site itself had not been formally investigated by a professional archaeologist.[8] Jones and his colleagues were later critical of this move; they believed it inadvertently confused the public who might have thought the site's significance was speleological not archaeological.[9]

The site was later renamed Kutikina, but at this time still went by its speleological club name of Fraser Cave (this appellation had nothing to do with the Prime Minister of the same name).[10] Kiernan rang Jones in the Northern Territory, where he was working on a site in Kakadu, and invited him to attend a second archaeological expedition to look specifically at the site. This March 1981 expedition therefore contained the same personnel as the first expedition, with the addition of Kiernan leading the way.[11]

By this time Jones's reputation from the film *The Last Tasmanian* and later media exposure was beginning to catch up with him. The Hydro and other opponents were trying to whip up public sentiment against him by describing the expedition as an archaeological stunt—the river bank site was salted or a hoax. Bob Burton remembers that Jones told him later that he was even challenged about it by a baggage handler at the airport, who asked whether he had 'planted it'.[12] It was in this contentious atmosphere that the second expedition revisited, excavated and affirmed the significance of Kutikina Cave.

Rhys Jones was keen not to have any more media contact until the 'real work' had been done, that is, the test excavation of the cave's floor. The group had only five or six days, during which it had to gain access to the site by climbing round rapids and complete the work in extreme wet and cold. Jones knew at first glance that it was 'a fantastic site' from the hundreds of stone artefacts scattered on the floor. The test excavation alone yielded the highest density of material, around 40 000 artefacts, he had even seen. Samples of charcoal were taken for carbon dating. Jones sieved most of the time while the others dug. As Jones was by then wary of the media, he was both surprised and disgruntled when a television crew flew in, led by journalist Henrik Gout, for Channel 6 (Tasmania). Nevertheless, the noise and excitement of helicopters in the wilderness somehow inspired Jones and he gave an interview anyway. He interpreted the site and theorised about the nature of the Pleistocene occupation. Jones's enthusiasm was clearly evident in the interview, and more importantly his conviction about the scientific importance of the site came across to the viewer as genuine.[13] He was confident, even without dates, that this site was not in a recent geomorphological context like the over-publicised chance find. That is, the archaeological material had been abandoned and then preserved in buried layers of soil. It was much much older than what he had seen on the first expedition. Within a few months, the radiocarbon dates for the site revealed that it was indeed an Ice Age or Pleistocene site with a most recent date of 14 840 ± 930 and a basal (lowest and oldest layer) date of 19 770 ± 850 BP.[14] Roughly speaking, it was between 15 000 and 20 000 years old.

At the time, Jones was still haunted by his image from the debate over *The Last Tasmanian* as a voluble and interfering scientist. It is possible he was relieved when John Mulvaney, still at the Australian National University, became involved. Mulvaney had a wide reputation as a respected archaeological authority (even before he became deeply involved in the debate over First Government House). He was the author of the first and most popular book about Australian archaeology, *The Prehistory of Australia* (it was later eclipsed by Josephine Flood's book *Archaeology of the Dreamtime* as essential reading for the interested public).[15] Mulvaney wrote in December 1981 to the Senate Select Committee on Southwest Tasmania, which had just been set up by the federal government.[16] Mulvaney brought to its attention the new evidence from Kutikina and the previous archaeological background, on which Jones had written an article for an archaeology journal.[17] Mulvaney also repeated the criticisms that Jones and other archaeologists had made of the archaeology in the Hydro's 1979 environmental impact statement.[18]

Without seeing the site, Mulvaney risked telling the media that it had great potential for research.[19] The development's proponents responded by claiming it could be salvaged before the dam was built. Their authority on the subject was the former television naturalist Harry Butler, the Bush Tucker Man, then a conservation consultant to the State government. Butler recommended that Aboriginal relics on the Franklin River be salvaged before the dam was built.[20] Mulvaney testily rebutted Butler's claims in the press that salvage was a practical solution and that it was appropriate in this case.[21]

President of the AAA, Sandra Bowdler, was also 'stunned beyond amusement by Harry Butler's blithe comment'.[22] Both she and Mulvaney emphasised in their rejoinders to Butler that the Pleistocene site of Kutikina was too important to flood, even after salvage excavation. Bowdler argued that such an excavation would need to be extended to at least nine other caves believed to be in the vicinity of Kutikina, and could cost up to $1 million. She stated it was not as simple as 'filling a few bags with stones and bones and bringing them back to the Tasmanian Museum to lie about'.[23]

The archaeologists from the Australian National University and TASNPWS decided that a third expedition should be made to the catchment area to put the site in context and verify archaeological claims of uniqueness. There was still an urgent need to undertake a systematic ground survey for further sites. The first priority was to revisit all the caves located during earlier speleological surveys. Lesser priority was given to more remote areas, which would be examined for caves if time was available.

The expedition located fifty new caves, most of which were of 'speleological interest only'.[24] That month, members of the Senate Select Committee who wished to see Kutikina were flown in by helicopter. Back in Hobart, they also visited the Tasmanian Aboriginal Centre and interviewed members who had made submissions to them on the matter. The AAA also presented submissions to the Select Committee. Mulvaney, as acting chair of the Australian Heritage Commission, and Dick Adams, the Tasmanian Minister for the National Parks and Wildlife Service, also visited the sites. Media interest was such that two television crews (ABC and Channel 6) attended these visits and meetings, broadcasting the material mid-March. Channel 6 completely filled one episode of *People, Politics and Places* with the topic.

The third expedition concluded that Kutikina:

> was not a unique phenomenon, but that its occupation was part of a systematic exploitation of the Franklin Valley by prehistoric hunters. Two major sites now show that this dated to the height of the last ice age, and we believe that many (or all?) of the caves were occupied during this phase ... All of the sites found in these expeditions would be drowned by the proposed hydro-electric scheme of the Gordon below Franklin.[25]

This conclusion, which was probably reached during the expedition, had serious implications for the proposed development. It meant that whole sections of the dam's proposed catchment could be considered to have archaeological significance, growing as it did out of the observations made by other scientists about palaeo-environments in the Southwest.

Meanwhile, the submission by Rhys Jones to the Senate Select Committee was read to federal parliament on 19 March 1982. While he did not include the latest information from the expedition described above, Jones still put the case for World Heritage status of archaeological resources in the Southwest based on existing information.[26] Mulvaney's submission was also tabled in parliament later in September.[27] Significantly, he noted the political pressure on the archaeologists as scientific researchers from all sides of the debate. It was mainly for this reason that twenty-five internationally prominent scholars appeared for the first time ever together in a full-page advertisement supporting the preservation of the Southwest. It ran with the headline 'Do people overseas care more about preserving Australia's treasures than our own Government?'[28] Even the nomination for World Heritage List inscription occurred under considerable pressure. The Labor Premier, Harry Holgate, signed it on his very last day in office in May 1982 before the newly elected, pro-dams Liberal government came into power. It was couriered out of Tasmania to Canberra by Rhys Jones that evening before the incoming Liberal Premier Robin Gray could rescind it.[29]

Mulvaney and Jones held a press conference at Parliament House in Canberra two days after the September advertisement appeared. They dwelt on the archaeological significance of the Tasmanian sites. The conference was well attended and exposed the issue further nationally. The pro-dam lobby still held the view that the archaeologists' claims were greatly exaggerated.[30] In November 1982 the Senate Select Committee presented its report, which contained sections on archaeology, to federal parliament.[31]

A fourth and final archaeological expedition was planned between 15 February and 5 March 1983.[32] The fieldwork had been discussed during the 1982 AAA conference in Hobart as many archaeologists vied to be included on the trip. No female archaeologists were considered and so it is possible that a *Boy's Own* adventure attitude reigned. It was not until the 1990s that male academic archaeologists directing excavations of Tasmanian Pleistocene sites commonly included female students or colleagues as fieldworkers.

The UNESCO World Heritage Commission in Paris accepted the Southwest Wilderness Area, including the area for dam development, for World Heritage inscription on 15 December 1982. The nomination needed high values for both the environmental and cultural criteria to be successful.[33] Just the day before the inscription was announced, the Tasmanian Wilderness Society began a three-month blockade of the Hydro's construction work on the development. Over 1200 people were arrested, including British media botanist David Bellamy and TWS director Bob Brown.[34] Archaeologists Betty Downie, Leslie Head, and Angela McGowan were also arrested.[35] Having been excluded from the archaeological expeditions, McGowan later commented wryly that 'the men went down the river and the women went to jail'.[36]

Filmmaker Tom Haydon, who had been following the debate, returned to Tasmania and shot extensive footage of the blockade. Only two films were publicly aired—*Beyond the Dam* (1985) and *The Fight for the Franklin* (1987).[37] Jones appeared briefly in the former film. Some of the locals were not pleased with Haydon's work, but the criticisms were from the conservationists and were very different to those made of *The Last Tasmanian*.

Fortunately for the Franklin, the federal elections were called early in 1983. The Labor Opposition, with Bob Hawke as its newly installed leader, campaigned on the issue with support from Bob Brown. Brown was an effective focus for the conservation movement on this issue and gathered much national support.[38] The campaign to 'vote for the Franklin' (and put Labor in the House of Representatives) was promoted widely in the media. The conservationists used full-page colour advertisements in all major news-papers across the country to get their message to the electorate.[39]

Prime Minister Malcolm Fraser became alarmed by the support Labor was gathering on the issue and in January 1983 offered the Tasmanian State government $500 million not to build the dam.[40] The State govern-ment refused the money and the federal Liberal government lost to Labor on 3 March 1983.[41] Despite its promise to stop the Hydro scheme, the new federal Labor government and the scheme's opponents still had to contend with a High Court challenge over State versus federal rights.[42]

The Hydro saw a last chance to undermine the archaeological evidence by conducting its own work for submission to the High Court. It spent $100 000 on a cave survey by its own geologists.[43] This work, however, did little to dissuade the court from accepting the archaeological evidence in the cultural significance assessment of the World Heritage inscription. After all the evidence was reviewed, the High Court decision (1 July 1983) supported federal government powers in this instance, and the scheme was stopped in August 1983.[44]

'Without first-class research, it's just a bullring'

The archaeologists of the Tasmanian National Parks and Wildlife Service were always aware of the difficult position they were in as public servants well before the State Liberal government came to power under Premier Gray. They might publish results of the expeditions in scientific journals, but were not able to participate in any public debate on the issue. The Hydro and its supporters, however, reserved their criticism for Jones and other mainland archaeologists. They thought that these archaeologists had worked closely with conservation groups against them throughout the whole process.[45] The archaeological profession, acting in unity through the AAA, advised against working for the Hydro.[46] This opposition to the Hydro grew out of a suspicion that such work would be selectively reinterpreted. Archaeologists were still wary of the Hydro because they believed that the writers of the 1979 environmental impact statement had misused Jones's Tasmanian research. The distrust that the AAA Executive Committee felt was transmitted to its members and made it impossible for the Hydro to employ its own archaeologists to verify the work of the expeditions.[47] This extraordinary example of the power of professional veto was only possible due to the small size of the discipline at that time. As a result, the Hydro had to rely on Harry Butler in 1982 and its own geologists in 1983 to refute the archaeological evidence and submissions.

The Hydro had been correct to be sceptical of the media claims that the first find was Pleistocene, and Jones himself always believed it was much younger. It was eventually dated to the late Holocene, that is, within the last few thousand years.[48] But the Hydro made itself even more unpopular with archaeologists by conducting a smear campaign against those who went on the four expeditions.[49] By attacking Jones and other researchers personally, the Hydro lost any remaining credibility with archaeologists whom it might have used as consultants and advisers. The Hydro really needed their advice, as the archaeological significance of the area was one issue of the debate that it never successfully grasped on its own.

The discovery of Kutikina Cave presented a major problem for the Hydro because it was impossible to minimise the impact of the development on the site. It would be flooded and destroyed by the dam. While Harry Butler advised that salvage was possible, the archaeologists argued that it was a poor strategy for such a significant site and region.[50] Not often are archaeological sites an 'insurmountable object to development'.[51]

Bob Burton recalls that the Hydro's engineers then tried to solve the Kutikina problem by producing a plan of a concrete bunker designed to protect the cave from the dam's rising waters. A funnel or chimney built above the rising waterline would allow access to the cave for archaeological researchers.[52] This interesting example of lateral or desperate thinking was never taken too seriously by any of the parties in the debate.

Finally, the Hydro felt it necessary to re-survey the limestone cave area using its own geologists to supply evidence to the High Court challenge. The Hydro thought this was the closest it could get to an archaeological survey. After all, it was Kevin Kiernan, a geomorphologist, who had first discovered Kutikina. The Hydro's aim was to prove that Pleistocene caves with archaeological deposits were common in the Southwest and that a few less sites here or there would not matter. They also tried to argue that the sites already located had less scientific world significance than those in France, such as Lascaux, because they did not have rock art.[53]

This argument is interesting because it illustrates the problems with assessing cultural sites for World Heritage List inscription. One problem, in particular, haunts cultural heritage managers and other heritage professionals when trying to decide what is eligible for a World Heritage inscription: what else is out there and how do these other cultural sites or landscapes rank in comparison?[54] Nevertheless, in answer to the Hydro's argument about Lascaux, rock art in the form of hand stencils was later found in a few Southwest rockshelters by TASNPWS in 1986.[55] The ranking of Aboriginal rock art against rock art elsewhere is a difficult issue; it is best contemplated in a research seminar, not a media frenzy.

The Hydro's final sally for the High Court challenge was left to its geologists, putting S. J. Patterson, Chief Geologist for the Hydro, in a difficult position. He led the team of five Hydro geologists that had completed the 1983 survey. Patterson told the *Hobart Mercury*,

> Clearly the attitude adopted [by archaeologists] lacked scientific objectivity, and emphasised the wide gap between truth and verisimilitude when science is subordinated to promoting a cause. The social and economic cost of influencing public opinion is great. Therefore, archaeologists can only continue to receive public support if the information the community receives is scientifically correct and sustainable.[56]

Patterson's comment could be interpreted as resentment after the High Court decision or just as grudging recognition of the major contribution that the archaeological evidence had made to the decision. Without its own archaeologists to review the evidence, it was certainly difficult for the Hydro to counteract the impact of the evidence and archaeological authority in the debate.

Most archaeologists interviewed for this book believe that the Franklin dam was the most publicly contentious issue that Australian archaeology has encountered. Many also believe that archaeology had a major role in saving the Franklin as the caves were critical for meeting the standards of cultural significance for inscription on the World Heritage List.[57] Malcolm Fraser commented once to Robin Williams of the ABC Radio Science Show 'that it was the archaeological research that made the difference in the Franklin decision. Without first-class research, it's just a bull-ring'.[58] Provision of the best possible scientific evidence when the debate was at its most contentious was crucial to justifying a World Heritage inscription and ongoing preservation. Once scientific justification had been established, the political factors then came into play. The credibility of the archaeologists who conducted the work was never seriously in doubt: the main figures in the discipline were supportive of them without necessarily taking part in the conservation movement's strategies and politics.[59]

What was the relationship between the conservationists and the archaeologists? How close were they? Only one archaeologist ever worked directly for the conservation movement for a short time and that was Angela McGowan. She was briefly employed as an office-manager for the Tasmanian Conservation Trust in Hobart. In 1980–81, she helped to organise meetings to discuss non-violent action and strategies for the Franklin campaign among other conservation concerns at the time. McGowan made a submission to the Senate Select Committee concerning the problems with the Hydro's 1979 environemental impact statement. Later she was one of many activists involved in planning and running the blockade and she was among those arrested. When McGowan was working at the trust, she never imagined the Franklin would become a national and international issue.[60]

Rhys Jones states that he did not go looking for sites hoping they would produce something important enough to stop the development. At first he doubted whether much would be located due to the poor ground surface visibility and difficult access in the area. He did, however, believe that the Hydro's environmental impact statement was inadequate and that some independent effort at survey should be made.[61] He did not meet Kevin Kiernan, discoverer of Kutikina Cave, until the second expedition. Jones was even nervous that he would be implicated in a 'Greenie Petrov Affair', but he went on the expedition anyway.[62] Mulvaney was similarly wary when asked to support Jones and TASNPWS archaeologists in proclaiming the significance of the site.[63] At no stage did the archaeologists sit down with conservationists and plan the discoveries step-by-step until they had enough evidence to stop the development as was implied by some of the Hydro's statements.

Mulvaney has since stated that mainland conservationists at the time had a 'marked lack of interest in the Aboriginal prehistory cause . . . the fact that humans occupied south-west Tasmania during ice-age times, *before* the forests developed their impenetrability, perhaps ruined their idealistic concept of a timeless Wilderness'.[64] It was biologist Tim Flannery who later made attacks on the popular concept of 'pristine wilderness'. He has popularised the idea (originally mooted by Jones) that much of the Australian environment has been modified by Aboriginal people in various ways, particularly by fire. These ideas, however, only started to attract conservationists when Flannery began to publish material on land-carrying capacity. His book *The Future Eaters* (1995) was favourably reviewed by Greenpeace, because it is relevant to concerns about rural landcare.[65]

Aboriginal consultation and involvement

The archaeologists did not consistently consult the Aboriginal community during the research in the Southwest. In February 1982 the president of the AAA, Sandra Bowdler, criticised the Hydro and the Australian National University archaeologists for not consulting the Tasmanian Aboriginal community during the debate. She stated that Tasmanian Aborigines had survived like many Aboriginal people in Victoria and New South Wales and should not still be considered a 'lost or extinct race'.[66] The archaeologists from the Australian National University, however, did not consult the Aboriginal community until later that year. The meeting occurred just before the fourth expedition and near the end of the work. This consultation was probably spurred by a paper by Tasmanian Aboriginal activist Ros Langford, which startled some of the participants at the 1982 AAA Hobart conference at the height of the Franklin debate.[67] Langford made scathing comments about the lack of involvement of Aboriginal people generally in archaeological research. Her arguments regarding Aboriginal custodianship of information and of archaeological material will be dealt with in the next chapter. Langford observed in her paper that she had not forgotten Rhys Jones's involvement with Haydon in *The Last Tasmanian*.[68] The Australian National University researchers and TASNPWS archaeologists recognised at the conference that they would need to keep in close contact with the Tasmanian Aboriginal Centre in Hobart. Barry Blain argued that they were not able to take Aboriginal representatives on the fourth expedition because of legislation passed by the State government to control protesters in the national park. They did, however, notify the centre of the expedition results and send it a report.[69]

The Franklin debate was the first issue directly concerning archaeological sites in which Aboriginal people in Tasmania became politically involved. At that stage, they had no Aboriginal site or project officers with experience in archaeological survey or excavation. It was difficult for them to assess what their involvement should be: no guidelines had been agreed upon and they received little recognition from any of the main parties in the debate. Jones maintained the same view that he and Haydon had promoted in *The Last Tasmanian*, that all Tasmanian Aboriginal people had been wiped out, in his submission to the Senate Select Committee.[70] The Tasmanian Aboriginal Centre had difficulties not only with the archaeologists, but also with the conservation movement concerning recognition of the centre's right to be involved in the debate.[71]

Nevertheless, the centre made a submission to the Senate Select Committee, and members of the Committee addressed this on their visit in March 1982. In July the Tasmanian Nomenclature Board agreed to the centre's request that Fraser Cave be renamed Kutikina, which means 'spirit' in one of the Tasmanian Aboriginal languages.[72] Mike Mansell and Ros Langford, representing the centre, visited the cave in late 1982 and were further impressed by its spiritual significance.[73]

The definition of an archaeological site as sacred was interpreted by many archaeologists as a direct challenge to their scientific authority, raising questions about custodianship and access. The Franklin River campaign provided a highly charged and complex backdrop to debate about these issues. The Tasmanian Aboriginal Centre quickly became alienated from the Tasmanian Wilderness Society and TASNPWS regarding its role in preserving the sites. The Tasmanian Aboriginal Land Council (known as TALC) has managed heritage matters for the Aboriginal community in Tasmania since its formation in the early 1990s. It has also acted on occasion as a bridge between the politically active Tasmanian Aboriginal Centre and other groups. The tensions between sacred/scientific and custodianship/access are still debated. They are discussed in depth, using mainly Australian case studies, in the next chapter on the management of human skeletal remains.

7

Trouble with bones

THE DEBATE CONCERNING the control and deposition of human skeletal remains is another example of an issue that was contentious for the archaeological community in the late twentieth century. It has served in some instances to galvanise Aboriginal and public opinion against some archaeologists. To meet this challenge, archaeologists need to display creativity and develop a new type of collaboration with other parties.

The history of Western scientific imperialism and of archaeologists' claims to objectivity was discussed in Chapter 2. It cannot be denied that the history of conquest and colonialism in this country has influenced the politicisation of Aboriginal and Torres Strait Islander viewpoints. Some archaeologists' lack of sensitivity to or understanding of the cultural continuity of particular indigenous groups has fanned this politicisation. The reburial debate in the late 1980s reignited the controversy regarding cultural continuity and self-determination which arose in the late 1970s in Tasmania, as discussed in Chapter 4.

This chapter examines the background to disagreements over the deposition and curation of indigenous human remains in Australia with reference to the ideological differences between the stakeholders. It explores the contrasts between Aboriginal and European concepts about the treatment of human remains and makes comparisons with a similar conflict of ideas in North America. Aboriginal and European ideas often conflict concerning time scales, the nature of origins, and acceptance of the need to conduct certain types of research on human remains.

The central question in these case studies is the benefits of maintaining burials *in situ* as against removing them and reburying them elsewhere or storing them in museums. Other questions are: Should ancient remains be treated differently to more recent remains? Should descendants of non-indigenous Australians expect researchers and others to show respect to a deceased ancestor's physical and cultural legacy? Are research restrictions associated with the curation of such a legacy warranted?

Indigenous and non-indigenous concepts

Indigenous and non-indigenous beliefs differ on the nature of time, on religion and on community politics, but is there a more fundamental cleavage? American archaeologist Larry Zimmerman argues that the differences between Native American and European concepts go deeper than these issues in North America.[1] Eric Willmot, Aboriginal analyst and former director of the Australian Institute of Aboriginal and Torres Strait Islander Studies, also believes that the differences are based on fundamental contrasts. In his 1989 David Unaipon lecture, Willmot suggested European 'societies built themselves upon the idea that social perfection could be best constructed by the human intellect. They created their societies upon this belief, and they were in a broad sense anti-nature societies'.[2]

The colonisation of Australia over the last two hundred years has resulted in great damage to the social fabric of indigenous Australia. Aboriginal and Torres Strait Islander people have been severely affected by this history and dislocation. Cultural continuity, however, is stronger in southeastern Australia than many non-Aboriginal people realise.[3] Aboriginal people claim a physical and cultural legacy and they feel an increasing responsibility and obligation towards their children to preserve this heritage.[4] Enough of this legacy is still visible for some people to persistently discriminate against indigenous people in many situations.[5]

Archaeologists and other researchers interested in analysing indigenous human remains have been negligent in understanding and exploring possible cultural differences as part of their work.[6] A second wave of researchers began to work more closely with indigenous people in the 1990s. This change is the result of a number of factors, including a greater interest in indigenous belief systems and contact history, social justice concerns, legislation favouring indigenous self-determination, and the development of a new confidence about dealing with indigenous interest groups.

It is not possible to go into all the indigenous beliefs about the past which conflict with the Western scientific model. As physical anthropologist Colin Pardoe observed, 'Aboriginal Australians have regularly objected to a European view of the past that makes a distinction between history and prehistory'.[7] In response, as we have seen, many archaeologists have adopted the terms 'pre-contact archaeology' or 'Aboriginal archaeology' to describe the type of archaeology that they practise.

Specific to the skeletal remains debate, many Aboriginal people do not distinguish between the Dreamtime and the recent past. They possibly see the past as compacted rather than linear, as do the Native Americans in the southwestern United States.[8] Aboriginal people who wish to rebury repatriated human remains do not agree with some archaeologists that these ancestors might have had different beliefs to Aboriginal groups today about burial practices.[9] Such groups sometimes state that they already know that they and their ancestors originated in Australia, and so archaeological research into human migration here is pointless.[10]

The conventional view of archaeologists and physical anthropologists concerning Aboriginal origins is generally that *Homo sapiens* did not evolve in Australia. There is an alternative possibility, though, that *Homo sapiens* developed from the Javanese *Homo erectus* and then migrated throughout the Pacific.[11] Some even argue that Asian *Homo erectus* may predate African specimens. In this case the 'out of Africa' notion—that *Homo sapiens* originated in Africa and dispersed from there—will have to be rethought. It has been receiving some competition from a 'multi-regional' model of species diffusion, which postulates that modern humans developed independently and almost concurrently from *Homo erectus* populations in a number of locations, including Indonesia.[12] Whether Australia could be one of the independent locations remains to be seen; no actual evidence of *Homo erectus* has ever been discovered here.

It is inevitable that politics and religion enter this debate. 'Whatever the reason, human bones have become symbols of power, both spiritual and political', according to Zimmerman.[13] Burials are symbolic to many Aboriginal people. Howard Creamer, an anthropologist, notes that 'they [the burials] stand for all ancestors: those who enjoyed the idyllic life before contact and those who endured the suffering of invasion'.[14] Consultant archaeologist Jeanette Hope takes this even further when she observes that the 'unknown Aboriginal dead [are] symbolic of Aboriginal cultural continuity, survival, fortitude and sacrifice'.[15]

Archaeological research prior to the late 1980s either ignored or avoided the implications of this symbolism. In the 1980s and early 1990s researchers were faced with the dilemma, like much of Australian society, about the rights of indigenous Australians. Eric Willmot noted that further research into human remains could not ethically continue unless Aboriginal people with degrees in archaeology and physical anthropology were available to work directly for communities.[16] This sentiment was echoed by many archaeologists, including John Mulvaney and Isabel McBryde.[17]

By 1995, a few such people had graduated and were available, including Robyne Bancroft, Steve Free, David Johnston and Sam Whiteman.

More have followed. What research questions are Aboriginal archaeologists interested in now? Have they borrowed the skills but refused to subscribe to the mainstream archaeological ideology? Can the rest of the discipline collaborate with Aboriginal communities and Aboriginal archaeologists successfully?

When interviewed for this book, Aboriginal archaeologists Robyne Bancroft and David Johnston said that they were drawn to archaeology because they wished to study their own heritage. Since graduating, Bancroft has worked for the Museum of Australia cataloguing repatriated skeletal remains. Johnston is a self-employed consultant. Bancroft has the qualifications and the interest to undertake postgraduate study of human remains to broaden her understanding of the Aboriginal past.[18]

To some extent, Bancroft and the others have picked up the skills but have refused some of the archaeological mainstream ideology. Their views on the future of the discipline include more collaboration with relevant local communities than many non-indigenous archaeologists would envisage. Other Aboriginal professionals would also like to see more collaboration between non-Aboriginal and Aboriginal archaeologists or communities in researching Aboriginal remains.[19] Examples and guidelines for such work are available in some of the literature for both communities and

Aboriginal archaeologist Robyne Bancroft attends a reburial of skeletal remains by an Aboriginal community near Cooma, NSW, in the early 1990s.

Wurundjeri Aboriginal community members excavate a test pit near Melbourne. Ringo Terrick (centre), Gary Hunter (right) and his son (left).

Wurundjeri Aboriginal community members, Brian Patterson and Tony Garvey, locating a surface artefact scatter in the Upper Yarra, near Melbourne.

Anonymous Aboriginal community members putting the fun back into archaeology while mucking around on a site survey, Victoria.

researchers.[20] Most consulting archaeologists, particularly those in Victoria, have been working closely with and for Aboriginal communities for a number of years. Nevertheless, a few mainstream academic archaeologists are still unable to fully grasp the concept.

Non-indigenous remains

Archaeologists in Australia are increasingly being asked to excavate non-indigenous burials or to be present at exhumations. Two cases are a nineteenth-century Maori political prisoner, Hohepa Te Umuroa, who was imprisoned in a convict settlement in Tasmania where he later died, and the relocation and reburial of a pioneer family cemetery at Melton, Victoria. In both cases, the closest relatives were consulted regarding whether the excavation should take place and how the remains should be reburied.

The exhumation of Hohepa's remains was carried out at the request of the New Zealand government with the approval of the federal and Tasmanian State governments. Descendants of Hohepa were directly involved in the exhumation on Maria Island and returned with the remains to New Zealand. Their trip to Tasmania was funded by the New Zealand Justice Department 'in a gesture aimed at correcting, as far as possible, an injustice perpetrated by the British 142 years ago'. A great deal of goodwill flowed from the work. Richard Morrison, the historical archaeologist who conducted the exhumation, said that he 'felt privileged to have assisted the Maori visitors in attaining their goal'.[21]

The Pinkerton family graves were exhumed at the request of the Shire of Melton Council, which wanted to build over the burial ground. Melton is 40 kilometres northwest of Melbourne and has a vigorous historical society. The graves were marked by a cairn and were well known to the local historical society and to the family's descendants. Gary Vines, consultant archaeologist, notes that the descendants did not agree to the proposed relocation of the remains until after several meetings had been held at the Shire of Melton offices. Those present at the meetings comprised the local council, the descendants, and representatives of the historical society and the State site protection authority (then the Victoria Archaeological Survey). The Cemeteries and Crematoria Section of the Victorian Department of Health was also contacted regarding the official requirements for exhuming graves. The Shire of Melton had to obtain five 'Licenses to Exhume a Body' from the department (one for each body). The remains were eventually excavated and interred at another location beneath the reconstructed cairn.[22]

The National Trust has made cemetery management and preservation an important part of its work. In 1987, the National Trust of Australia (New South Wales) produced a policy paper which identified for the first time the types of burials related to European settlement and their historical significance.[23] The Heritage Council of New South Wales has also produced some guidelines for their conservation.[24] In Victoria the National Trust of Australia (Victoria) and the Ministry of Planning have produced publications on the history and management of the State's cemeteries.[25] Other States have followed suit.

Comparing indigenous and non-indigenous attitudes in Australian society

In summary, a number of factors arise in deciding what reaction people have to excavation, research and relocation of burials. These include the characteristics of the group of people:

- their mobility: 'Do they still live near where their ancestors were buried?'
- their religious beliefs and mortuary practices
- their moral values
- their belief about human origins
- their beliefs about the role of science.

Many non-indigenous people do not want to donate their bodies to science and want to be buried; would they welcome the thought that their remains might be removed and researched by future archaeologists? It is possible that they would rather be cremated. A person who places restrictions on the use of their personal papers or does not want their body parts used and includes these wishes in their will, is saying to their descendants that they wish to be remembered in a certain way. In the case of some famous people, their wishes have not always been placed above those of journalists, historians, relatives and public libraries.

Social justice and human remains 'North American Style'

Since the late 1970s, indigenous groups around the world have pressured the scientific community and museums to return or repatriate indigenous skeletal remains as well as body parts. It is relevant here to make some comparisons between the social justice meted out to two indigenous groups, Native Americans and Australian Aboriginal people. Although collections of human remains were made for similar reasons, the outcome of the re-patriation debate for the two groups has differed.

As a result of activism by indigenous groups, a partially public debate has occurred in both countries about legislation, consultation and policy for undertaking repatriation. It is a mistake to see this as a separate issue from those of self-determination and social justice. The history of the develop-ment of legislation, policies and codes of ethics for the treatment of human remains in America and Australia is outlined below.

Native American burials receive protection from federal law on federal and Native American lands only. The main federal legislation that protects all sites on federal and Native American lands is the *Archaeological Resources Protection Act 1979*.[26] There are statutes for twenty seven States, few of which protect unmarked burials on private land. A number of tribes have also enacted their own ordinances and tribal codes. These laws and codes allow them to offer protection not only to burials on tribal lands, but also to those in traditional areas where they have allowed non-Native Americans to settle.[27]

The United States has a severe problem with looters of archaeological sites, particularly those that contain burial items as well as skeletal remains. Despite some tightening of legislation, most burials on private land are not protected. Unlike many other countries, America does not have com-prehensive federal statutes that protect significant and known cultural resources regardless of land tenure. It is unlikely to change its position on this in the future because of pressure from Anglo-American civil rights groups. Archaeologists believe that the best way to overcome the looting problem is through other strategies to raise public sympathy, including edu-cation programmes.[28]

Mechanisms for repatriation in the United States were not formalised by federal legislation until the 1990s. Native American groups have applied political pressure on Congress over a number of years, and as a result it passed the *Native American Graves and Repatriation Act* in November 1990. This Act has already proved useful in stopping the unpleasant activities of bone-sellers. In Virginia, Richard Maniscalo tried to sell a leg bone to an undercover agent from the Bureau of Land Management. Maniscalo was the first person to be charged under the Act for buying and selling Native American human remains. He was fined US$2000 and was also required to pay the cost of returning the bone to the Northern Cheyenne in Montana.[29] Other prosecutions and actions under the Act are regularly reported in the National Parks Service publication, *Common Ground*.

The US government has funded the establishment of a new national museum in Washington and has directed the Smithsonian Institute to repatriate Native American skeletal material and grave goods that it has in its possession to the museum.[30] The Institute and many members of the Society for American Archaeology were not pleased with this directive and argued that their own policies should be acknowledged.[31] Bennie Keel believes that archaeologists and other researchers should 'pay more attention to the rights and desires of the legitimate Native Americans and do our best to find a way out of this morass'.[32] No doubt Native Americans will continue to have to prove this legitimacy, which has been defined by non-indigenous Americans.[33] Jane Hubert takes the position that common ground can be reached and that 'both archaeologists and indigenous people would then be in a position to recognise their genuine common interest in the preservation and protection of the evidence of the past'.[34] Canadian archaeologist George Nicholas also notes that there has been an increase in indigenous and co-authored publications that indicate an emerging interest in new ways of thinking about the past and protecting it. He views this as a result of the change brought about by the *Native American Graves and Repatriation Act*.[35]

Social justice and human remains in Australia

By the early 1980s, most Australian archaeologists accepted that repatriation of skeletal remains to Aboriginal communities was inevitable, providing it was on their conditions, in line with the AAA's skeletal remains policy. However, opinion was divided as to whether Aboriginal communities should rebury skeletal remains of high scientific significance and of some antiquity. The debate over the role of indigenous self-determination in this issue continued for some time into the 1990s.

State rather than federal legislation has shaped most archaeological practices in Australia. Burials are generally considered archaeological sites or 'relics' and were protected under State laws passed in the late 1960s and early 1970s. Most laws have been reviewed since then to include the option of negotiating heritage agreements to protect sites, rather than reserving land outright. Two federal laws impinge on the issue, but are not the mainstay of protection for burials. They are the *Aboriginal and Torres Strait Islanders Heritage Protection Act 1984* and the *Protection of Movable Cultural Heritage Act 1986*. These Acts can be called on by Aboriginal and Torres Strait Islander people in cases where significant cultural sites and property are about to be damaged or exported.[36] Many of the older State laws, however, still nominate the State museum as the ultimate repository of archaeological relics. Aboriginal groups in New South Wales were critical of the *National Parks and Wildlife Service Act 1974* for this reason. Robert Lester of the NSW Aboriginal Land Council was concerned that 'if someone exhumed reburied remains, further down the track, they could end up back in the museum'.[37]

Most collections of indigenous human skeletal remains in Australian museums and overseas were collected before burial sites were protected by any legislation. At the time they were not claimed by, or associated with, any present Aboriginal community organisation. Aboriginal heritage organisations have only been established in the last twenty-five years. Repatriation of human remains has been fought for most actively by Aboriginal community groups in southeastern Australia, with Tasmania leading the way. On 30 April 1976, Truganini's remains were returned to the Tasmanian Aboriginal community by the State government. Under police guard the ashes were taken for safe keeping until the next morning. Premier Doug Lowe formally handed the ashes to Roy Nichols, State Secretary of the Tasmanian Aboriginal Information Service in a special ceremony that was held at Oyster Cove, where her cremated remains were scattered into the sea[38].

Benjamin Duterrau's painting of Truganini or 'Trugernana', 1834.

Throughout the 1980s the Tasmanian Aboriginal community continued to push for Aboriginal rights in relation to heritage. As we saw in the previous chapter, Ros Langford sent a strong message to archaeologists in her paper to the AAA conference in 1982[39] and it was later reinforced in the Federal Court.[40] The question of repatriation was also addressed as part of the motion passed by AAA members at the 1982 annual general meeting supporting Aboriginal people's aspirations and ownership of heritage.[41]

In July 1984 the Tasmanian government announced that it would allow all Aboriginal remains in State depositories to be transferred to Aboriginal communities, even if they wished to cremate them.[42] Tasmanian Aboriginal community activists, in conjunction with people from northern Australia, continued their efforts overseas. They succeeded in locating collections in the University of Edinburgh and the British Natural History Museum. The former collection is in the process of being returned to Aboriginal communities throughout Australia. This process is slow because communities who wish to rebury remains need to find appropriate areas which will not be disturbed by future development. A joint statement recently by the Australian and British prime ministers promised to increase efforts to repatriate human remains to Australian indigenous communities and to provide catalogues of the collection held by the Natural History Museum to the Australian government. It also noted that other British institutions had already negotiated agreements with indigenous communities for the release of significant remains.[43]

The prospect of regaining custody of human remains in Australia by using the federal *Aboriginal and Torres Strait Islander Heritage Protection Act 1984* or a new State heritage law encouraged Victorian Aboriginal people to act in relation to local museums. Jim Berg organised a conference on skeletal remains at the Victorian State Museum in July 1984 to discuss the issue. Later in the year, the AAA became alarmed that the government in Victoria would allow repatriation without due thought to how the remains would be curated.

Some leading archaeologists of the time formed an AAA sub-committee to create a policy on skeletal remains on behalf of the discipline. It comprised Alan Thorne (chair), Jack Golson, Neville White and Betty Meehan.[44] They wrote to Evan Walker, Victorian Minister for Planning and Environment, stating it was important to distinguish between remains like those in the Crowther Collection and others of unknown individuals from the distant past such as Pleistocene burials. The former contained mostly individuals who had died during the contact period and could be considered recent ancestors of the living indigenous population. In this they were closely following the line of the Society for American Archaeology and the

Smithsonian Institute in America.[45] The AAA also objected to Aboriginal communities reburying material of scientific significance. The solution of underground keeping places was raised for the first time. The sub-committee suggested that the State government should support Aboriginal keeping places and fund training for Aboriginal people working in them.

The sub-committee did not mention the cultural value to Aboriginal people of the remains. Nor were Aboriginal people consulted when either the policy or the letters were produced. Although a semi-professional body with a particular mindset, they would only have consulted professional Aboriginal archaeologists about this, but none of these existed at the time.

Meanwhile in South Australia, Aboriginal groups regained four embalmed bodies from the South Australian Museum. The State Coroner, Sir John Cleland, had preserved these remains over sixty years ago.[46] Communities in other states also began to show an interest in the Murray Black Collection, so named after the collector, engineer George Murray Black, who had an amateur interest in anatomy. He was active removing bones from burials along the Murray River Valley between 1929 and 1951. The collection comprised over 1600 individuals who were buried between the contact period and 14 000 years ago[47]. The Murray Black Collection began the repatriation process from the McKenzie Institute of Anatomy in Canberra through the Victorian State Museum in December 1988, using some selected advice from AAA. If the AAA sub-committee thought it could relax, it was wrong. Two far more controversial repatriations were not far away. In November 1989 Aboriginal representatives at a workshop on research at Willandra Lakes on the Darling River, western New South Wales, raised concerns about the control of archaeological heritage and the conduct of research. Archaeologists were to hear much more from these communities over the next four years, as we shall see later in this chapter.

Repatriation of human remains from museums and research collections in Australia and overseas did not receive recognition in broader cultural policies until the 1990s. Policies and programmes were considered the best avenue to follow, rather than passing specific legislation as in the United States.[48] The Council of Australian Museum Associations generated a repatriation policy in 1993. It states that museums should finally recognise the 'fundamental links between cultural heritage, traditional belief and land [and] rights to self-determination and basic human rights, as set out in the United Nations Declaration of Human Rights'.[49] Critics of museum policy at the time had observed that many institutions still operated under a system of internal colonialism and values that excluded indigenous people and their views.[50] The council's policy declares that as 'a moral imperative', such colonialist values should replaced with those which are more sensitive to indigenous peoples' concern for their heritage.[51] Hence State museum policies changed and human remains were removed from display, and more research was conducted to identify and return named individuals.[52]

In the lead-up to the 1993 federal election, Robert Tickner, Minister for Aboriginal and Torres Strait Islander Affairs in the Labor government, produced a policy recognising that the sale of Aboriginal arts and crafts was worth an estimated $30 million per annum. It also stated that 'Aboriginal arts and culture enrich the culture of all Australians'.[53] After recognising this financial and cultural enrichment contributed by Aboriginal Australians, the Labor Party promised to 'continue to support the return of cultural property to Aboriginal and Torres Strait Islander people, giving priority to the immediate return of human remains to their rightful owners'.[54] The Creative Nation cultural policy expanded and modified this view with provisos about keeping places and the training of indigenous people in curation techniques such as collection management, interpretation and display. Human remains are not referred to specifically, but it is assumed that they are part of the Return of Cultural Property Programme that was part of the policy. After Labor left government this programme continued until 1997, when it was partially replaced by the Return of Indigenous Ancestral Remains and Secret/Sacred Objects Programme. It grants museums and organisations funding under two sub-programmes, museum support and community support. The former assists museums to prepare collections for return; the latter helps with resources for communities needing to travel to the museums, pack their cultural property safely and accompany it home.[55]

The Aboriginal and Torres Strait Islander Commission, which is responsible for the repatriation of overseas collections, became uneasy about the funding levels and self-sufficiency of such programmes. It commissioned a report entitled the *Resourcing Indigenous Development and Self-determination: A Scoping Paper*, in September 2000. The paper aimed to assist the commission in the formulation of future policy regarding funding relationships between indigenous Australia and federal and State governments. The commission sees the 'current funding arrangement is one of dependence, based on the historical relationship between coloniser and colonised, and does not encourage Indigenous self-determination. In order for the commission to achieve our vision of self-determining communities this relationship needs to change'.[56]

The differences between the United States and Australia concerning indigenous burials and repatriation of human remains reflect a different contact history and a different view of social justice. Australia has stronger protective legislation for archaeological remains, more promotion of indigenous culture in cultural tourism, less trouble with looting, and a different situation concerning reconciliation and self-determination. The approach to repatriation in the 1990s as part of a reconciliation process in museum and cultural policies indicates that at some levels Australian society is sincere about rejecting scientific imperialism. The positions of all government agencies and museums on this issue has changed, partly as a result of the High Court decision in June 1992 (*Mabo v Queensland*, no. 2), which recognised that indigenous people held native title over land at the time of British colonisation in 1788 and hence it still exists unless extinguished by freehold acquisition. This court decision was followed by the enactment of the *Native Title Act* in 1993.[57]

A survey of the views of Aboriginal communities about archaeology and ownership of cultural heritage was conducted by Steve Free in early 1993, before the policies outlined above were officially adopted and the *Native Title Act* was passed. The World Archaeology Congress's Code of Ethics on indigenous consultation by archaeologists, was adopted and adapted to local conditions by the AAA, and it appears to have made some difference to the relationship between archaeologists, physical anthropologists and indigenous people. However, further surveys of indigenous communities Australia-wide need to be carried out to confirm or deny this view and to ascertain whether repatriation policies are satisfying the needs of indigenous communities with regard to the control of cultural property. Forums to discuss these issues have been mooted by various authorities, such as the Tasmanian Aboriginal Centre, but so far nothing has eventuated.[58]

Negotiating the public interest

A problem arises with burials that does not occur with any other type of Aboriginal site or landscape. This occurs when police or other government authorities decide to act in the public interest. Most State site authorities have had problems in the past with overzealous police treating isolated finds of Aboriginal burials as potential murder victims and have produced policies on this in conjunction with the police force.[59] There are still grey areas even where these policies and legislation apply to protect burials. One such grey area appeared after the NSW State Coroner seized Aboriginal human remains from Angophora Shelter in Sydney.

When human skeletal material was identified by police at Angophora Reserve rockshelter, archaeologists encountered problems with the Coroner's Court, not the Aboriginal community. The initial find of a piece of mandible was made by a schoolboy in March 1988 and was reported immediately to the police, who contacted the State Coroner. The Coroner

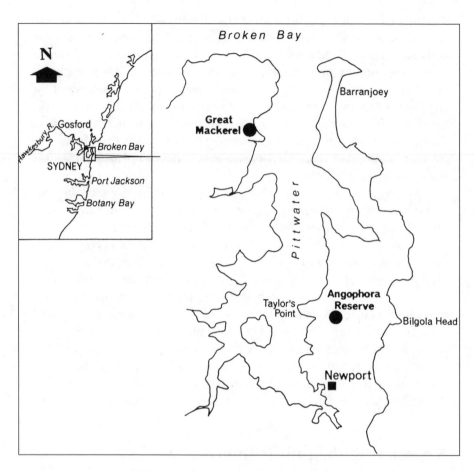

Angophora Reserve Rockshelter, Sydney. Adapted from Josephine McDonald, The Archaeology of the Angophora Reserve Rockshelter, *NSW National Parks and Wildlife Service, Sydney, 1992, p. 11.*

directed police to sift through the soil deposit on the floor of the rockshelter in order to reveal possible clues. Without contacting the archaeologists of the relevant site authority or Aboriginal group, as required by NSWNPWS policy, the Coroner had the original find examined by a dental pathologist at the University of Sydney. He identified one of the teeth as having dentine like that of a living or recently deceased human with dental preservation consistent with fluoridation of water.[60] The NSWNPWS, the relevant site authority, came to hear of the investigation. Its archaeologist, Bronwyn Connors, visited the reserve and identified the rockshelter as an Aboriginal archaeological site.

The Coroner still believed, however, that the rockshelter was the site of a recent murder. The NSWNPWS archaeologists assisted the police in the rockshelter until the Coroner directed that a larger area of the rockshelter would need to be examined for clues. Josephine McDonald was contracted to undertake the work as it was beyond the Service's resources. Members of the police force also assisted in the archaeological excavation during May and June 1988.[61]

While the Coroner was still convinced that the remains were of a five-year-old white child who had died in the last two years, a re-examination by a physical anthropologist, Colin Pardoe, indicated otherwise.[62] He identified it as the skeleton of an Aboriginal child of three or four years of age. The initial excavation uncovered the remains of two more pre-contact children, according to the stratigraphy. Excavation of the deposit below the midden layer discovered three individuals, including one female adult with a six-month-old baby in close proximity in an undisturbed context. Pardoe considered these remains to be 'indisputably Aboriginal'.[63] Archaeologists interpreted the woman and baby as a mother and child burial, which is known in the ethnographic literature. In cases where a mother and child both die when the child is very young, the baby is buried at the breast of its mother.[64]

As well as the burials, archaeologists removed and examined hearths, burnt bones, shell and stone artefacts during the excavation.[65] It soon became abundantly clear that this was an Aboriginal site. The excavation worked well as a public relations exercise with the local police, who had not heard of NSWNPWS policy concerning Aboriginal burials or the manual on handling skeletal remains by Thorne and Ross, which had been published two years before these events.[66]

Returning to the politics concerning the site, the Metropolitan Local Aboriginal Land Council was unhappy about the excavation and the removal of the burials. Nevertheless, they allowed the police the latitude to investigate in case a child had been murdered. McDonald and Ross note that they supported the 'scientific' excavation 'so that a full history of the site could be revealed . . . [Otherwise they] were saddened by the discovery of the burial of the mother and baby, and angered by the insensitive action of the [Government Medical Officer] towards these people.'[67]

The Government Medical Officer had incurred much criticism from the Aboriginal community by attempting to remove bones from the baby's skeleton without consulting their representative body, the Metropolitan Local Aboriginal Land Council. He was prevented from this action by the consultant archaeologists and by the Aboriginal representative of the community (who had been present throughout the excavation). The land council then refused permission to the Coroner's expert to conduct detailed research on the skeletons and demanded the return of the remaining bones held by the Coroner.

McDonald and Ross fear part of the reason for the Coroner's behaviour lies in his belief in the inalienable right of the Coroner's Court to follow an investigation despite trampling on other sensitivities or legislation.[68] The *Coroner's Act 1980* can override legislation and policies which protect burials and other sites from disturbance. The Coroner can also ignore Aboriginal concerns in the name of the 'public interest'.

Aboriginal communities and reburial—three cases

Aboriginal people in southeastern Australia often consider burial sites to be one of the most important links to the past and of high social value. Since the Victorian government adopted the federal *Aboriginal and Torres Strait Islander Heritage Protection Act 1984* as part of the State legislation protecting Aboriginal cultural heritage in 1987, Victorian Aboriginal people have been given more responsibility in deciding the ultimate fate of sites than their counterparts in any other State or Territory. The repatriation and reburial debates concerning the Murray Black Collection, the Kow Swamp Collection and Mungo Woman demonstrate interesting differences between Victoria and other States.

The Murray Black Collection of human remains was sanctioned and funded by two institutions, the Institute of Anatomy in Canberra and the University of Melbourne.[69] Little information accompanied much of the collection and the lack of systematic recording during excavation reduced its scientific value. The burials were disturbed without archaeological or local Aboriginal participation.

This lack of participation and consultation occurred because the collections were made earlier in the twentieth century when there was no government protection policy or legislation. A feeble joke, typical of the racist humour of the time, arose because Murray Black chose to concentrate on raiding burial mounds in the Murray River Valley to uncover the bones of over 1800 Murray 'blacks'. The collection included remains as recent as eighty years and others which were 14 000 years old.[70] The collection therefore comprised a mixture of recent and distant Aboriginal ancestors from Victoria, New South Wales and South Australia.

By 1984, the pendulum had begun to swing in favour of Victorian Aboriginal people gaining control over their heritage. Jim Berg, an Aboriginal originally from Framlingham Aboriginal Station (then with the Koori Legal Service), pressured the government to allow the part of the Murray Black Collection held by the University of Melbourne to be transferred to the Museum of Victoria preparatory to its repatriation. In 1988, the process of repatriation of the material to Victorian communities began, despite objections from AAA. The repatriation of NSW remains previously held by the Canberra Institute of Anatomy was accomplished via the Museum of Australia.[71]

Some archaeologists and physical anthropologists mourned the return and reburial of the remains, fearing that it was the end of human biological research in Australia.[72] John Mulvaney went as far as to accuse the Aboriginal communities involved of 'gross insecurity' and 'equally aggressive cultural imperialism' in choosing to destroy ancient scientific evidence.[73] Nevertheless, some archaeologists and physical anthropologists realised, as a result of this reburial, that they had an ethical obligation to explain the relevance of their research to the Aboriginal communities.[74]

The repatriation of the Kow Swamp remains in 1990 for reburial further split the discipline. It also gave the media the opportunity to goad Aborigines and archaeologists into incompatible positions on the issue. It was the most extreme example witnessed in Australia of a conflict of cultural values concerning skeletal remains between these two groups.

The reburial option for the Kow Swamp remains came as a shock to the archaeological community because the collection had been made by professional archaeologists, not collectors. It was the result of excavations in the 1960s and 1970s and were dated to between 9000 and 15 000 years in age.[75] Alan Thorne, physical anthropologist and archaeologist, was responsible for the generation of the major part of the collection with assistance from Alan West, Museum of Victoria.[76] The museum loaned the collection to Thorne to conduct research, much of which was important to his interest in Aboriginal origins.[77]

Thorne did not consult with local Aboriginal communities until after the collection was proposed for return. Both he and Mulvaney have found difficulties with the Aboriginal view that there was no difference between the Murray Black and Kow Swamp collections. Their delay in putting their ideas to the Echuca Aboriginal community and asking for a collaborative approach to further research did not help. Sandra Bowdler, another

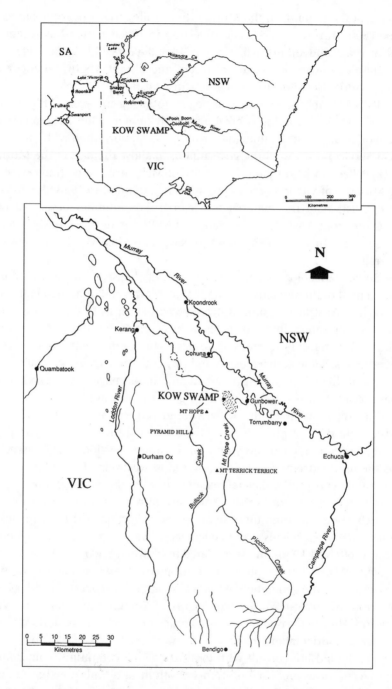

Approximate location of Kow Swamp, Victoria. Adapted from Colin Pardoe, 'The Cemetery as a Symbol: The Distribution of Aboriginal Burial Grounds in Southern Australia', Archaeology in Oceania, *vol. 23, p. 4.*

archaeologist who has worked in the area, argues that by 1990 it was too late for consultation with the Aboriginal community; it should have been conducted much earlier.[78] Such consultation could still have occurred after Aboriginal communities in Victoria were named as bodies responsible for Aboriginal heritage in the amended version of the federal *Aboriginal and Torres Strait Islander Heritage Protection Act 1984*. But, to be fair, Echuca was not named as the relevant community for Kow Swamp area until disputes were settled over community areas according to the 1989 regulations attached to this Act. However, Victorian Aboriginal people were showing an interest in consulting with archaeologists as early as 1986 when they attended the AAA conference in Lorne, Victoria. There was much talk about proposed changes under the new federal and State Act, and perhaps if Thorne had seen this as a signal he could have liaised with them before 1990 and worked out a compromise.

The discipline split into three camps over the Kow Swamp issue. These viewpoints divided into those who:

- were strongly against reburial
- wished to see Aboriginal wishes respected but would prefer reburial not to occur if possible
- were ready to accept local Aboriginal community policy.

Among the archaeologists whom I interviewed for this book, these positions had continued into the 1990s. Most of them fell into the last category. Bowdler summarises the dilemma as 'a conflict between archaeologists claiming a professional hegemony over what they consider a scientific resource, and Aboriginal people asserting a more significant and spiritual custodianship sanctioned by their history and tradition'.[79]

John Mulvaney[80] has been critical of the attitude of younger colleagues. Mulvaney insists that reburial would cause destruction and disagreed with it for two reasons: that both research questions and research techniques are always changing. He has argued that techniques are always improving and that future Aboriginal archaeologists will want to research questions using the remains; and that the remains are of world significance because of their uniqueness and it should not be the decision of any one group to destroy them.

Mulvaney suggested a keeping place with an underground vault, instead of reburial, to the Aboriginal community, but they rejected it. Again, it is likely that the timing was bad, because keeping places of various kinds have been popular with most communities since. The Kow Swamp collection was claimed by the Echuca Aboriginal Co-operative (Yorta Yorta tribe) for reburial for spiritual reasons. As they had not been involved closely in any of the previous analysis, they did not see the point in a keeping place, which would preserve the remains for future researchers. The Yorta Yorta have made extensive efforts to maintain elements of their cultural heritage by recording oral history and archaeological sites within their territory.[81]

By the end of the debate, Mulvaney was particularly bitter about the politics which led to the reburial of the Kow Swamp remains.[82] He criticised the State government for making a quick and easy decision under pressure from city-based activists in order to show the public that they were committed to social justice. Mulvaney saw the government's decision to repatriate the material unconditionally as an attempt 'to disguise government inactivity on the social and economic cause of Land Rights'. While this is perfectly possible, it is unlikely that the Minister for Aboriginal Affairs was acting from a position of 'crass ignorance and total misinformation', as Mulvaney claims.[83]

In his role as an intellectual activist, Professor John Mulvaney supported the return of the Crowther Collection, but was against the reburial of the older Murray Black and Kow Swamp remains because of their continuing value to science. Although he has never personally worked on human remains, he was cited and portrayed in media reports on the debate as the (evil) opposition to Aboriginal wishes.[84] The more stimulating aspects of his argument were sensationalised by journalists hoping to further polarise the debate. In the initial 1984 media debate on 'cross-cultural values or racial monopoly' Mulvaney was also quoted as attacking the views of Aboriginal activists with examples of ethnography recorded in the mid-twentieth century by Ronald Berndt in northern Australia.[85]

Mulvaney's activism failed in the Kow Swamp debate, although as we have seen it had succeeded in the early 1980s when it was instrumental in the debates over the Tasmanian Southwest and First Government House. This failure, with the lack of backing from an increasingly disunited discipline of archaeology, may have led him to become less intensely involved in future debates. Increasingly, Mulvaney found that his ideas concerning the role of archaeology in Australian society did not have the same impact or authority as they had previously.

Mulvaney's argument that the remains are of world significance and therefore belong to the wider community may be easy to argue in the media, but is deadly in the context of past and present race relations. It is probable that many of his colleagues were also aware of this and that greater sensitivity was needed. In disagreeing with Mulvaney, they are more likely following the tide of social change that resulted in the *Native Title Act* in 1993 and current moves towards reconciliation. Their attitude, which acknowledges indigenous self-determination, has also made a difference to the Aboriginal communities concerned with the repatriation of Mungo Woman and her ultimate deposition in a more positive way than Mulvaney's arguments.

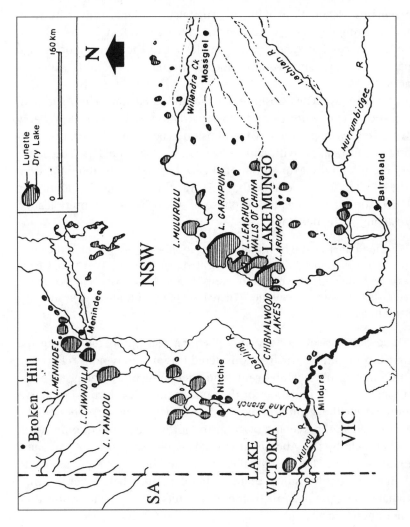

Lake Mungo, New South Wales. Adapted from J. Flood, Archaeology of the Dreamtime, p. 40.

In relation to Lake Mungo, the issue of control of archaeological heritage was raised initially by Aboriginal participants at a 1989 workshop at Willandra Lakes. Both archaeologists and Aboriginal people agreed on a formal statement affirming Aboriginal custodianship of Willandra's archaeological heritage. This heritage is inscribed on the World Heritage List and comprises the 25 000-year-old cremation burial of Mungo Woman, among other remains. Negotiations with the Australian National University were conducted through NSWNPWS Aboriginal Site Officer, Badger Bates. It was agreed that researcher Alan Thorne would return the remains of Mungo Woman to the Aboriginal communities of western New South Wales on 11 January 1992.[86]

Cultural analyst Olga Gostin notes that the *ad hoc* nature of Australian social justice was at work behind this repatriation decision (as it probably was with Kow Swamp). She saw the decision as being made abruptly, without proper consultation with all the relevant Aboriginal elders. The handover of the title of the Mungo National Park had been scheduled for 1992 and she thought it was possible that this was the major factor behind the quick decision. She quotes the response of Aboriginal community leader, Mary Pappin, to the decision:

> We don't understand why it is all coming together so fast one after the other [the return of Mungo National Park and of Mungo Woman]. Why were we not asked whether it is convenient to receive her now. And who is to receive her and what are we to do with her? There is no time to breathe, to think out the right thing to do.[87]

Three possible solutions to this dilemma were proposed among the Aboriginal community. The first considered was an anonymous reburial so that 'no one can dig her up again [and] her spirit can be at peace'. The second solution was cremation for the same reason. The third solution was propounded by the geomorphologist Jim Bowler, who first located the burial.[88] His idea of a keeping place in the form of an underground vault with a key held by the Aboriginal custodians was said to have had some Aboriginal support. The Aboriginal communities, however, were unable to agree on an option that suited them for her deposition before her return.[89] The remains were put in a safe by the community, who are happy now they have her on 'home ground'.

While Gostin believes the decision by the Australian National University to return Mungo Woman was political expediency,[90] Aboriginal archaeologists disagree. Aboriginal archaeologist Stephen Free saw the event as significant because it followed the repatriation and reburial of Murray Black and Kow Swamp collections. He hails it as the first example of a compromise between the two parties, Aborigines and archaeologists, who until then, when taken to their extremes, were incompatible. Free notes that the

Mungo return shows that there is some middle ground. Firstly, Mungo Woman remains in safe keeping by the Aboriginal community in an underground keeping place. Secondly, he observes that the return ceremony was something that had to be experienced. It took place in 1992 at the burial site near the area known as the Walls of China, where the remains were first discovered, at Lake Mungo. Archaeologists and Aboriginal people may look at sites of ancient occupation in different ways, but on this occasion, Free could see that the entire group of people present felt very much the same about it. This return of Mungo Woman's remains stimulated deep emotional feelings.[91]

The future repatriation of scientifically significant collections for reburial or for cremation is unpredictable. Free states that 'one cannot expect a result similar to Mungo Woman in every case, given the diversity of Aboriginal and scientific opinion on the issue'.[92] This diversity is evident in the policies followed for the previous examples of the Murray Black and Kow Swamp collections. After repatriation these collections were being reburied only 200 kilometres away from Lake Mungo, also during 1992.

Finally, in this post-modernist world we are left with competing claims to analyse. Post-modernist theory is of little use in assessing competing claims such as social significance versus scientific significance. It tends to reduce all claims to equal value, which is fine if consensus can then be reached. When conflicting claims are presented in the media, as can be seen in the case of the reburial of the Kow Swamp collection, much of the rational debate disappears. Some Aboriginal people and archaeologists will never be able to collaborate on projects because their positions are too polarised. Increasingly, however, public archaeologists, museum workers and many academics are trying to involve indigenous people at every stage of their work. Policies and legislation may aid them in this process, as far as the *ad hoc* nature of social justice in Australia allows any progress towards indigenous self-determination and reconciliation.

It is inevitable that greater understanding of indigenous, history, culture and customs will have an impact on the way research is conducted and the beliefs about human remains in general. This change will occur as non-indigenous people question and contrast their own beliefs. Two books (one by the archaeologist and priest Eugene Stockton) show that the non-indigenous community in Australia is interested in such self-reflection and spirituality.[93] Several of the people interviewed for this book noted that people in general had a responsibility to the dead, and one ventured that 'families should be consulted [regarding personal papers] like Aboriginal communities'. It is possible that a concern is growing in sections of the wider community about the sanctity of an individual's physical and cultural legacy. These concerns for privacy after death and for burials of pioneer ancestors resemble the concerns felt by indigenous people for their ancestors.

8

The future of
Australian archaeology

AUSTRALIAN ARCHAEOLOGY has generated many great discoveries over the past few decades and now it is coming to terms with their socio-political repercussions. For instance, indigenous cultural identity has been influenced to a large extent by the early dates identified for human occupation. But the devil is in the detail; the diversity of human experience in this country, from 60 000 years ago to the present, needs to become part of the Australian cultural identity as perceived by both insiders and outsiders. Chinese people in Southeast Asia, for example, often see Australia as having a lot of very early archaeological evidence, a big gap, and then some discoveries related to white settlement and the gold rush, with nothing much in between. I fear that many people in Australia perceive the archaeological record in a similar way, despite being physically closer to the sites.

For instance, the realisation that it has not been one long homogenous journey for indigenous culture here is yet to get through to mainstream Australia. Most people still tend to see indigenous culture as remaining static across time and space. The belief that indigenous archaeological remains are the same no matter when and where they originate in Australia is still current. Understandably, Aboriginal and Torres Strait Islander people and others are concerned about this perception and want archaeologists, museum curators, educators and the media to focus more on the richness and diversity of their cultures. No doubt the more involved indigenous people become in proposing and undertaking research, the better such concerns will be answered.

Archaeologists and historians are also worried that the complexities of the recent period (before, during and after contact between indigenous people and others) are not well understood by non-indigenous people. They would like to see the issues associated with colonial and post-colonial management of Australia researched and interpreted for more people to

142

grasp. Accordingly, archaeologists need to work with non-archaeologists, heritage professionals, and indigenous community members in different and challenging ways in order to generate such knowledge and bring it to the attention of a wider public. Australian archaeology is entering a period where the provocation of the earlier debates is beginning to lead to a 'new professionalism', with more attention to ethical and political issues.

Archaeological authority and the 'new professionalism'

Why is archaeology adopting a 'new professionalism' in its approach to research and practice? The short answer is that there has been a dawning realisation both inside and outside the discipline that more is going on here than discovering lots of stones and bones. In the production and subsequent use of archaeological knowledge, archaeologists have experienced much more controversy than they did thirty years ago. Overall, heritage professionals have been reviewing the ethical basis of their professions and updating various codes and charters created earlier; for instance, Australia ICOMOS has recently reviewed the Burra Charter and rewritten some of its heritage conservation principles. Pre-contact archaeology is ahead of the crowd: the AAA adopted a Code of Ethics for Australian archaeologists working with Aboriginal and Torres Strait Islander peoples' heritage in 1992. More attention to consultation is needed to realise a better model of co-operation between archaeologists, indigenous people and local communities (for contact, historical and maritime archaeology). Very few archaeology students are trained in the methods of consulting stakeholders, although they are becoming more aware of the importance of involving indigenous and non-indigenous community groups in archaeological endeavours.

What is more difficult to teach and to learn is the best way to approach controversial situations where archaeologists are just one of the many authorities called upon to resolve an issue. As we have seen in some of the case studies, a successful tactic for locally based archaeologists conducting actual research in such a situation is to call in outside archaeological authorities to speak on archaeological matters. Archaeologists have been more effective when they have maintained some independence from other lobby groups. Working with peers or other heritage professionals has been the best way in the past for archaeologists to have their views heard. This has been difficult where the sheer multiplication of issues requiring the attention of such a professional lobby group has reduced its effectiveness. For instance, the timely support of the AAA was instrumental in the controversies over the Franklin River and First Government House, but since then the organisation has found it trickier to respond quickly to, for example, calls for submissions on proposed changes to important State and federal heritage protection legislation.

How far can individual archaeologists go to raise and comment publicly on such issues? Not many archaeologists in consulting practice feel comfortable about criticising development decisions, while government archaeologists are unable to comment publicly on government policy. The establishment of a well-organised, highly professional and politically motivated group to speak for archaeologists could be one solution. Alternatively, archaeological organisations could become part of a larger umbrella organisation for heritage protection, as has been mooted by members of the AAA. One such association might be Australia ICOMOS. Linkage to such an organisation, which is well respected and has international connections, could be a direction taken in future.

Archaeologists have realised (some belatedly) that archaeological authority and calls to further scientific research for its own sake are not the only claims receiving attention in public affairs. Priorities have changed since the early 1970s, when archaeologists could dominate the proceedings in terms of negotiating preservation and ownership of archaeological material, as demonstrated in the clashes with indigenous groups and with public officials over human remains. The more controversial the issue, the harder it is for all parties to communicate well and negotiate. These and other tactics were previously outside the professional experience of archaeologists. The increase in such issues, a general middle-class concern about reconciliation, and the greater feeling of public scrutiny are causing archaeologists to rapidly acquire those skills. Otherwise, they risk being left behind by those whose ethical stance already requires them to represent a 'new professionalism' in their approach.

Research, be silent, die

In the style of the famous Sydney railway graffiti 'Consume, be silent, die', this maxim is being taken seriously by many archaeologists. If they stay silent and do not publish finished results, archaeologists cannot expect their work and archaeology to retain support over the long-term. The four most important questions about research now are:

- Who is research for?
- Why should it happen?
- What is a worthwhile research question?
- Who decides?

These issues are linked directly to perceptions of archaeological authority and professionalism. Hopefully, greater specificity in ethical concerns will provide the momentum to explore these issues in depth with a confidence that has so far been lacking. If archaeologists develop a good understanding of the socio-political context of their discipline, then much of the uncertainty is taken out of doing research with community involvement. I suspect that it is this uncertainty about the reception of archaeological research proposals and interpretations that causes some archaeologists to leave community consultation of any kind out of their programme until the very last minute. It should become an important maxim that community or stakeholder consultation is an on-going process; like heritage conservation, it should be seen as part of any project from the beginning. By building relationships with stakeholders, ideas about what to research and how it should be conducted can be exchanged without the fear of total rejection.

Researchers who return to the same area time after time to carry out fieldwork are in a good position to establish a long-term relationship with local communities. Much consulting work is unfortunately short-term in nature, although a lot of small jobs in one area can result in an archaeological consultant knowing local Aboriginal community groups well. The same can be true of non-indigenous communities where archaeologists have taken the trouble to contact local heritage societies and libraries for information. In all cases, it is important to try to return information to the community in the form of non-technical presentations, community reports, or some other medium.

A more demanding audience for future archaeological interpretations will require more complex and sophisticated communication, and with that comes the need to work with professionals in other disciplines. The movement towards multidisciplinary research projects, which incorporate archaeology but are not dominated by it, has been slow in Australia. Inadequate funding hampers most attempts. Aside from some of the Sydney excavations and heritage management plans that put archaeology alongside a whole range of disciplines (and archaeological sub-disciplines), not much has occurred with a landscape or neighbourhood focus. The Cumberland–Gloucester Street neighbourhood study did this well for non-indigenous history and archaeology for a section of The Rocks, but more ambitious studies integrating all sub-disciplines of archaeology should be attempted in the future. One approach might be to take landscape types such as the Cape York Peninsula, the Western Australian coastline or volcanic plains of Western Victoria and synthesise all existing work into a CD-ROM, television documentary or book that will assist the public in understanding the cultural significance of these places.

For studies requiring an approach that is broader than archaeology, a multi-skilled team can be drawn from the disciplines such as history, museum studies, materials conservation, anthropology, architecture, zoology, botany, geomorphology or whatever each case requires. Successful projects of this kind remain rare, which causes discouragement, despite the general consensus that this is the right direction for heritage projects.

They blinded me with science!

One aspect of archaeology that can alienate non-archaeologists is the proposed use of new technology in research and management projects. It is important to emphasise that such projects should not have the testing of technological wonders as their main aim. Technological devices and approaches reliant on technology for results should still have a focus that aids in the understanding of the human past; they should not be undertaken merely for their own sake or for some kind of aggrandisement in the eyes of peers. New technology can offer a lot to both archaeologists and the community, but it must support the main aim of the research or management practices, such as compiling site registers or mapping, and not dominate it.

Technology can be useful for answering research questions of the present and can assist with much that is desperately needed in the management of archaeological heritage. Besides expected improvements in dating methods, other methods that may make their presence felt inside and outside archaeology are DNA testing of archaeological remains, Geographic Information Systems databases, and computer reconstruction or simulation based on archaeological and other evidence.

DNA testing and residue analyses are already being used on samples from human remains and organic products associated with artefacts or rock art. There has been an on-going battle in the mass media, as mentioned in the previous chapter, between the proponents of the two theories of human species development and dispersal, the 'out of Africa model' and 'multi-regional model', respectively. The debate concerns DNA drawn from skeletal remains for a variety of studies of different chromosomes. It is likely that the debate will continue for at least another decade before it reaches a conclusion that most authorities will accept. Indigenous communities in Australia will probably be barracking for the multi-regional model as their creation myths tell them that they have always been here. Asian and Pacific peoples also find this model of considerable interest, and further research into this debate will assist in understanding Australia's past relationship with the Asia-Pacific region.

Other less contentious projects will also develop a use for this technology, particularly for the understanding of migrations and movements of populations within Australia. Analyses of residues (of substances such as resin, ground seeds and blood found on stone tools) and use-wear (as in the microscopic examination of stone tool working surfaces) are still of great interest. Such studies are important for determining the usage of stone tools and may be combined with DNA testing of blood residue to discover new facts, such as the gender of tool users. DNA testing can be applied to rock art, analysing, for instance, blood mixed with pigment that is common in some wall paintings.

Geographic Information Systems (GIS) have already been adopted by some universities and government heritage agencies to organise geographic data in a way that aids in the interpretation of archaeological landscapes. GIS can be used to locate archaeological features and evidence both within a site (to plan the spatial distribution of stone artefacts discarded at a quarry site) and within a neighbourhood, landscape or region (to compile a site register). It will eventually become integral to understanding cultural land-scapes of all kinds and will hopefully aid researchers in linking or super-imposing such landscapes as a series of dimensions that make up the diverse aspects of the human journey through Australia's past. Currently GIS is neither simple nor cheap, but its application in research into and manage-ment of archaeological heritage is rapidly becoming essential. The most common application of GIS is as a way of computerising archaeological site lists spatially to aid in their protection by government agencies. As more indigenous people become computer-literate it could also become an im-portant management tool for larger indigenous organisations, such as the Central Aboriginal Land Council. World Heritage sites overseas are already starting to rely on such databases as a management tool in cases where information on a great number of features needs to be recorded and their condition monitored. GIS is more flexible than normal mapping, which cannot be added to or updated as neatly when new information becomes available, such as that from new finds. Accordingly, it has great appeal to those working with historical sites and landscapes, particularly goldfields and the distribution of shipwrecks.

Computer reconstruction or simulation of an ancient or historic place could become a powerful interpretive tool for archaeologists in the future. So far it has had little application in Australia, although it is becoming more common in the interpretation of complex sites overseas. An example is the computer-generated reconstruction of the burial mound of China's first emperor and of Native American sites available on the Internet. Virtual archaeological displays may have a role in museums and in the production of other media such as educational CD-ROMs. They will never completely replace the evocative qualities of seeing the real thing, but they can be used to complement the display of such objects or structures and to assist in

Open area excavation of foundations of stables at Roxborough Park, near Melbourne. Remains such as these could form the basis of computer simulations or reconstructions of the original buildings.

giving contextual information. A computer-generated simulation of the consecutive phases of the development of a site or landscape can present a compelling picture of its physical change over time.

Those funding blues

Funding remains a central issue for archaeological fieldwork, whether it occurs as part of academic research or of conservation and heritage management projects. Resources are needed to carry out the work, interpret its results for the public, and manage any collections or on-site remains afterwards. Funding is also important for the general management of archaeological heritage, whether it will be the subject of future research or not. Tourism is often hailed as a possible source of financial support for on-going maintenance of or research into the archaeological past, but gate fees and other levies may be insufficient to cover the cost of conserving the heritage on display. If core funding cannot be found, it is better to limit access rather than let the cultural values of the attraction decay from poorly managed visitation. Dependence on tourism raises the spectre of the argument that the only worthwhile heritage is that which has an economic value.

A new generation of government heritage grants are currently being developed with a view to managing conservation of a wide range of heritage assets, including those that are archaeological. An appeal to philanthropic organisations (such as the American Express Foundation) may be another direction that will be followed in the future, but most archaeologists are wary of corporate aid that could dominate their research agendas. Do not expect to see a McDisneyfication of archaeological excavations, sites or collections anywhere soon.

How people can get more out of archaeology in Australia

Even without using theme parks to popularise archaeology in this country, it should be possible to balance education and entertainment in the way archaeology is experienced by non-archaeologists. Taking a lesson from past archaeological debates and the public intellectuals involved in them, archaeologists could cultivate a specialised interest in archaeological issues among the mass media in particular. Press releases and information sheets should be directed to influential individuals in the media, education and the Internet in a way which will encourage them to take more than a passing interest in Australian archaeology. Such people are the information gatekeepers between archaeologists and non-archaeologists and they must be drawn in if archaeology is to increase its public profile. Better communication skills in the areas of writing press releases and establishing useful web sites may be on the agenda for many archaeologists in an update of the advice given by Clark back in the 1950s, that the perfect archaeologist needs a 'flair for journalism'. An increase in its public profile would aid Australian archaeology to grow and garner more community support. Allowing for more opportunities for public participation, as described in the success stories in Chapter 3, would assist this aim.

The reconciliation process is also offering a chance at last for non-indigenous non-professionals to become more involved in research into indigenous heritage. For instance, the gathering of historical information prior to some archaeological research is a stage when non-indigenous heritage enthusiasts have a role to play. Information in diaries and personal papers belonging to the non-indigenous ancestors of families still resident in a district can give useful clues to the indigenous usage of that place many years ago. When it is combined with archaeological evidence, it can tell a

'White Australia has a black heart', wall mural done by schoolchildren for the
Aboriginal Reconciliation Conference held in Melbourne in 1997.

cogent story about the cultural landscape of an area. The Macedon Ranges Pre-contact Pilot Study and the Nillumbik Aboriginal Heritage Study, both carried out in Victoria, employed extensive consultation with the non-indigenous and indigenous communities. Fieldworkers sought information about the contact history and Aboriginal presence by a series of interviews with long-term residents and heritage societies, and they publicised the study and its results widely within these areas. Although not originally intended, both studies complemented efforts at reconciliation between Aboriginal and non-Aboriginal sections of the community that were being facilitated by the local shire councils. The Macedon study was nominated in the local government section of the inaugural Council for Aboriginal Reconciliation Awards as an example of how local government and archaeology can support the reconciliation process.

Improved opportunities for meaningful involvement in archaeological fieldwork can discourage destructive practices like metal detecting and shipwreck bashing. A significant number of people undertake these practices out of curiosity about the past rather than hope of financial gain. Although legal prosecution of those who desecrate archaeological sites on land and sea is still the most effective measure for deterring looters, the curious should be encouraged to participate in understanding the past in a more constructive way, rather than destroying it. They are a readymade audience and voluntary workforce for archaeological research. It is hoped that more effort by archaeological heritage managers and others will be put into luring or converting them to archaeology so that more archaeological remains will be conserved and researched properly. Archaeology is about much more than stones and bones. It gives us ways of understanding the past in the present and enables us to imagine multiple futures.

APPENDIX I

Australia International Council on Monuments and Sites: Burra Charter for the Conservation of Places of Cultural Significance, 1983 version

This version was the one in use between 1981 and 1988, the period of most of the action described in the case studies.

Preamble

Having regard to the International Charter for the Conservation and Restoration of Monuments and Sites (Venice 1966), and the Resolutions of 5th General Assembly of ICOMOS (Moscow 1978), the following Charter has been adopted by Australia ICOMOS.

Definitions

Article 1. For the purpose of this Charter:

1.1 *Place* means site, area, building or other work, group of buildings or other works together with pertinent contents and surroundings.

1.2 *Cultural significance* means aesthetic, historic, scientific or social value for past, present or future generations.

1.3 *Fabric* means all the physical material of the *place*.

1.4 *Conservation* means all the processes of looking after a *place* so as to retain its *cultural significance*. It includes *maintenance* and may according to circumstance include *preservation, restoration, reconstruction and adaptation* and will be commonly a combination of these.

1.5   *Maintenance* means the continuous protective care of the *fabric,* contents and setting of a *place* and is to be distinguished from repair. Repair involves *restoration* or *reconstruction* and it should be treated accordingly.

1.6   *Preservation* means maintaining the *fabric* of a *place* in its existing state and retarding deterioration.

1.7   *Restoration* means returning the EXISTING *fabric* of a *place* to a known earlier state by removing accretions or by reassembling existing components without the introduction of new material.

1.8   *Reconstruction* means returning a *place* as nearly as possible to a known earlier state and is distinguished by the introduction of materials (new or old) into the *fabric*. This is not to be confused with either re-creation or conjectural reconstruction, which are outside the scope of this Charter.

1.9   *Adaptation* means modifying a *place* to suit proposed compatible uses.

1.10 *Compatible use* means a use which involves no change to the culturally significant fabric, changes which are substantially reversible, or changes which require a minimal impact.

Conservation Principles

Article 2. The aim of *conservation* is to retain or recover the *cultural significance* of a *place* and must include provision for its security, its *maintenance* and its future.

Article 3. *Conservation* is based on a respect for the existing *fabric* and should involve the least possible physical intervention. It should not distort the evidence provided by the *fabric*.

Article 4. *Conservation* should make sure of all the disciplines which can contribute to the study and safeguarding of a *place*. Techniques employed should be traditional but in some circumstances they may be modern ones for which a firm scientific basis exists and which have been supported by a body of experience.

Article 5. *Conservation* of a *place* should take into consideration all aspects of its *cultural significance* without unwarranted emphasis on any one at the expense of others.

Article 6. The conservation policy appropriate to a *place* must first be determined by an understanding of its *cultural significance* and its physical condition.

Article 7. The conservation policy will determine which uses are compatible.

Article 8. *Conservation* requires the maintenance of an appropriate visual setting, e.g. form, scale, colour, texture and materials. No new construction, demolition or modification which would adversely affect the settings should be allowed. Environmental intrusions which adversely affect the *place* should excluded.

Article 9. A building or work should remain in its historical location. The moving of all or part of a building or work is unacceptable unless this is the sole means of ensuring its survival.

Article 10. The removal of contents which form part of the *cultural signifi- cance* of the *place* is unacceptable unless it is the sole means of ensuring their security and *preservation*. Such contents must be returned should changed circumstances make this practicable.

Conservation Processes

Preservation

Article 11. *Preservation* is appropriate where the existing state of the *fabric* itself constitutes evidence of specific *cultural significance*, or where insufficient evidence is available to allow other conservation processes to be carried out.

Article 12. *Preservation* is limited to the protection, maintenance and where necessary, the stabilisation of the existing *fabric* but without the distortion of its *cultural significance*.

Restoration

Article 13. *Restoration* is appropriate only if there is sufficient evidence of an earlier state of the *fabric* and only if returning the *fabric* to that state recovers the *cultural significance* of the *place*.

Article 14. *Restoration* should reveal anew cultural significant aspects of the *place*. It is based on respect for all the physical, documentary and other evidence and stops at the point where conjecture begins.

Article 15. *Restoration* is limited to the reassembling of displaced com- ponents or removal of accretions in accordance with Article 16.

Article 16. The contributions of all periods to the *place* must be respected. If a *place* includes the *fabric* of different periods, revealing the *fabric* of one period at the expense of another can only be justified when what is removed is of slight *cultural significance* and the *fabric* which is to be revealed is of much greater *cultural significance*.

Reconstruction

Article 17. *Reconstruction* is appropriate where a *place* is incomplete through damage or alteration and where it is necessary for its survival, or where it recovers the *cultural significance* of the *place* as a whole.

Article 18. *Reconstruction* is limited to the completion of a depleted entity and should not constitute the majority of the *fabric* or *place*.

Article 19. *Reconstruction* is limited to the reproduction of *fabric* the form of which is known from the physical and/or documentary evidence. It should be identifiable for inspection as being new work.

Adaptation

Article 20. *Adaptation* is acceptable where the *conservation* of the *place* can not otherwise be achieved, and where the *adaptation* does not substantially detract from its *cultural significance*.

Article 21. *Adaptation* must be limited to that which is essential to a use for the *place* determined in accordance with Articles 6 and 7.

Article 22. *Fabric* of *cultural significance* unavoidably removed in the process of *adaptation* must be kept safely to enable its future reinstatement.

Conservation Practice

Article 23. Work on a *place* must be preceded by professionally prepared studies of the physical, documentary and other evidence, and the existing *fabric* recorded before any disturbance of the *place*.

Article 24. Study of a *place* by any disturbance of the *fabric* or by archaeological excavation should be undertaken where necessary to provide data essential for decisions on the *conservation* of the *place* and/or to secure evidence about to be lost or made inaccessible through necessary *conservation* or other unavoidable action. Investigation of a *place* which requires physical disturbance and which adds substantially to a scientific body of knowledge may be permitted, provided that it is consistent with the conservation policy for the *place*.

Article 25. A written statement of conservation policy must be professionally prepared setting out the *cultural significance*, physical condition and proposed *conservation* process together with justification and supporting evidence, including photographs, drawings and all appropriate samples.

Article 26. The organisation and individuals responsible for policy decisions must be named and specific responsibility taken for each such decision.

Article 27. Appropriate professional direction and supervision must be maintained at all stages of the work and a log kept of new evidence and additional decisions recorded as in Article 25 above.

Article 28. The records required by Articles 23, 25, 26 and 27 should be placed in a permanent archive and made publicly available.

Article 29. The items referred to in Article 10 and Article 22 should be professionally catalogued and protected.

APPENDIX II

Excerpts from the Statement of Cultural Significance regarding First Government House, 1983

The following passages are the parts of the First Government House Site Statement of Cultural Significance (pp. 6–9, 15–16) that are most relevant to the discussion in Chapter 5. The statement was written by Anne Bickford, Robert Irving, Michael Pearson, Helen Proudfoot, Meredith Walker and Peter White for submission to the debate by the Australian Archaeological Association in November 1983. The authors deal with the cultural significance of the site for the period covered by the Museum of Sydney (1788–1845). The statement also discussed all the phases of the site in line with the principles embodied in the Burra Charter (Appendix 1), including the lack of evidence for Aboriginal occupation of the site before 1788 and the significance of the phases after 1845.

The significance of the site and its evidence comprises:

(a) Social:

- ■ it is a cultural landmark and focus of sentiment for all Australians and for particular majority and minority groups throughout Australia. These groups include persons of English, Irish and Scots descent, First Fleeters and Aboriginal people. For Aboriginal people the site is significant both as the focal point for the invasion of their country and because of its association with historic Aboriginal persons.

- ■ it is of *perpetual* significance as the first evidence for and a symbol of European settlement on the Australian continent.

- ■ it is of *current* significance to the Bicentennial in that it is the only *in situ* physical evidence from the first year of European occupation.

- ■ it was of significance in the *past* as the centre of the colony until 1845. For example, acceptance of emancipists at First Government

House significantly affected the colony's social and political structure. The markers erected by the RAHS in 1917 and the Sydney City Council in the 1960s are later expressions of social significance.

■ it is, and always will be, of great educational value as a vehicle for learning and teaching and a trigger to the imagination.

(b) Historic:

■ association with historic persons, such as governors, foreign visitors, explorers, Aboriginals, merchants, settlers and statesmen.

■ association with historic events, such as the first European settlement, the beginnings of the press, the Rum Rebellion and the meeting of the first Legislative Council.

■ association with a major phase in Australia's governmental and administrative history. First Government House was the umbilical cord with the U.K. through which government flowed until the governor moved to the current government house (circa 1842). First Government House was the centre of the government power throughout its life.

■ as an exemplar of architectural history. The *in situ* works and structures and the associated documentary evidence demonstrate that the first building was of high standard, beyond that of the other, domestic architecture of the period. The changes in the building over time show the influence of overseas architectural trends, and the need for more space for administrative and residential purposes. The site's evolution further demonstrates architectural adaptations to the Australian environment, notably in the use of verandahs and covered ways. In its final form the building became a synthesis of diverse elements, echoing the European Picturesque style.

■ as an exemplar of building technology. The footings and drainage systems show the high standards which could be obtained in early European Australia. The remains demonstrate difficulties which had to be overcome in the use of building materials available in the Australian environment, and the resolution of these. The technology used in later buildings was being developed from the start of settlement.

■ as an example of how local environment and topography were considered and used, shown in the aspects and locations of the buildings and the placement of rooms, structures, spaces and gardens.

■ association with the history of art. In a very large number of the paintings and drawings of Sydney before 1845 the House and its setting figured prominently, signifying the fact that it was a vital focus and major landmark of the town.

- association with the history of printing, publishing and newspapers. The first Government Orders (1795) and *Sydney Gazette* (1803) were printed here. Works associated with the printing office in the services wing, and some metal printing type, have been found.

(c) Scientific:

First Government House is of archaeological significance in that it is the locus for many historical and scientific questions which can be solved only by archaeological techniques. This significance is both proven, in the areas already excavated, and potential, in all unexcavated areas of the First Government House site. The site provides rare opportunities for research into aspects of Sydney's 200 years of history. These include issues in archaeology, history, architecture, soil science, building technology, manufacturing processes, environmental adaptation and taphonomic processes. First Government House has potential to provide further information on these and other scientific problems depending on the questions asked of it.

(d) Aesthetic:

The aesthetic integrity of the First Government House site will ultimately depend on:

- the retention of an appropriate visual setting without environmental intrusions which adversely affect appreciation or enjoyment of the place, and
- direct visibility of the remains, since only if they are visible can their form, scale, material, texture and three-dimensional qualities be appreciated.

There are three aspects to the aesthetic significance of First Government House:

- within the site the remains themselves, both *in situ* and removed, have unique qualities of form, scale and texture.
- within the townscape of Bridge and Phillip Streets, the site contributes both variation in terms of space and scale, and continuity in the use and scale of materials.
- within the city of Sydney the site provides a balance to the dominant, verticality of the city buildings, and evokes the form of the city.

Summary statement of cultural significance

The most important fact about the First Government House site is that it contains the remains of the administrative and social centre of the first permanent European occupation of Australia. It contains the only remains from 1788 known to survive in 1983. The remains have been in the past, are now and will be in the future seen as a cultural and historical landmark and focus of sentiment for the Australian community and for individual groups within it. This value of the site depends to a large extent on the visible presence and form of the remains from the period 1788–1845.

First Government House site has a series of historic associations, which combine to give the place a unique historic significance. These historic associations include:

- the use of the site by a large number of prominent historic figures, both European and Aboriginal, of the eighteenth and nineteenth centuries,
- the role of the site and its inhabitants in events of major historical importance,
- the association with a number of major formative phases in Australian history and the administration of the colony of New South Wales,
- evidence of the formative phase of Australian architectural history and building technology, of which the site and its remains are an exemplar.

The potential of the site to answer research questions in these and other fields gives the place great scientific significance.

The buildings at 39–47 Phillip Street and 36–42 Young Street, which flank and partly cover the 1788–1845 remains, are important in their own right. They have historic value. The former are rare survivors of residential use in this part of the city, and included among their residents several historically important figures; the latter is a probably unique example of office accommodation in the terrace style. These buildings have townscape value.

The streets adjoining the site of the 1788–1845 remains are of primary importance in that they may be assumed to cover a further substantial proportion of such remains. They also embody evidence of 140 years of street construction and use.

The First Government House site is the most tangible link with the foundation of white settlement on this continent and, as such, is of the greatest symbolic importance to the Australian community.

Notes

1 What is Australian archaeology?

[1] Prehistoric Lithic Resource Utilitisation, p. 1.

[2] Thomas, *Archaeology*, p. 167.

[3] Pearson and Sullivan, *Looking after Heritage Places*, p. 84.

[4] Instead, see books such as Merrillees, *Living with Egypt's Past in Australia*.

[5] M. Truscott and L. Smith, 'Women's Roles in the Archaeological Workforce', pp. 217–21.

[6] Staniforth, 'A Future for Australian Maritime Archaeology?', p. 92.

[7] Hermes, 'Developing a Course in Australian Prehistory', pp. 1–4.

[8] Birckhead, 'Traditional Aboriginal Land Management Practices', pp. 297–300.

[9] 'Cultural Resource Management as Archaeological Housework', p. 191.

[10] du Cros, 'Popular Archaeology', pp. 190–1.

[11] du Cros, 'To See Ourselves as Others See Us', pp. 243–5.

[12] du Cros, 'Popular Archaeology', p. 192.

[13] Weissensteiner, Indiana Jones Fantasy vs Archaeological Reality, pp. 30–6.

[14] Lucasfilm Pty Ltd, *Indiana Jones and the Last Crusade*; Weissensteiner, Indiana Jones Fantasy vs Archaeological Reality, pp. 3–36.

[15] Communications and Entertainment Pty Ltd, *Robbers of the Sacred Mountain*.

[16] Weissensteiner, Indiana Jones Fantasy vs Archaeological Reality, p. 20

[17] Wood Jones, 'Tasmania's Vanished Race', 3AR lecture broadcast 26 May 1935.

[18] See the discussion of Tom Haydon's work in Chapter 4.

[19] Williams, *This is The Science Show*, pp. 3–10

[20] See 1990s reports in the Audio-visual References.

[21] Richard I. Ford in Thomas, *Archaeology*, p. 138.

[22] Clark, *Archaeology and Society*, pp. 17–18.

[23] du Cros, 'To See Ourselves as Others See Us', pp. 243–5.

[24] Gero, 'Producing Prehistory, Controlling the Past', pp. 89–95.

[25] Gero, 'Producing Prehistory, Controlling the Past', p. 98.

[26] See White, *The Past Is Human*.

[27] White, *The Past Is Human*, p. 1.

[28] *Australian*, 4 February 1992.

[29] *Australian*, 4 February 1992, p. 31.

[30] *Australian*, 1 March 1993.

[31] See du Cros, 'To See Ourselves as Others See Us', pp. 243–5; Weissensteiner Indiana Jones Fantasy vs Archaeological Reality, p. 20.

32 Creamer, 'Aboriginal Perceptions of the Past', p. 130; Gostin, 'Accessing the Dreaming', p. 63; Free, 'The Return of Mungo Woman', p. 37; Flood, *Archaeology of the Dreamtime*, p. 15.

2 Australian developments and discoveries

1 Phillip, *The Voyage of Governor Phillip to Botany Bay*, pp. 137–9.
2 Daniel, *150 Years of Archaeology*, pp. 16–25; Trigger, *A History of Archaeological Thought*, pp. 45–52.
3 du Cros, 'Skeletons in the Closet', pp. 11–23.
4 Griffiths, *Hunters and Collectors*, pp. 9–86.
5 Davison, 'A Brief History of the Australian Heritage Movement', pp. 14–27.
6 Proudfoot et al., *Australia's First Government House*, pp. 150–1.
7 du Cros, 'Skeletons in the Closet', pp. 30–1.
8 du Cros, 'Female Skeletons in the Closet', pp. 239–44.
9 du Cros, 'Skeletons in the Closet', pp. 36–7.
10 du Cros, 'Skeletons in the Closet', pp. 24–34.
11 du Cros, *The Otways Regional Archaeological Study Stage 1*, pp. 1–10; Robinson, 'Selling our National Heritage', pp. 41–3; Griffiths, *Hunters and Collectors*, pp. 82–6.
12 du Cros, 'Skeletons in the Closet', p. 63.
13 du Cros, 'The Burrill Lake Rockshelter', pp. 1–7.
14 Mulvaney, 'The Australian Aborigines 1606–1929', pp. 297–314; White and O'Connell, *Sunda and Sahul*, p. 28.
15 du Cros, 'The Burrill Lake Rockshelter', pp. 1–7.
16 du Cros, 'Skeletons in the Closet', pp. 11–22.
17 Pulleine, 'The Tasmanians and their Stone Culture', p. 310; du Cros, 'Skeletons in the Closet', p. 5.
18 Mulvaney, 'The Australian Aborigines 1606–1929', pp. 297–314, and 'The Stone Age of Australia', pp. 56–107.
19 See Glover, 'Scientific Racism, the Australian Aboriginal 1865–1915, and the Logic of Evolutionary Anthropology', pp. 1–30; Willmot, 'Dilemma of Mind', pp. 1–10.
20 Trigger, *A History of Archaeological Thought*, p. 145
21 *Sydney Morning Herald*, 14 July 1930; du Cros, 'Skeletons in the Closet', pp. 37–44.
22 Mulvaney, 'The Stone Age of Australia', pp. 56–107, and 'Prehistory from Antipodean Perspectives', pp. 228–312.
23 Horton, *Recovering the Tracks*, pp. 4–5.
24 Mulvaney, 'The Stone Age of Australia', pp. 56–107.
25 Trigger, *A History of Archaeological Thought*, p. 145.
26 Murray and White, 'Cambridge in the Bush?', pp. 255–63; du Cros, 'Skeletons in the Closet', p. 7; Moser, 'Archaeology and its Disciplinary Culture', p. 108.
27 Moser, 'Archaeology and its Disciplinary Culture', p. 110.
28 Isobel McBryde quoted in Moser, 'Archaeology and its Disciplinary Culture', p. 131.
29 Moser, 'Archaeology and its Disciplinary Culture', pp. 21, 196 and 198.
30 McCarthy, 'The Australian Institute of Aboriginal Studies, p. 307.
31 Moser, 'Archaeology and its Disciplinary Culture', p. 219.
32 Pearson and Sullivan, *Looking after Heritage Places*, p. 4.
33 See McKinlay and Jones, *Archaeological Resource Management in Australia and Oceania*; Sullivan and Bowdler, *Site Survey and Significance Assessment*, 1984.
34 Pearson and Sullivan, *Looking after Heritage Places*, p. 4.
35 Mackay and Karskens, 'Historical Archaeology in Australia', pp. 110–14.
36 Apologies to Anne Summers' inspirational feminist work, *Damned Whores and God's Police*, 1975.
37 Greenwood, *Australia*, pp. 1–10.
38 Scenery Preservation Board, 'Report of the Chairman for the Year 1937–8'.
39 Temple, 'Historical Archaeology and its Role in the Community', p. 41.

[40] See Baker, 'The Preservation Movement in Australia', 1969.

[41] Temple, 'Historical Archaeology and its Role in the Community', pp. 42–3.

[42] du Cros, 'Skeletons in the Closet', p. 61.

[43] Moser, 'Archaeology and its Disciplinary Culture', p. 114.

[44] Mulvaney, 'Two Remarkable Careers', pp. 96–101.

[45] Moser, 'Archaeology and its Disciplinary Culture', p. 90.

[46] See Pearson and Sullivan's *Looking after Heritage Places* for more information on the development of legislation, and see web sites of various heritage agencies for the most up-to-date information as many State acts were being reviewed or amended at the time of writing.

[47] Pearson and Sullivan, *Looking after Heritage Places*, pp. 79–80.

[48] Barker, *Techniques of Archaeological Excavation*, pp. 11–12.

[49] Pearson and Sullivan, *Looking after Heritage Places*, pp. 79–80.

[50] Henderson, *Maritime Archaeology in Australia*, pp. 1–5.

[51] Terry Arnott, interviewed by Mary McKell, on ABC Radio's *Science Show*, 1993.

[52] Bannear, 'North Goldfields Project', p. 25.

[53] S. Cheney, 'Turner's Paddock: Nineteenth Century Refuse and the Growth of Consumer Society'.

[54] In the 1990s it became the Australasian Society for Historical Archaeology with the inclusion of historical archaeologists from New Zealand.

[55] Moser, 'Archaeology and its Disciplinary Culture', p. 90.

[56] Mulvaney, 'Preface', in J. Mummery (ed.) *Prehistory and Heritage*, p. v; Arnold and Morris, *Monash Bibliographic Dictionary of 20th Century Australia*; and Moser, 'Archaeology and its Disciplinary Culture', pp. 108–10.

[57] Graham Clark quoted in Moser, 'Archaeology and its Disciplinary Culture', p. 108.

[58] Moser, 'Archaeology and its Disciplinary Culture', pp. 108–10.

[59] Trigger, *A History of Archaeological Thought*, pp. 1–3; Gero, Producing Prehistory, Controlling the Past, pp. 89–95; and 'The Social World of Prehistoric Facts', pp. 31–40.

[60] Trigger, *A History of Archaeological Thought*, pp. 144–5.

[61] Moser, 'Archaeology and its Disciplinary Culture', pp. 108–20; Smith, 'What is this Thing called Post-processual Archaeology?', pp. 28–31.

[62] Attenbrow and Meehan, 'Editorial', p. 1.

[63] Moser, 'Archaeology and its Disciplinary Culture', pp. 238–9.

[64] See for example, Bowler et al., 'Pleistocene Human Remains for Australia', 1970, and 'Pleistocene Man in Australia', 1972; Bowler and Thorne, 'Human Remains from Lake Mungo', 1976; Thorne, 'Mungo and Kow Swamp', 1971; Webb, *The Willandra Lakes Hominids*, 1989; Hope, 'Pleistocene Archaeological Sites in the Central Murray-Darling Basin', 1993; Johnston, 'Pleistocene Shell Middens of the Willandra Lakes', 1993; Mulvaney and Kamminga, *Prehistory of Australia*, 1999.

[65] *National Times*, 10 January 1988.

[66] See White and O'Connell, *Sunda and Sahul*, 1982.

[67] Lilley, 'Australian Archaeologists in the Pacific', pp. 46–53.

[68] Horton, *Recovering the Tracks*, pp. 301–9; Allen, 'Notions of the Pleistocene in Greater Australia'; pp. 139–51.

[69] Allen, 'Notions of the Pleistocene in Greater Australia', pp. 139–51; Bowdler, 'Views of the Past in Australian Archaeology', pp. 123–38.

[70] Meehan and Jones, *Archaeology with Ethnography*; Thomas, 'Models and Prima-donnas in Southwest Tasmania, pp. 21–3; and Cosgrove et al., 'Late Pleistocene Human Occupation in Tasmania', pp. 28–35.

[71] Moser, 'Archaeology and its Disciplinary Culture', p. 163.

[72] Lourandos and Ross, 'The Great Intensification Debate', p. 55.

[73] See Lourandos, 'Forces of Change', 1980; Ross, If There Were Water, 1984; Williams, *Complex Hunter-Gatherers*, 1988.

[74] Bird and Frankel, 'Chronology and Explanation in Western Victoria and South-east Australia', pp. 1–16.

75 Hiscock, 'Technological Change in the Hunter River Valley', pp. 40–50.

76 Lourandos and Ross, 'The Great Intensification Debate', p. 59.

77 See Birmingham and Murray, *Historical Archaeology in Australia*, 1987.

78 Egloff, 'From Swiss Family Robinson to Sir Russell Drysdale', pp. 1–8.

79 See Birmingham and Murray, *Historical Archaeology in Australia*, 1987; Connah, *The Archaeology of Australia's History*, 1988.

80 Birmingham and Jeans, 'The Swiss Family Robinson Model and the Archaeology of Colonisation', pp. 3–14.

81 Bairstow, 'Historical Archaeology at the Crossroads', pp. 32–9; Egloff, 'From Swiss Family Robinson to Sir Russell Drysdale', pp. 1–8.

82 Bickford, 'The Patina of Nostalgia', pp. 5–6.

83 Burke et al., 'Beyond the Looking Glass', pp. 13–22; Pearson and Sullivan, *Looking after Heritage Places*, p. 130.

84 See Birmingham and Murray, *Historical Archaeology in Australia*, 1987.

85 Birmingham et al., *Archaeology and Colonisation*, p. 5.

86 See Birmingham et al., *Australian Pioneer Technology, 1979*, and *Industrial Archaeology in Australian Rural Industry*, 1983.

87 Murray, 'Relativism, Conservation Philosophy and Historical Archaeology', pp. 1–19; Birmingham, 'A Decade of Digging', pp. 13–22; Lydon, 'Sites: Archaeology in Conext'; Mackay and Karskens, 'Historical Archaeology in Australia', pp. 110–12.

88 Bairstow, 'Urban Archaeology', pp. 52–8; Karskens, 'Engaging Artefacts', pp. 8–11.

89 Henderson, *Maritime Archaeology in Australia*, pp. 1–5; Hosty and Stuart, 'Maritime Archaeology over the Last Twenty Years', pp. 9–19.

90 Henderson, *Maritime Archaeology in Australia*, pp. 1–20.

91 Connah, *The Archaeology of Australia's History*, pp. 12–19.

92 Hosty and Stuart, 'Maritime Archaeology over the Last Twenty Years', pp. 9–19.

93 Hosty and Stuart, 'Maritime Archaeology over the Last Twenty Years'.

94 Muckelroy, 'Maritime Archaeology', 1978.

95 Burke et al., 'Beyond the Looking Glass', pp. 13–22.

96 See Mansell, 'The Last Tasmanian', p. 2; Bickford, 'The Last Tasmanian', pp. 11–14; Langford, 'Our Heritage—Your Playground' pp. 1–8; Fourmile, 'The Need for a National Inquiry into State Collection of Aboriginal and Torres Strait Islander Cultural Heritage', pp. 3–4; Field et al., 'Coming Back', pp. 39–42.

97 Fullagar et al., 'Early Human Occupation of Northern Australia', pp. 751–5.

98 Spooner, 'Human Occupation at Jinmium, Northern Australia', pp. 173–8; *Sydney Morning Herald*, 1 June 1998; Owen, 'Potential Errors in the Dating at the Jinmium Site, in Northwestern Australia', pp. 32–6.

99 The Piltdown Hoax involved the discovery of some human and animal remains from some gravels in Sussex between 1905 and 1915. The human remains were considered to be a 'missing link' in human evolution. In 1953 they were revealed to be a hoax when fluorine dating and other methods showed that the skull was *Homo sapiens* and the jaw was orangutang: Bray and Trump, *The Penguin Dictionary of Archaeology*, p. 179.

1 See du Cros and Smith (eds), *Women in Archaeology*, 1993; Beck and Balme (eds), *Gendered Archaeology*, 1994; Casey et al., *Refining Archaeology*, 1998.

2 Wylie, 'The Complexity of Gender Bias', p. 53.

3 du Cros and Smith, 'Introduction', pp. xii–xx.

4 Clarke, 'Cultural Resource Management as Archaeological Housework', pp. 191–4; Hope, 'Double Bind', pp. 175–90; Beck and Balme, 'Introduction', pp. 1–6.

5 Smith, 'What is this Thing called Post-processual Archaeology?', pp. 28–31.

6 Pearson and Sullivan, 'Looking After Heritage Places,' p. 14.

7 Bodycoat et al., 'The Swan Brewery, Perth', pp. 22–4; Askew, 'Editorial', p. 4; Vinnicombe, 'An Aboriginal Site Complex at the foot of Mount Eliza that includes the Old Swan Brewery', pp. 53–62.

[8] Egloff, 'Old Cloth for a New Suit: Training for Archaeological Heritage Management in Australia', 'The Return of Mungo Woman', 1993; Truscott, 'Indigenous Cultural Heritage Protection Programme', 1994; Blair and Feary, 'Regional Assessment of Cultural Heritage', 1995, pp. 15–21.

[9] Henderson, 'Current Approaches to the Underwater Cultural Heritage', pp. 5–8; Hosty and Stuart, 'Maritime Archaeology over the Last Twenty Years', pp. 9–19; Mackay and Karskens, 'Historical Archaeology in Australia', pp. 110–12.

[10] Mulvaney in Connah, *The Archaeology of Australia's History*, pp. xiii–iv; I. Jack, 'Historical Archaeology and the Historian', pp. 130–6; S. Jack, 'Divorce or Reconciliation', p. 124.

[11] I. Jack, 'Historical Archaeology and the Historian', p. 131.

[12] Godden Mackay Logan Ltd and Grace Karskens, 'The Cumberland /Gloucester Streets Site, The Rocks', pp. 1–3.

3 The dig, diggers and the community

[1] Denis Gojak, interview by author, Sydney, 14 March 1995.

[2] Chris Tilley, 'Excavation as Theatre', p. 278.

[3] For instance, Grace Karskens *The Rocks: The Life in Early Sydney*, 1997 and *Inside The Rocks*, 1999; Jane Lydon, *Many Inventions: The Chinese in The Rocks*, 1999.

[4] Department of Planning, *Historical Sites Investigation and Conservation Guidelines*, p. 31.

[5] Tilley, 'Archaeology as Theatre', pp. 275–80.

[6] Department of Planning, *Guidelines*, p. 31.

[7] Davies and Buckley, *Port Arthur Conservation Development Project: Archaeological Procedures Manual*, pp. 3–4.

[8] du Cros and Rhodes, 'Commonwealth/Telecom Sites: Artefact Cataloguing and Analysis Methods', pp. 17–20; and my own recent observations.

[9] For local examples see Mulvaney, *Archaeology Manual No. 4*, 1968; Connah, *Australian Field Archaeology: A Guide to Techniques*, 1983; Green, *Maritime Archaeology: A Technical Handbook*, 1990.

[10] As part of excavation permits issued by most government heritage agencies. For an example of policy precedent see Department of Planning, *Guidelines*, pp. 35–6.

[11] Anne Bickford, interview by author, Sydney, 15 March 1995.

[12] Tilley, 'Archaeology as Theatre', pp. 275–80.

[13] Hodder, 'Interpretive Archaeology and its Role', pp. 7–18; Hodder, *The Archaeological Process*, pp. 62–5.

[14] Moser, 'Archaeology and its Disciplinary Culture', pp. 237–8; Gero, 'Excavation Bias and Woman-at-Home Ideology', pp. 37–42.

[15] Gero, 'Excavation Bias and Woman-at-Home Ideology'; Yellen, 'Women, Archaeology, the National Science Foundation', pp. 53–8.

[16] Beck, 'Women in Archaeology', p. 99.

[17] Anne Bickford, interview by author, Sydney, 15 March 1995.

[18] See Hoffman and Lerner, 'Arizona'; Lange, 'A Role for Avocationalists and Volunteers'.

[19] Tilley, 'Archaeology as Theatre', p. 279.

[20] Department of Planning, *Guidelines*, p. 39; Australian Archaeological Association, 'Code of Ethics', p. 129.

[21] For example, *Inherit*, Heritage Victoria's newsletter; *Heritage NSW*, NSW Heritage Office's newsletter; and *In Place*, Australian Heritage Commission's occasional newsletter.

[22] Godden Mackay Ltd, 'Conservation and Management Report', p. 16.

[23] Karskens, *Inside the Rocks*, pp. 12–17.

[24] Wayne Johnson, interview by author, Sydney, February 1995.

[25] See Kelly, *Anchored in a Small Cove: A History and Archaeology of The Rocks, Sydney*, 1997; Karskens, *The Rocks: Life in Early Sydney*, 1997; Karskens, *Inside the Rocks*, 1999.

[26] Godden Mackay Logan Ltd and Karskens, 'National Trust Energy Australia Heritage Awards Report', pp. 1–4.

[27] Godden Mackay Ltd, 'Conservation and Management Report', p. 16.

[28] Brown, 'The Rocks Revealed', p. 1.

[29] Brown, 'The Rocks Revealed'; Godden Mackay Ltd, 'Conservation and Management Report', p. 16.

[30] Godden Mackay Ltd, 'Conservation and Management Report'.

[31] Geraldine O'Brien, interview by author, Sydney, 12 April 1995.

[32] Godden Mackay Ltd, 'Conservation and Management Report', p. 16.

[33] Karskens, *The Rocks*, p. 17.

[34] Anne Bickford, interview by author, Sydney, 15 March 1995.

[34] K. C. Smith, 'By Land or by Sea', pp. 13–17.

[36] Jean Longpre, interview by author, Fort Chambly, Montreal, 4 January 1994.

[37] It was the State government body concerned with the administration of archaeological protection legislation at the time; it has since been restructured and absorbed into several different departments, including Heritage Victoria and Aboriginal Affairs Victoria.

[38] Victoria Archaeological Survey Press Release, January 1988.

[39] *Weekend Australian*, 9–10 January 1988, p. 3; *Age*, 9 January 1988, p. 1.

[40] *Age*, 3 February 1988, p. 1; *Herald*, 4 February 1988, p. 3.

[41] *Age* 12 February 1988.

[42] See Annear, *Bearbrass*; *Age* 25 March 1995.

[43] Richard Lange, Arizona State Museum, interview by the author, December 1991.

[44] *ASHA Newsletter*, 28 April 1998.

[45] *Sydney Morning Herald*, 15 February 1993.

[46] McDonald et al., 'The Rouse Hill Infrastructure Project (Stage 1)', pp. 259–63.

[47] McDonald et al., 'The Rouse Hill Infrastructure Project (Stage 1)'.

[48] McDonald et al., 'The Rouse Hill Infrastructure Project (Stage 1)'.

[49] Josephine McDonald, interview by author, Sydney, 8 March 1995.

[50] *Hills Shire Times*, 24 November 1992, 19, 22 October, 23 November 1993.

[51] See the *Hills Shire Times*, 15 June 1993.

[52] *Rouse Hill Infrastructure News*, 1993, 1994.

[53] McDonald, letter 10 May 2000.

[54] Lange, 'A Role for Avocationalists and Volunteers'.

[55] Gojak, 'Presenting Archaeology to the Public'.

[56] Gojak, 'Presenting Archaeology to the Public'; Denis Gojak, interview by author, Sydney, 14 March 1995.

[57] *Archaeology Abroad*, Bulletin, May 1999.

[58] Lange, 'A Role for Avocationalists and Volunteers'.

[59] Richard Mackay, interview by author, Sydney, 13 March 1995.

[60] Interview by author, Sydney, 15 March 1995.

[61] Interview by author, Sydney, 13 March 1995.

[62] Anne Bickford, interview by author, Sydney, 15 March 1995.

[63] Riemer Knoop, 'Public Awareness and Archaeology', p. 444.

[64] *Australia ICOMOS News*, April 1999.

4 Romancing the stones

[1] Jones, 'Tom Haydon, 1938–1991', p. 51.

[2] Jones, 'Tom Haydon, 1938–1991'.

[3] See Haydon, *Dig a Million, Make a Million*, 1969.

[4] See Haydon, *The Last Tasmanian*, 1977.

[5] Jones, 'Tom Haydon, 1938–1991', p. 51.

[6] Macintosh always published under the initials N. W. G. He was known to his medical peers as 'Black Mac' because of his interest in Aboriginal human remains and Australian physical anthropology.

[7] See Haydon, *Fossil Man in Australia*, 1967.

[8] Flood, 'Archaeology of the Dreaming', pp. 55–6.

[9] See Haydon, *The Talgai Skull*, 1969; Jones, 'Tom Haydon, 1938–1991', p. 53.

[10] See Haydon, *The Long Long Walkabout*, 1975.

[11] Jones, 'Tom Haydon, 1938–1991', pp. 54, 55, 62.

[12] Unfortunately this scene has been cut from the shorter 55-minute version shown on Australian television. It is present in the original 109-minute version held by the Australian National Library.

[13] Jones, 'Tom Haydon, 1938–1991', pp. 55, 59.

[14] Jones, 'Tom Haydon, 1938–1991', p. 59; Bickford, 'The Last Tasmanian', pp. 11–14.

[15] See Artis Film Productions, *The Last Tasmanian*, 1977.

[16] Jones, 'Tom Haydon 1938–1991', pp. 59–60.

[17] Published as *The Aboriginal Tasmanians*, it ran into two editions, which have a decidedly different slant on the question of Tasmanian Aboriginal identity—see 2nd edn, pp. 254–5.

[18] Reynolds, *Fate of a Free People*, 1995.

[19] Reynolds, *Fate of a Free People*, p. 194.

[20] See Hawker, *The Resurrection of the Batavia*, 1995.

[21] Unfortunately this scene has been cut from the shorter 55-minute version.

[22] *Australian*, 25 May 1978; *Saturday Evening Mercury*, 27 May 1978.

[23] Haydon, 'The Last Tasmanian—Educational Guide', pp. 1–2.

[24] *Sunday Times*, 28 May 1978.

[25] *Australian*, 20 June 1978.

[26] *Sunday Press*, 20 August 1978.

[27] Attwood, *The Making of the Aborigines*, pp. x–xi.

[28] *National Times*, 22 July 1978.

[29] *National Times*, 29 July 1978.

[30] *National Times*, 3 August 1978.

[31] See Gaby and Marion, 'Racism in Tasmania', 1978.

[32] See Moore, *Monday Conference*, 4 September 1978.

[33] See Moore, *Monday Conference*, 4 September 1978.

[34] Jones, 'Tom Haydon, 1938–1991', pp. 59–60.

[35] Rosenthal, *The Documentary Conscience*, pp. 1–10; Lloyd-James, 'Television Documentary', pp. 113–16.

[36] Haydon produced two films on the Franklin campaign, one of which also featured Jones (see Chapter 6).

[37] See Haydon, 'The Last Tasmanian—Educational Guide'.

[38] See Haydon, *Fossil Man in Australia*, 1967, *The Talgai Skull*, 1969, and *The Long Long Walkabout*, 1975; Raymond, *The Origin of the Australians*, 1972; Thorne and Raymond, *Man on the Rim*, 1989.

[39] *Screen International*, 18 May 1978.

[40] See Haydon, *The Long Long Walkabout*, 1975.

[41] See Thorne and Raymond, *Man on the Rim*, 1989.

[42] Shields in *Bulletin*, 12 November 1991.

[43] See Garrett, *From Mungo to Makaratta*, 1983; see also Chapter 7.

[44] BBC Discovery Communications Inc., *The Sands of Dreamtime*, 1997.

5 Exposing First Government House

[1] Quoted in Connah, *The Archaeology of Australia's History*, p. 27.

[2] Proudfoot et al., *Australia's First Government House*, pp. 78–80, 106.

[3] Connah, *The Archaeology of Australia's History*, p. 27.

[4] Proudfoot et al., *Australia's First Government House*, pp. 124–7.

[5] See Appendix 2; Connah, *The Archaeology of Australia's History*, p. 27.

[6] Proudfoot et al., *Australia's First Government House*, p. 1.

[7] Connah, *The Archaeology of Australia's History*, p. 28.

8 Helen Temple, interview by author, Sydney, 11 April 1995.

9 Temple, 'Historical Archaeology and its Role in the Community', p. 80.

10 Connah, *The Archaeology of Australia's History*, p. 26.

11 Heritage Council of New South Wales, *Annual Report*, 1982. Names have changed since 1982: the Heritage Branch is now the Heritage Office, within the Ministry of Urban Affairs and Planning. The Heritage Council of New South Wales, however, remains the same in name and function (although it now oversees a heritage fund that can be used to fund Aboriginal heritage projects along with non-Aboriginal ones).

12 Historic Houses Trust of New South Wales, *Hyde Park Barracks Museum Plan*, p. 26.

13 Whitehouse, 'Future Management Options', pp. 32–8.

14 Helen Temple, interview by author, Sydney, 11 April 1995.

15 Helen Temple, interview by author, Sydney, 11 April 1995.

16 Heritage Council of New South Wales, *Annual Report*, 1982.

17 Denis Gojak, interview by author, 14 March 1995, and later comments April 2000.

18 Proudfoot et al., *Australia's First Government House*, p. 16.

19 Robyn Stocks, interview by author, Sydney, 8 February 1995.

20 Proudfoot et al., *Australia's First Government House*, p. 16.

21 Judy Birmingham, interview by author, Sydney, 12 April 1995.

22 David Rhodes, interview by author, Melbourne, 4 May 1995.

23 Egloff and Smith, 'Analysis of Glass Artefacts from the Excavation of First Government House, Sydney', p. 44.

24 This information is based on Proudfoot et al., *Australia's First Government House*; Denis Gojak's newspaper clipping collection; the author's own recollections.

25 Proudfoot et al., *Australia's First Government House*, p. 3; Temple, interview by author, Sydney, 11 April 1995; and Bickford, interview by author, Sydney, 15 March 1995.

26 Proudfoot et al., *Australia's First Government House*, p. 8.

27 Bickford, 'Background Paper on First Government House', pp. 4–13; Gojak, interview by author, Sydney, 14 March 1995; Bickford, interview by author, Sydney, 15 March 1995.

28 Proudfoot et al, *Australia's First Government House*, p. 52.

29 Bickford, interview by author, Sydney, 15 March 1995.

30 Descendants of James Bloodworth, an early pioneer who was credited with the construction of First Government House—see Proudfoot et al, *Australia's First Government House*, p. 55

31 *Daily Telegraph*, 19, 20 September 1983.

32 *Daily Telegraph*, 6 October 1983.

33 *Sydney Morning Herald*, 4 October 1983.

34 *Sydney Morning Herald*, 30 September 1983.

35 *Sydney Morning Herald*, 13 October 1983.

36 Gojak, interview by author, Sydney, 14 March 1995; Temple, interview by author, Sydney, 11 April 1995.

37 Temple, interview by author, Sydney, 11 April 1995.

38 Proudfoot et al., *Australia's First Government House*, p. 12.

39 Denis Gojak, interview by Joy Hughes, Sydney, 7 November 1994.

40 *Weekend Australian*, 25–26 January 1985.

41 Conybeare, Morrison and Partners Pty Ltd, 'First Government House Site Survey Draft Conservation Plan', p. 250.

42 *Sydney Morning Herald*, 8 January 1986.

43 Proudfoot et al., *Australia's First Government House*, pp. 18–19.

44 *Sunday Telegraph*, 9 August 1987.

45 Conybeare, Morrison and Partners Pty Ltd, 'First Government House Site Survey Draft Conservation Plan', p. 250.

46 Temple, interview by author, Sydney, 11 April 1995; Watt, 'Welcome to Delegates', Seminar 1995.

47 *Sydney Morning Herald*, 30 June 1990.

48 Kevin Williams, NSW Historic Houses Trust, interview by author, 11 November 1995.

49 See Proudfoot et al., *Australia's First Government House*.
50 Stocks, interview by author, Sydney, 8 February 1995.
51 *Sydney Morning Herald*, 20 November 1993.
52 *Sydney Morning Herald*, 4 July 1983.
53 Bickford, interview by author, Sydney, 15 March 1995.
54 Bickford, 'Encounters in Places', pp. 126–31.
55 *Sydney Morning Herald*, 8 January 1986.
56 *Sydney Morning Herald*, 2 June 1983.
57 *Sydney Morning Herald*, 2 June 1983.
58 Many thanks go to Denis Gojak for the loan of his extensive collection of media pieces and ephemera on which this analysis is based.
59 *Daily Telegraph*, 10 July 1983.
60 Temple, interview by author, Sydney, 11 April 1995.
61 *Daily Telegraph*, 10, 21 July 1983.
62 Bickford, interview by author, Sydney, 15 March 1995.
63 *Daily Telegraph*, 10 July 1983.
64 Bickford, interview by author, Sydney, 15 March 1995.
65 Temple, interview by author, Sydney, 11 April 1995.
66 Temple, interview by author, Sydney, 11 April 1995.
67 *Daily Telegraph*, 16 June 1983.
68 Bickford, interview by author, Sydney, 15 March 1995.
69 Judy Birmingham, interview by author, Sydney, 12 April 1995.
70 *Sunday Telegraph* 9 October 1983.
71 Mulvaney, 'A Good Foundation,' 1985.
72 *Friends of First Government House Newsletter*, October 1986.
73 See Proudfoot et al., *Australia's First Government House*.
74 Bickford, interview by author, Sydney, 15 March 1995.
75 McBryde, *Guests of the Governor*, 1989.
76 Glascott, interview by author, Sydney, 9 May 1995.
77 *Daily Mirror*, 9 August 1983; *Australian*, 29 September 1983.
78 Bickford, interview by author, Sydney, 15 March 1995.
79 Temple, interview by author, Sydney, 11 April 1995.
80 *Financial Review*, 16 September 1983.
81 *Sydney Morning Herald*, Letters to the Editor, 15 September 1983.
82 *Sydney Morning Herald*, Letters to the Editor, 26 September 1983.
83 *Sydney Morning Herald*, 13 September 1997.
84 Lydon, 'Sites: Archaeology in Context'; Richard Mackay, interview by author, Sydney, 13 March 1995; David Rhodes, interview by author, 4 May 1995.
85 Karskens, *The Archaeology of a Neighbourhood*, pp. 14–20.
86 Bickford, 'Romantic Ruins', p. 82.
87 Bickford 'Romantic Ruins', p. 82.
88 Bickford, 'The Australia ICOMOS Charter (the Burra Charter) and First Government House', pp. 38–42.
89 McBryde, 'Archaeology of the Metropolis'.
90 Proudfoot et al., *Australia's First Government House*, p. 9; Sullivan, 'A New Wave on the Oceans of Time'.
91 *Sydney Morning Herald*, 26 September 1983.
92 *Daily Telegraph*, 25 November 1983.
93 *Sydney Morning Herald*, 7 July 1994.
94 McBryde, *Guests of the Governor*, pp. 1–14.
95 Museum of Sydney, web site <www.mos.nsw.gov.au>, 21 July 1999.
96 Sullivan, 'Report of the Archaeological Advisory Panel', p. 29.
97 Sullivan, 'Report of the Archaeological Advisory Panel', p. 29.
98 Quoted in J. F. Whitehouse, 'Future Management Options', p. 33.

[99] Zdenowski, 'Civil Liberties', pp. 145–73; Glascott, interview by author, Sydney, 9 May 1995.
[1] *Australian Heritage Commission Act 1975*, Section 4(1).
[2] Sullivan, 'Report of the Archaeological Advisory Panel', pp. v–x.
[3] Bickford, 'Romantic Ruins', pp. 77–90.
[4] Bickford, 'Romantic Ruins', p. 82.
[5] *Friends of First Government House Newsletter*, February–March 1994; Emmett, 'WYSIWYG on the Site of First Government House'; Ireland, 'Excavating National Identity'; Brereton, 'The Sydney Museum: Digitising Our Past for the Future', at web site <www.arrakis.com.au/content/magazine/brereton/future1.html>, 21 July 1999.
[6] Museum of Sydney, web site <www.mos.nsw.gov.au>, 21 July 1999.
[7] Linda Young, 'Museum of Sydney, on the Site of First Government House Exhibition Review', pp. 666–7.
[8] *Sydney Morning Herald*, 17 October 1983; Bickford, *Encounters in Places*, pp. 117–33.
[9] Ireland, Excavating National Identity.
[10] Temple, phone conversation, February 2001.
[11] Karskens, 'Engaging Artefacts', p. 15.

6 The battle for Southwest Tasmania

[1] Lister, 'A Submission from the Tasmanian Archaeological Society', pp. 1–7.
[2] She later reverted to her married name, McGowan.
[3] Angela McGowan, interview by author, 18 September 1994.
[4] Jones, 'Submission to the Senate Select Committee on Southwest Tasmania', pp. 96–106.
[5] Lister, ' A Submission from the Tasmanian Archaeological Society', pp. 1–7, and 'Submission concerning the Gordon River Power Development Stage 2'; Jones, 'Submission to the Senate Select Committee on Southwest Tasmania', pp. 96–106.
[6] Jones, 'Submission to the Senate Select Committee on Southwest Tasmania', pp. 96–106.
[7] Jones, 'Submission to the Senate Select Committee on Southwest Tasmania', pp. 96–106; Kiernan et al., 'New Evidence from Fraser Cave for Glacial Age Man in Southwest Tasmania', pp. 28–32.
[8] *Hobart Mercury*, 17 February 1981.
[9] Jones et al., 'The Australian National University – Tasmanian National Parks and Wildlife Service Archaeological Expedition to the Franklin River', pp. 57–70.
[10] Bob Burton, email, 17 March 2001.
[11] Jones, 'Submission to the Senate Select Committee on Southwest Tasmania', pp. 96–106.
[12] Bob Burton, interview by author, 19 September 1994.
[13] *News*, Channel 6, 19 March 1981.
[14] Jones et al., 'The Australian National University – Tasmanian National Parks and Wildlife Service Archaeological Expedition to the Franklin River', pp. 57–70; Kiernan et al., 'New Evidence from Fraser Cave for Glacial Age Man in Southwest Tasmania', pp. 28–32.
[15] Mulvaney, *The Prehistory of Australia*; Flood, *Archaeology of the Dreamtime*.
[16] Letter reprinted in Mummery, *Prehistory and Heritage*, pp. 319–24.
[17] Jones, 'Submission to the Senate Select Committee on Southwest Tasmania', pp. 96–106.
[18] Letter reprinted in Mummery, *Prehistory and Heritage*, pp. 319–24.
[19] *Canberra Times*, 3 January 1982.
[20] *Examiner*, 5 February 1982; *Herald*, 5 February 1982; Jones et al., 'The Australian National University – Tasmanian National Parks and Wildlife Service Archaeological Expedition to the Franklin River', pp. 57–70.
[21] *Hobart Mercury*, 6 February 1982.
[22] *Sydney Morning Herald*, Letters to the Editor, 13 February 1982.
[23] *Sydney Morning Herald*, Letters to the Editor, 13 February 1982; Jones et al., 'The Australian National University – Tasmanian National Parks and Wildlife Service Archaeological Expedition to the Franklin River', pp. 57–70.

24 Jones et al., 'The Australian National University – Tasmanian National Parks and Wildlife Service Archaeological Expedition to the Franklin River', pp. 63–9.

25 Jones et al., 'The Australian National University – Tasmanian National Parks and Wildlife Service Archaeological Expedition to the Franklin River', p. 69.

26 Jones, 'Submission to the Senate Select Committee on Southwest Tasmania', pp. 96–106.

27 *Commonwealth Parliamentary Debates*, Senate, 1982, pp. 3493–5.

28 *Weekend Australian*, 4–5 September 1982.

29 Stephen Harris, interview by author, 22 May 1995.

30 Jones et al., 'The Australian National University – Tasmanian National Parks and Wildlife Service Archaeological Expedition to the Franklin River', pp. 57–70.

31 *Commonwealth Parliamentary Debates*, Senate, 1982, pp. 2852–5.

32 Blain et al., 'The Australian National University – Tasmanian National Parks and Wildlife Service Archaeological Expedition to the Franklin and Gordon Rivers', pp. 71–83.

33 Ranson et al., 'Australia's Prehistory Uncovered', pp. 83–7.

34 Bowman and Grattan, *Reformers*, pp. 200–2.

35 Angela McGowan, interview by author, 18 September 1994; Downie, 'Vehicles Churn up Evidence of Prehistoric Tasmanians', pp. 84–6.

36 McGowan, interview by author, 18 September 1994.

37 Haydon, *Beyond the Dam*, 1985, and *The Fight for the Franklin*, 1987.

38 Thompson, *Bob Brown and the Franklin River*, pp. 10–15.

39 Batchen, *Terrible Prospects*, pp. 46–9.

40 *Australian*, 21 January 1983.

41 Thompson, *Bob Brown and the Franklin River*, pp. 10–15; Bowman and Grattan, *Reformers*, pp. 200–2.

42 Thompson, *Bob Brown and the Franklin River*, pp. 10–15.

43 Patterson et al., 'Hydro-Electric Commission of Tasmania Gordon River Power Development —stage 2 Cave Survey Geological Report', pp. 1–15.

44 Bowman and Grattan, *Reformers*, pp. 200–2.

45 *Hobart Mercury*, 1 September 1983.

46 Allen, 'Aborigines and Archaeologists in Australia', pp. 7–10.

47 Allen, 'Aborigines and Archaeologists in Australia', pp. 7–10.

48 Jones, 'Submission to the Senate Select Committee on Southwest Tasmania', pp. 96–106.

49 Mulvaney, 'Submission to the Senate Select Committee on Southwest Tasmanian Prehistory'.

50 *Sydney Morning Herald*, Letters to the Editor, 13 February 1982.

51 Bowdler, 'The ICOMOS Approach to the Archaeological Resource,' p. 22.

52 Bob Burton, interview by author, 19 September 1994.

53 Patterson et al., 'Hydro-Electric Commission of Tasmania Gordon River Power Development —stage 2 Cave Survey Geological Report', pp. 1–15.

54 McBryde, 'Those Truly Oustanding Examples', pp. 15–19.

55 Ranson and Harris, 'Maxwell River Archaeological Survey', pp. 1–10.

56 *Hobart Mercury*, 1 September 1983.

57 *Bulletin*, 1 February 1983; Allen, 'The Rise of Public Archaeology', pp. 8–9; Bowdler, 'The ICOMOS Approach to the Archaeological Resource,' p. 22.

58 Williams, *This is the Science Show*, p. 286.

59 Mulvaney, 'Towards a New National Consciousness', pp. 88–9.

60 McGowan, interview by author, 18 September 1994.

61 Jones, 'Submission to the Senate Select Committee on Southwest Tasmania', pp. 96–106.

62 Jones et al., 'The Australian National University – Tasmanian National Parks and Wildlife Service Archaeological Expedition to the Franklin River', pp. 57–70.

63 Mulvaney 'Towards a New National Consciousness', pp. 88–9.

64 Mulvaney, 'Reflections on a Future of Past Cultural Landscapes', p. 2.

65 Flannery, *The Future Eaters*; *Greenpeace Australia Newsletter*, Winter 1995, p. 10.

66 *Sydney Morning Herald*, 31 March 1982, p. 21.

[67] Allen, 'Aborigines and Archaeologists in Australia', pp. 7–10.

[68] Langford, 'Our Heritage—Your Playground', pp. 1–8.

[69] Blain et al., 'The Australian National University – Tasmanian National Parks and Wildlife Service Archaeological Expedition to the Franklin and Gordon Rivers', pp. 71–83.

[70] Jones, 'Submission to the Senate Select Committee on Southwest Tasmania', pp. 96–106.

[71] Griffiths, 'History and Natural History', pp. 16–32.

[72] Jones et al., 'The Australian National University – Tasmanian National Parks and Wildlife Service Archaeological Expedition to the Franklin River', pp. 57–70.

[73] Mansell in McQueen, *The Franklin*, pp. 40–50; Mansell, 'Comrades or Trespassers on Aboriginal Land?', pp. 101–6.

7 Trouble with bones

[1] Zimmerman, 'Made Radical by My Own', pp. 60–7; 'Human Bones as Symbols of Power', pp. 211–16.

[2] Willmot, 'Dilemma of Mind', p. 3.

[3] Attwood, *The Making of the Aborigines*, p. xi; Bowdler, 'Unquiet Slumbers', pp. 103–6; Reynolds, *Fate of Free People*, p. 5.

[4] Bates and Witter, 'Cultural Tourism at Mutawintji and Beyond', pp. 215–20; Xiberras and du Cros, 'Aboriginal Involvement in Monitoring and Protecting Cultural Sites within the Melbourne Area', p. 226; Gostin, *Accessing the Dreaming*, pp. 1–10; Free, 'The Return of Mungo Woman', pp. 1–5.

[5] Moore, ABC 4 September 1978; *Royal Commission into the Aboriginal Deaths in Custody*, 1991; Tickner, 'Distinctly Australia', 1991–2; Dodson, 'Social Justice for Indigenous Peoples', 1994.

[6] See Langford, 'Our Heritage—Your Playground' pp. 1–8; Webb, 'Reburying Australian Skeletons', pp. 292–6; Zimmerman, 'Made Radical by My Own', pp. 60–7, and 'Human Bones as Symbols of Power', pp. 211–16; Willmot 'The Dragon Principle', pp. 41–8; Creamer, 'Aboriginal Perceptions of the Past', pp. 130–40; Fourmile, 'The Need for an Independent National Inquiry into State Collection of Aboriginal and Torres Strait Islander Cultural Heritage', pp. 3–4; Free, 'The Return of Mungo Woman', pp. 1–5; Council of Australian Museums Association, 'Previous Possessions, New Obligations'; Burke et al., 'Beyond the Looking Glass', pp. 13–15.

[7] Pardoe, 'Sharing the Past', p. 208.

[8] Zimmerman, 'Made Radical by My Own', pp. 60–7.

[9] Free 'The Return of Mungo Woman', pp. 1–5.

[10] See Garrett, *From Mungo to Mackaratta*, 1983; Creamer, 'Aboriginal Perceptions of the Past, pp. 130–40; Gostin, *Accessing the Dreaming*, pp. 1–10; Free, 'The Return of Mungo Woman', pp. 40–5.

[11] Thorne and Raymond, *Man on the Rim*.

[12] Lewin, 'Human Origins', p. 39, and recent discoveries by Alan Thorne.

[13] Zimmerman, 'Human Bones as Symbols of Power', p. 211.

[14] Creamer, 'Aboriginal Perceptions of the Past', p. 134.

[15] Hope, 'Aboriginal Burial Conservation in the Murray–Darling Basin', p. 58.

[16] Garrett, *From Mungo to Mackaratta*.

[17] Mulvaney, 1985, 'A Question of Values', pp. 63–71, 'Reflections on the Murray Black Collection', pp. 66–73, and 'Past Regained and Future Lost', pp. 12–21; Sullivan, The Custodianship of Aboriginal Sites in Southeastern Australia, pp. 136–40; McBryde, 'The Past as a Symbol of Identity', pp. 261–6, and 'Dream the Impossible Dream?', pp. 8–14.

[18] Bancroft, interview with author, 19 April 1995; Johnston, interview with author, 14 March 1995.

[19] Willmot, 'The Dragon Principle', pp. 41–8; Richardson, 'The Acquisition, Storage and Handling of Aboriginal Skeletal Remains in Museums', pp. 185–8; Fourmile, 'The Need for an Independent National Inquiry into State Collection of Aboriginal and Torres Strait Islander Cultural Heritage', pp. 3–4; Free 'The Return of Mungo Woman', pp. 1–5.

20 Pardoe, 'Sharing the Past', pp. 220–2; Xiberras, 'Aboriginal Skeletal Remains at VAS', p. 11; Council of Australian Museums Association, 'Previous Possessions, New Obligations', 1993. See also individual policies regarding the treatment of indigenous human remains followed by various State heritage agencies and museums.

21 *Tasmanian Archaeological Society Newsletter*, 1989, p. 13–14.

22 Vines, 'Pinkerton Graves, Melton', pp. 1–21.

23 National Trust of Australia, NSW, 'Cemeteries: A Policy Paper', pp. 1–10.

24 See Department of Planning, *Historical Archaeological Sites Investigation and Conservation Guidelines*, Heritage Council of NSW, Sydney, 1993; Bickford et. al., 'Guidelines for the management of Human Remains under the NSW Heritage Act, 1977', 2001.

25 See Sagazio (ed.), *Cemeteries: Our Heritage*, 1992; Ministry of Planning, *Cemeteries of Victoria: Guidelines for Management, Maintenance and Conservation*.

26 Carnett, *Legal Background of Archaeological Resources Protection*, pp. 1–5.

27 Anyon, 'Protecting the Past, Protecting the Present', pp. 215–22.

28 Stuart, 'Conclusion', pp. 243–52; Anyon, 'Protecting the Past, Protecting the Present', pp. 215–22; Keel, 'The Future of Protecting the Past', pp. 291–6; Rogers and Grant, 'Model State/Tribal Legislation and Jury Education', pp. 47–64.

29 *Archaeology*, 'Field Notes', July–August 1995, p. 26.

30 Keel, 'The Future of Protecting the Past' pp. 291–6.

31 Hubert, 'A Proper Place for the Dead', pp. 131–65.

32 Keel, 'The Future of Protecting the Past' p. 294.

33 Hammil and Cruz, 'Statement of American Indians Against Desecration Before the World Archaeology Congress', pp. 195–200; Moore, 'Federal Indian Burial Policy', pp. 201–10.

34 Hubert, 'A Proper Place for the Dead', p. 163.

35 Nicholas, 'Education and Canadian Archaeology', pp. 129–30.

36 Truscott, 'Repatriation of Indigenous Cultural Property in Australia', pp. 1–2.

37 *Sydney Morning Herald*, 18 March 1995.

38 Lexi Clark, Tasmanian Museum and Art Gallery, fax, 12 July 2001.

39 Langford, 'Our Heritage—Your Playground', pp. 1–8.

40 Allen, 'A Short History of the Tasmanian Affair', pp. 43–7; *Australian*, 25 July 1995; *Koori Mail*, 9 August 1995; *Weekend Australian*, Letters to the Editor, 9–10 September 1995; Harris, 'Scientific and Cultural Vandalism', pp. 28–32; Australian Institute of Aboriginal and Torres Strait Islander Studies, 'Our Culture, Our Future', p. 53.

41 Allen, 'Aborigines and Archaeologists in Tasmania', pp. 7–10.

42 Mulvaney, 'A Question of Values, Museums as Cultural Property', pp. 63–71.

43 British and Australian governments, joint statement, 26 January 2001.

44 Meehan, 'Aboriginal Skeletal Remains', pp. 122–42.

45 See Meehan, 'Aboriginal Skeletal Remains', pp. 122–42; Hubert, 'A Proper Place for the Dead', p. 163.

46 Richardson, 'The Acquisition, Storage and Handling of Aboriginal Skeletal Remains in Museums', pp. 185–8.

47 Griffiths, 'Hunters and Collectors', p. 81.

48 Truscott, 'Repatriation of Indigenous Cultural Property in Australia', p. 2.

49 Council of Australian Museums Association, 'Previous Possessions, New Obligations', p. 1.

50 Marrie, 'Museums and Aborigines', pp. 63–80; Fourmile, 'The Need for an Independent National Inquiry into State Collection of Aboriginal and Torres Strait Islander Cultural Heritage', pp. 3–4.

51 Council of Australian Museums Association, 'Previous Possessions, New Obligations', p. 7.

52 Truscott, 'Repatriation of Indigenous Cultural Property in Australia', p. 2.

53 Tickner, *Distinctly Australia—the Future for Australia's Cultural Development*.

54 Australian Labor Party, *Creative Nation*, p. 18.

55 Lori Richardson, email, 26 February 2001.

56 ATSIC website, <www.atsic.gov.au/default_ns.asp>, 22 February 2001.

57 Truscott, 'Repatriation of Indigenous Cultural Property in Australia', p. 2.

[58] Lori Richardson, email, 26 February 2001.

[59] See Thorne and Ross, *The Skeletal Manual*; Aboriginal Affairs Victoria, 'Advice About the Discovery of Aboriginal Human Remains. Treatment of Any Suspected Aboriginal Remains'; Hope and Littleton, 'Finding out About Aboriginal Burials'.

[60] McDonald, and Ross, 'Helping the Police with Their Inquiries', pp. 114–21.

[61] McDonald, and Ross, 'Helping the Police with Their Inquiries', pp. 114–21.

[62] Pardoe, 'Report on Human Skeletal Material Recovered Before 8 June 1988', p. 2.

[63] Pardoe, 'Report on Human Skeletal Material Recovered Before 8 June 1988', p. 177.

[64] McDonald and Ross, 'Helping the Police with Their Inquiries', pp. 114–21; McDonald, *The Archaeology of the Angophora Reserve Rockshelter*, pp. 1–20.

[65] See Wood, 'Angophora Reserve Rockshelter: A Faunal Analysis'; McDonald, *The Archaeology of the Angophora Reserve Rockshelter*, pp. 1–20.

[66] See Thorne and Ross, *The Skeletal Manual*.

[67] McDonald and Ross, 'Helping the Police with Their Inquiries', p. 119.

[68] McDonald and Ross, 'Helping the Police with Their Inquiries', p. 120.

[69] Wettenhall, 'The Murray Black Collection Goes Home', pp. 17–19; Mulvaney, 'Reflections on the Murray Black Collection', pp. 66–73.

[70] Mulvaney, 'Reflections on the Murray Black Collection', pp. 66–73.

[71] Wettenhall, 'The Murray Black Collection Goes Home', pp. 17–19.

[72] Pardoe, 'Farewell to the Murray Black Australian Aboriginal Skeletal Collection', pp. 119–21.

[73] Mulvaney, 'Reflections on the Murray Black Collection', p. 72.

[74] Webb, 'Reburying Australian Skeletons', pp. 292–6; Pardoe, 'Competing Paradigms and Ancient Human Remains', pp. 79–85.

[75] See Horton, *Recovering the Tracks*; Moser, 'Building the Discipline of Australian Archaeology', pp. 17–29.

[76] Thorne and Macumber, 'Discoveries of Late Pleistocene Man at Kow Swamp, Australia', pp. 316–19; West, 'Aboriginal Man at Kow Swamp, Northern Victoria', pp. 19–30.

[77] Thorne, 'Mungo and Kow Swamp', pp. 85–9, and 'Kow Swamp and Lake Mungo: Towards an Osteology of Early Man in Australia'.

[78] Bowdler, 'Unquiet Slumbers', pp. 103–6.

[79] Bowdler, 'Repainting Australian Rock Art', p. 523.

[80] Mulvaney, 'Past Regained and Future Lost', pp. 12–21.

[81] Ken Atkinson, interview with author, 1994.

[82] Mulvaney, 'Past Regained and Future Lost', pp. 12–21.

[83] Mulvaney, 'Past Regained and Future Lost', p. 20.

[84] *Bulletin*, 21 August 1984, 11 October 1988; *Age*, 31 August 1990; *Canberra Times*, 8 September 1990.

[85] *Bulletin*, 4 September 1984.

[86] McBryde, 'The Past as Symbol of Identity', pp. 261–6.

[87] Quoted in Gostin, 'Accessing the Dreaming', p. 77.

[88] Quoted in Gostin, 'Accessing the Dreaming', p. 77.

[89] Free, 'The Return of Mungo Woman', p. 3; Gostin, 'Accessing the Dreaming', p. 78.

[90] Gostin, 'Accessing the Dreaming', pp. 76–7.

[91] Free, 'The Return of Mungo Woman', p. 3.

[92] Free, 'The Return of Mungo Woman', p. 3.

[93] Tacey, *Edge of the Sacred*, pp. 129–30; Stockton, *The Aboriginal Gift*, pp. 77–89.

Glossary

Aborigines or Aboriginal people: The terms used to describe people who identify themselves as Aboriginal, are acknowledged by the Aboriginal community and are not of Torres Strait Island descent.

archaeological landscape: A discrete geographical area that shows particular evidence of a complex series of past human activities; examples are the Ballarat gold-mining area in Victoria or the Willandra Lakes system in New South Wales.

archaeological site: A site is generally defined as a locus of past human activity within boundaries distinguished by the presence of physical remains of that activity. Archaeology in Australia tends to focus on particular sites rather than on clusters of sites or regions.

contact archaeological site or landscape: An Aboriginal site or landscape with a documented historic context, such as a mission station or provisioning point; or a site which shows evidence of Aboriginal use of European or other non-Aboriginal materials and ideas. The latter may include artefact scatter sites, which contain artefacts made, for example, from glass, metal or ceramics.

contact archaeology: A new branch of archaeology that uses written records as well as oral history to complement information collected by archaeologists. It approximately covers the 'frontier' period of contact and following phases for both Aboriginal and non-Aboriginal cultures.

cultural (or archaeological) heritage management: The practice of working to conserve cultural heritage for both present and future generations.

cultural landscapes: Similar to an archaeological landscape, but includes some non-archaeological features of cultural significance, such as bridges or sacred trees, as well as archaeological remains.

cultural tourism: The act of visiting a cultural site for aesthetic pleasure, entertainment, confrontation, education or enlightenment. Cultural tourism often entails a merging of specific disciplines on sites and a widening of concepts concerning site interpretation, so that a 'site' might include an archaeological exhibit, art exhibition space, a souvenir shop and even a sound and light show. Like eco-tourism, cultural tourism relies on a resource—in this case, cultural heritage—to make a product such as a tour package for tourists to consume.

historical archaeology: The study of archaeological sites and landscapes which were formed after cultural contact; together with research using written records and/or oral history, site recording, excavating and artefact analysis.

Holocene: Recent geological time period, covering the last 10 000 years.

in situ: Literally, in place. In archaeology it refers to the practice of leaving exposed physical remains as they were first found during an excavation or survey.

intensification: The idea that hunter-gatherers can be responsive in relationship with their environment, that they can 'intensify' productivity by a range of techniques such as those that harness or increase sources of food. Researchers argued that one clear example of this was the fish-traps, weirs and channels constructed in some in swampy areas of Western Victoria and New South Wales.

keeping place: A repository for indigenous cultural property and human remains managed and owned by an indigenous community group.

maritime archaeology: The study of archaeological material occurring underwater (such as shipwrecks), extending to include sites on water margins associated with shipping. It can also be undertaken in inland rivers and lakes, not just along the coast. The material is generally historical; no pre-contact sites (e.g. waterlogged Pleistocene sites) have been excavated so far in Australia. Maritime archaeology employs the same skills as historical archaeology, including historical research, site recording, excavation and artefact analysis.

megafauna: Large extinct animals and birds, including varieties of kangaroos and wombats.

multi-regional model: A theory of human origins which argues that regional populations of *Homo erectus* may have evolved into *Homo sapiens* while intermingling with one another in places such as China, Indonesia and the Middle East (away from Africa).

'out of Africa' model: A theory of human origins which argues that both *Homo sapiens* and its predecessor *Homo erectus* originated in Africa. From there they spread to other continents, *Homo sapiens* eventually reaching every continent on Earth.

Pleistocene: Geological period preceding the Holocene, extending back from 10 000 years to three million years approximately.

pre-contact archaeology: The study of physical evidence of past indigenous inhabitants of Australia, such as a stone artefact scatters, scarred trees, burials or rock paintings, dating to either before or not long after European arrival. If such evidence shows indications that contact has occurred with non-Aboriginal people, including Macassans (Indonesians), it should be considered from the later, contact period. Such a site or landscape is usually investigated using an archaeological approach—site recording, excavation and artefact or rock art analysis—as it is difficult for non-Aboriginal researchers to discover much information without it. In some future cases, linguistic and oral history data may also complement archaeological means in researching this period.

public archaeology: Archaeology conducted for non-academic and/or regulatory purposes, carried out by consulting archaeologists (who are mostly engaged by government authorities) and archaeologists employed by site protection authorities, heritage organisations, museums and government authorities that manage or develop large tracts of land, such as Forestry Tasmania and Pacific Power. See also **cultural (or archaeological) heritage management**.

radiocarbon dating: The method of dating organic fossil remains based on how much of the radioactive isotope carbon-14 can measured in their fabric. It is most accurate within the range of a few hundred to 40 000 years, but is often calibrated with tree ring dating for the most accuracy for the last thousand years.

rockshelter: A naturally formed overhang in a cliff face or boulder.

stone artefact: In Australia, an Aboriginal stone artefact is usually the result of the process of manufacturing stone tools. It is a general term for both the debris and the finished product, the stone tool.

stone tool: Any stone object that indigenous people used in their daily lives. The study of stone technology is an important part of **pre-contact archaeology**.

stratigraphy: Layering of sediments which may sometimes also contain artefacts. A well-stratified archaeological site has clear boundaries between consecutively laid down layers of soil. The oldest are usually at the bottom and the youngest at the top.

Torres Strait Islanders: The indigenous inhabitants of the islands to the north of Australia, which are nominally part of Queensland. The late Eddie Mabo was a famous Torres Strait Islander.

Sources

Audio-visual materials

ABC TV. *7.30 Report* (Victoria) 30 July 1995. La Trobe University expired permits (8 minutes).

ABC TV. *Quantum*, 15 November 1995. La Trobe University expired permits (15 minutes).

ABC TV. *Quantum*, 19 October 1994. Auto-cad on The Rocks—Cumberland and Gloucester Street Excavation (8 minutes).

ABC TV. *Quantum*, 25 May 1995. La Trobe University expired permits (8 minutes).

ABC TV. *Quantum*, 26 October 1995. Dating Aboriginal rock art (7 minutes).

ATSIC web site: <www.atsic.gov.au/default_ns.asp>, 22 February 2001.

BBC/Discovery Communications Inc. *The Sands of Dreamtime* (55 minutes), 1997.

Brereton, K. 'The Sydney Museum: Digitising Our Past for the Future', listed at web site <www.arrakis.com.au/content/magazine/brereton/future1.html>, 21 July 1999.

Communications and Entertainment Ltd. *Robbers of the Sacred Mountain* (98 minutes), 1982.

Garrett, K. *From Mungo to Mackaratta: Australian Prehistory*, Science Unit ABC Radio National, Sydney (180 minutes), 1983.

Hawker, P. *The Resurrection of the Batavia*, ABC/Dutch Production, ABC TV, Sydney (55 minutes), 1995.

Haydon, T. ANZAAS Lecture, 'Fossil Man in Australia' by Professor N. W. G. Macintosh, ANZAAS 39th Congress, University of Melbourne, telecast ABC TV Sydney (55 minutes), 1967.

—— *Dig a Million, Make a Million*, ABC TV Production, Melbourne (55 minutes), 1969.

—— *The Talgai Skull*, Film Documentary produced for the National Museum of Victoria and the Australian Institute of Aboriginal Studies, Canberra (55 minutes), 1969.

—— *The Long Long Walkabout*, Film Documentary, ABC–BBC TV Co-production, Sydney (55 minutes), 1975.

—— *Beyond the Dam*, Artis Film Productions, North Sydney (55 minutes), 1985.

—— *The Fight for the Franklin*, Artis Film Productions, North Sydney (55 minutes), 1987.

Haydon, T. and Jones, R. *The Last Tasmanian: A Documentary Film on the Genocide of the Tasmanian Aborigines (English Version)*, Artis Film Productions, North Sydney (109 minutes), 1978.

Lucasfilm Pty Ltd. *Indiana Jones and the Last Crusade* (122 minutes), 1989.

McKell, M. *Maritime Archaeology in Australia*, Science Unit, ABC Science Show, Radio National, Sydney (84 minutes), 1993.

Moore, B. *Monday Conference on 'The Last Tasmanian'*, ABC TV, Hobart (55 minutes), 4 September 1978.

Museum of Sydney web site: <www.mos.nsw.gov.au>, 21 July 1999.

Raymond, R. *The Origin of the Australians*, Channel 7, Sydney (56 minutes), 1972.

SBS Television. *Imagine*, Review of Museum of Sydney (6 minutes), 31 May 1995.

Thorne, A. and Raymond, R. *Man on the Rim*, six-part TV series, Angus and Robertson and ABC TV, Sydney (336 minutes), 1989.

Wood Jones, F. *Tasmania's Vanished Race*, lecture series broadcast 26 February, 6 and 12 March 1935, National Talks, 3AR Radio Melbourne, Australian Broadcasting Commission.

Archival and other unpublished materials

Aboriginal Affairs Victoria. Advice About the Discovery of Aboriginal Human Remains: The Treatment of Any Suspected Aboriginal Remains Discovered in the Course of Development Work, Notes to Consultants, 1995.

Bannear, D. North Central Goldfields Project: Historic Mining Sites in the Dunolly Mining Division, report to the Department of Conservation and Natural Resources, Northwest Area, 1993, pp. 1–62.

Bickford, A. Lavelle, S. and Donlon, D. Guidelines for the Management of Human Remains under the NSW Heritage Act, 1977, Heritage Office, forthcoming.

Cheney, S. Turners Paddock: Nineteenth Century Refuse and the Growth of Consumer Society, paper given at the Australasian Association of Historical Archaeology Conference, Adelaide, 1993.

Conybeare Morrison and Partners Pty Ltd. First Government House Site Survey Draft Conservation Plan, report to the Department of Environment and Planning, 1985, pp. 1–250.

Egloff, B. Old Cloth for a New Suit: Training for Archaeological Heritage Management in Australia, notes for a conference paper, n.d.

Egloff, B. and Smith, J. Analysis of Glass Artefacts from the Excavation of First Government House, Sydney, report by ANUTECH Pty Ltd to the Department of Planning, 1987, pp. 1–44.

Godden Mackay Ltd. Cumberland Gloucester Street Site, Conservation and Management Report, report to the Sydney Cove Authority, Sydney, 1994.

Godden Mackay Logan Ltd and G. Karskens. The Cumberland/Gloucester Streets Site, The Rocks: National Trust Energy Australia Heritage Awards Report on Publications, report to the National Trust, 2000.

Ireland, T. Excavating National Identity, paper given at the Sites Seminar, Museum of Sydney, Sydney, 1995.

Lange, R. A Role for Avocationalists and Volunteers: A View from the Academic World, paper given at the Society for American Archaeology Annual Meeting, New Orleans, 1991.

Lister, A. A Submission from the Tasmanian Archaeological Society Concerning the Hydro-Electric Commission's Report on the Gordon River Power Development, Stage 2 and the Draft Environmental Impact Statement (Appendix 5), report to Tasmanian State Government Review, 1980, pp. 1–7.

—— Submission Concerning the Gordon River Power Development, Stage 2, report to the Tasmanian State Government, 1980, pp. 1–6.

Lydon, J. Sites: Archaeology in Context, paper given at the Sites Seminar, Museum of Sydney, Sydney, 1995.

McBryde, I. Archaeology in the Metropolis: the Investigation of the First Government House Site and its Implications for the Practice of Archaeology in Urban Contexts, paper given at the Sites Seminar, Museum of Sydney, Sydney, 1995.

Mulvaney, J. Submission to the Senate Select Committee on Southwest Tasmanian Prehistory, 1982.

Pardoe, C. Report on Human Skeletal Material Recovered Before 8 June 1988, report to Brayshaw McDonald Pty Ltd, 1988.

Patterson, S. J., Underwood, R., Tarvydes, R. K., Wilson, D. R. and Baynes, F. J. Hydro-Electric Commission of Tasmanian Gordon River Power Development— Stage 2 Cave Survey Geological Report No. 644-94-23, report to Hydro-Electric Commission of Tasmania, 1983, pp. 1–15.

Ranson, D. and Harris, S. Maxwell River Archaeological Survey, report to Tasmanian National Parks and Wildlife Service, 1986.

Sullivan, S. A New Wave on the Ocean of Time: Archaeology, Places and Museums, paper given at the Sites Seminar, Museum of Sydney, Sydney, 1995.

Truscott, M. Repatriation of Indigenous Cultural Property in Australia, paper given at a South African Seminar on Cultural Property, 2000, pp. 1–4.

Vines, G. Pinkerton Graves, Melton, report to the Shire of Melton Council, 1992, pp. 1–21.

Watts, P. Welcome to Delegates, Sites Seminar, Museum of Sydney, Sydney, 1995.

Books, articles and theses

Allen, J. 'Aborigines and Archaeologists in Tasmania', *Australian Archaeology*, vol. 16, 1983, pp. 7–10.

—— 'The Rise of Public Archaeology', *Natuni*, vol. 6, 1987, pp. 8–9.

—— 'Notions of the Pleistocene in Greater Australia', in M. Spriggs, D. Yen, W. Ambrose, R. Jones, A. Thorne, and A. Andrews (eds), *A Community of Culture: The People and Prehistory of the Pacific*, Department of Prehistory, Research School of Pacific Studies, the Australian National University, Canberra, 1993, pp. 123–38.

—— 'A Short History of the Tasmanian Affair', *Australian Archaeology*, vol. 41, 1995, pp. 43–7.

Annear, R. *Bearbrass: Imagining Early Melbourne*, Mandarin Books, Melbourne, 1995.

Anyon, R. 'Protecting the Past, Protecting the Present: Cultural Resources and American Indians', in S. Smith and J. E. Ehrenhard (eds), *Protecting the Past*, CRC Press, Boston, 1991, pp. 215–22.

Archaeology Abroad, May Bulletin, 1999.

Arnold, J. and Morris, D. *Monash Bibliographical Dictionary of 20th Century Australia*, Reed Reference Publishing, Melbourne, 1994.

Askew, M. 'Editorial', *Historic Environment*, vol. 9 (1 & 2), 1992, p. 4.

Attenbrow, A. and Meehan, B. 'Editorial', *Australian Archaeology*, vol. 30, 1990, p. 1.

Australasian Society for Historical Archaeology Newsletter, April 1998.

Australia ICOMOS News, April 1999.

Australian Archaeological Association, 'Code of Ethics of the Australian Archaeological Association (Members' obligations to Australian Aboriginal and Torres Strait Islander People)', *Australian Archaeology*, vol. 39, 1994, p. 129.

Australian Institute of Aboriginal and Torres Strait Islander Studies, *Our Culture, Our Future. Proposals for the recognition and protection of Indigenous Cultural and Intellectual Property*, Michael Frankel Company Solicitors, AIATSIS, and ATSIC, Canberra, 1997.

Australian Labor Party *Creative Nation: Commonwealth Cultural Policy, October 1994*, Commonwealth of Australia, Canberra, 1994.

Bairstow, D. 'Historical Archaeology at the Crossroads: An Appraisal of Theoretical Considerations', *Australian Archaeology*, vol. 18, 1984, pp. 32–9.

—— 'Urban Archaeology: American Theory, Australian Experience', *Australian Archaeology*, vol. 33, 1991, pp. 52–8.

Baker, H. The Preservation Movement in Australia, Master of Town and Country Planning, University of Sydney, 1969.

Balme, J. and Beck, W. (eds). *Gendered Archaeology: The Second Australian Women in Archaeology Conference, Armidale*, Research School of Pacific and Asian Studies, Australian National University, Canberra, 1994.

Barker, P. *Techniques of Archaeological Excavation*, 2nd edn, Batsford, London, 1982.

Batchen, G. 'Terrible Prospects', in A. Shiell and A. Stephen (eds), *The Lie of the Land*, Ideas for Australia Programme 1991–92, National Centre for Australian Studies, and the Powerhouse Museum, Sydney, 1992, pp. 46–9.

Bates, B. and Witter, D. 'Cultural Tourism at Mutawintji—and Beyond', in J. Birckhead, T. de Lacy and L. Smith (eds), *Aboriginal Involvement in Parks and Protected Areas*, Aboriginal Studies Press, Canberra, 1992, pp. 215–20.

Beck, W. 'Women in Archaeology: Australia and the United States', in M. Nelson, S. Nelson and A. Wylie (eds), *Equity Issues for Women in Archaeology*, Archaeological Papers No. 5, American Anthropological Association, Washington, 1994, pp. 99–104.

Bickford, A. 'The Last Tasmanian: Superb Documentary or Racist Fantasy?', *Film News*, January 1979, pp. 11–14.

—— 'The Patina of Nostalgia', *Australian Archaeology*, vol. 13, 1981, pp. 1–7.

—— 'Background Paper on First Government House Site: Extracts from Progress Report on First Government House Site 4/3/84', in H. Temple and S. Sullivan (eds), *First Government House Site, Sydney: Its Significance and Future*, Proceedings of Seminar No. 2, Department of Environment and Planning, Sydney, 1985, pp. 4–13.

—— 'Romantic Ruins' and 'The Australian ICOMOS Charter (the Burra Charter) and First Government House', in G. Davison and C. McConville (eds), *A Heritage Handbook*, Allen & Unwin, Sydney, 1991, pp. 38–42, 77–90.

—— 'Encounters in Places', in T. Bonyhady and T. Griffiths (eds), *Prehistory to Politics: John Mulvaney, the Humanities and the Public Intellectual*, Melbourne University Press, Melbourne, 1996, pp. 117–35.

Birckhead, J. 'Traditional Aboriginal Land Management Practices at Charles Sturt University—The Cultural Politics of a Curriculum Innovation', in J. Birckhead, de T. Lacy and L. Smith (eds), *Aboriginal Involvement in Parks and Protected Areas*, Aboriginal Studies Press, Canberra, 1992, pp. 297–306.

Bird, C. Prehistoric Lithic Resource Utilisation: A Case Study from the Southwest of Western Australia, PhD thesis, University of Western Australia, 1985.

Bird, C. and Frankel, D. 'Chronology and Explanation in Western Victoria and South-east South Australia', *Archaeology in Oceania*, vol. 26, 1991, pp. 1–16.

Birmingham, J. 'A Decade of Digging: Deconstructing Urban Archaeology', *Australian Journal of Historical Archaeology*, vol. 8, 1990, pp. 13–22.

Birmingham, J. and Jeans, D. 'Swiss Family Robinson and the Archaeology of Colonisation', *Australian Journal of Historical Archaeology*, vol. 1, 1983, pp. 3–14.

Birmingham, J. and Murray, T. *Historical Archaeology in Australia: A Handbook*, Birmingham & Murray, Sydney, 1987.

Birmingham, J., Bairstow, D. and Wilson, A. *Archaeology and Colonisation: Australia in the World Context*, Australian Association for Historical Archaeology, Sydney, 1988.

Birmingham, J., Jack, I. and Jeans, D. *Australian Pioneer Technology*, Heinemann, Melbourne, 1979.

Birmingham, J., Jack, I. and Jeans, D. *Industrial Archaeology in Australian Rural Industry*, Heinemann, Melbourne, 1983.

Blain, B. et al. 'The Australian National University – Tasmanian National Parks and Wildlife Service Archaeological Expedition to the Franklin and Gordon Rivers, 1983: A Summary of Results', *Australian Archaeology*, vol. 16, 1983, pp. 71–83.

Blair, S. and Feary, S. 'Regional Assessment of Cultural Heritage. A New Approach Based on Community and Expert Partnerships', *Historic Environment*, vol. 11 (2 & 3), 1995, pp. 15–21.

Bodycoat, R., Hocking, I. and Staples, A. C. 'The Swan Brewery, Perth', *Heritage Australia*, vol. 4 (2), 1985, pp. 22–4.

Bowdler, S. 'Repainting Australian Rock Art', *Antiquity*, vol. 62, 1988, pp. 517–23.

—— 'The ICOMOS Approach to the Archaeological Resource', *Historic Environment*, vol. 9 (3), 1992, pp. 20–2.

—— 'Unquiet Slumbers: The Return of the Kow Swamp Burials', *Antiquity*, vol. 66, 1992, pp. 103–6.

—— 'Views of the Past in Australian Prehistory', in M. Spriggs, D. Yen, W. Ambrose, R. Jones, A. Thorne, and A. Andrews (eds), *A Community of Culture: The People and Prehistory of the Pacific*, Department of Prehistory, Research School of Pacific Studies, Australian National University, Canberra, 1993, pp. 123–38.

Bowler, J. and Thorne, A. 'Human Remains from Lake Mungo: Discovery and Excavation of Lake Mungo III,' in R. L. Kirk and A. Thorne (eds), *The Origin of the*

Australians, Australian Institute of Aboriginal Studies, Canberra, 1976, pp. 127–38.

Bowler, J., Jones, R., Allen, H. and Thorne, A. 'Pleistocene Human Remains from Australia: A Living Site and Human Cremation from Lake Mungo, Western New South Wales', *World Archaeology,* vol. 2, 1970, pp. 39–60.

Bowler, J., Thorne, A. and Polach, N. 'Pleistocene Man in Australia: Age and Significance of the Mungo Skeleton', *Nature,* no. 240, 1972, pp. 48–50.

Bowman, M. and Grattan, M. *Reformers: Shaping Australian Society from the 60s to the 80s,* Collins Dove, Melbourne, 1989.

Bray, W. and Trump, D. *The Penguin Dictionary of Archaeology,* Penguin Reference Books, London, 1970.

British and Australian Government Joint Statement, 'Australia Day Statement on the Repatriation of Indigenous Human Remains from British Museums', 26 January 2000.

Brown, M. 'The Rocks Revealed', *Heritage NSW,* vol. 1 (3), 1994, p. 1.

Burke, H., Lovell-Jones, C. and Smith, C. 'Beyond the Looking-Glass: Some Thoughts on Sociopolitics and Reflexivity in Australian Archaeology', *Australian Archaeology,* vol. 38, 1994, pp. 13–22.

Carnett, C. *Legal Background of Archaeological Resources Protection,* Technical Brief No. 11, National Parks Service, US Department of the Interior, Washington, 1991.

Casey, M., Donlon, D., Hope, J. and Welfare, S. *Refining Archaeology: Feminist Perspectives,* Research Papers No. 29, Archaeology and Natural History Publications, Australian National University, Canberra, 1998.

Clark, G. *Archaeology and Society,* Methuen, London, 1957.

Clarke, A. 'Cultural Resource Management (CRM) as Archaeological Housework: Confining Women to the Ghetto of Management', in H. du Cros and L. Smith (eds), *Women in Archaeology: A Feminist Critique,* Australian National University, Canberra, 1993, pp. 191–4.

Connah, G. *Australian Field Archaeology: A Guide to Techniques,* Australian Institute of Aboriginal Studies, Canberra, 1983.

—— *The Archaeology of Australia's History,* Cambridge University Press, Cambridge, 1988.

Cosgrove, R., Allen, J. and Marshall, B. 'Late Pleistocene Human Occupation in Tasmania,' *Australian Archaeology,* vol. 38, 1994, pp. 28–35.

Council of Australian Museum Associations. *Previous Possessions, New Obligations: Policies for Museums in Australia and Aboriginal and Torres Strait Islander People,* Council of Australian Museum Associations, Melbourne, 1993.

Creamer, H. 'Aboriginal Perceptions of the Past: The Implications for Cultural Resource Management in Australia', in P. Gathercole and D. Lowenthal (eds), *The Politics of the Past,* Unwin Hyman, London, 1990, pp. 130–40.

Daniel, G. *150 Years of Archaeology,* Duckworth, London, 1975.

Davies, M. and Buckley, K. *Port Arthur Conservation Development Project,* Archaeological Procedures Manual, Occasional Paper No. 13, Department of Lands, Parks and Wildlife, Tasmania, 1987.

Davison, G. 'A Brief History of the Australian Heritage Movement', in G. Davison and C. McConville (eds), *A Heritage Handbook,* Allen & Unwin, St Leonards, NSW, 1991, pp. 14–27.

Department of Planning, *Historical Archaeological Sites Investigation and Conservation Guidelines,* Heritage Council of New South Wales, Sydney, 1993.

Dodson, M. *Social Justice for Indigenous Peoples,* Third David Unaipon Lecture, Aboriginal Research Institute Publications, University of South Australia, Underdale, SA, 1994.

Downie, J. E. 'Vehicles Churn up Evidence of Prehistoric Tasmanians', *Australian Archaeology,* vol. 16, 1983, pp. 84–6.

du Cros, H. Skeletons in the Closet. A History of the Prehistoric Archaeology of New South Wales. (c. 1890–1940), BA (Hons) thesis, University of Sydney, 1983.

—— 'Burrill Lake Rockshelter: An Early Use of a Research Design in Australian Prehistory', *Australian Archaeology,* vol. 19, 1984, pp. 1–7.

—— *The Otway Region Archaeological Study, Stage 1,* Victoria Archaeological Survey Occasional Report Series No. 28, Department of Conservation and Environment, Melbourne, 1990.

—— To See Ourselves as Others See Us: Australian Archaeology's Value to Australian Contemporary Culture, unpublished proceedings of the Archaeology in the Early 1990s Seminar, University of New England, Armidale, NSW, 1992, pp. 230–45.

—— 'Female Skeletons in the Closet,' in H. du Cros and L. Smith (eds), *Women in Archaeology: A Feminist Critique,* Research School of Pacific, Asian and Australian Studies, Australian National University, Canberra, 1993, pp. 195–205.

—— 'Popular Archaeology', *Journal of Australian Studies,* vol. 62, 2000, pp. 190–7.

du Cros, H. and Rhodes, D. 'Commonwealth/Telecom Sites: Artefact Cataloguing and Analysis Methods', *Australian Archaeology,* vol. 32, 1991, pp. 17–20.

du Cros, H. and Smith, L. (eds). *Women in Archaeology: A Feminist Critique,* Research School of Pacific, Asian and Australian Studies, Australian National University, Canberra, 1993.

Egloff, B. 'From Swiss Family Robinson to Sir Russell Drysdale: Towards Changing the Tone of Historical Archaeology in Australia', *Australian Archaeology,* vol. 39, 1994, pp. 1–8.

Emmett, P. 'WYSIWYG on the Site of First Government House', Paper given at the Sites Seminar, Museum of Sydney, Sydney, 1995.

Field, J., Barker, J., Barker, R., Coffey, E., Coffey, L., Crawford, E., Darcy, L., Fields, T., Lord, G., Steadman, B. and Colley, S. 'Coming Back: Aborigines and Archaeologists at Cuddie Springs', *Public Archaeology,* vol. 1 (1), 2000, pp. 39–42.

Flannery, T. *The Future Eaters,* Reed, Port Melbourne, Vic., 1995.

Flood, J. *Archaeology of the Dreamtime: The Story of Prehistoric Australia and its People,* 2nd edn, Angus & Robertson, Sydney, 1995.

Fourmile, H. 'The Need for an Independent National Inquiry into State Collection of Aboriginal and Torres Strait Islander Cultural Heritage', *Aboriginal Law Bulletin,* vol. 2 (56), 1992, pp. 3–4.

Free, S. The Return of Mungo Woman: An Act of Reconciliation? BA (Hons) thesis, Australian National University, Canberra, 1993.

Fullagar, R., Price, D., and Head, L. 'Early Human Occupation of Northern Australia: Archaeology and Thermoluminescence Dating in Jinmium Rockshelter, Northern Territory,' *Antiquity,* vol. 70, 1996, pp. 751–73.

Gaby, – and Marion, – (eds), *Racism in Tasmania*, Australian Union of Students, Carlton, Vic., 1978.

Gero, J. 'Producing Prehistory, Controlling the Past: the Case of the New England Beehives', in V. Pinsky and A. Wylie (eds), *Critical Traditions in Contemporary Archaeology*, Cambridge University Press, Cambridge, 1989, pp. 89–95.

—— 'The Social World of Prehistoric Facts: Gender and Power in Palaeoindian Research', in H. du Cros and L. Smith (eds), *Women in Archaeology: A Feminist Critique*, Research School of Pacific, Asian and Australian Studies, Australian National University, Canberra, 1993, pp. 31–40.

—— 'Excavation Bias and the Women-at-home Ideology', in M. Nelson, S. Nelson and A. Wylie (eds), *Equity Issues for Women in Archaeology*, Archaeological Papers No. 5, American Anthropological Association, Washington, 1994, pp. 37–42.

Glover, R. Scientific Racism, the Australian Aboriginal 1865–1915, and the Logic of Evolutionary Anthropology, BA (Hons) thesis, University of Sydney, 1982.

Gojak, D. 'Presenting Archaeology to the Public: Lessons from the Cadmans Cottage Archaeological Project', forthcoming in *Australian Archaeology*.

Gostin, O. *Accessing the Dreaming: Heritage, Conservation and Tourism at Mungo National Park*, Aboriginal Research Unit Publications, University of South Australia, Underdale, SA, 1993.

Green, J. N. *Maritime Archaeology: A Technical Handbook*, Academic Press, New York, 1990.

Greenwood, G. *Australia: A Social and Political History*, Angus & Robertson, Sydney, 1977.

Griffiths, T. 'History and Natural History: Conservation Movements in Conflict?', in J. Richard and P. Spearritt (eds), *Packaging the Past? Public Histories*, Melbourne University Press and Australian Historical Studies, Melbourne, 1991, pp. 16–32.

—— *Hunters and Collectors: The Antiquarian Imagination in Australia*, Cambridge University Press, Melbourne, 1996.

Hammil, J. and Cruz, R. 'Statement of American Indians Against Desecration Before the World Archaeology Congress', in R. Layton (ed.), *Conflict in the Archaeology of Living Traditions*, One World Archaeology Series No. 8, Unwin Hyman, London, 1989, pp. 195–200.

Harris, M. 'Scientific and Cultural Vandalism', *Alternative Law Journal*, vol. 21 (1), 1996, pp. 28–32.

Haydon, T. *The Last Tasmanian: Educational Guide*, Artis Film Productions, North Sydney, 1990.

Henderson, G. *Maritime Archaeology in Australia*, University of Western Australia, Nedlands, WA, 1986.

—— 'Current Approaches to the Underwater Cultural Heritage—Strengths and Weaknesses: The International Perspective', *Historic Environment*, vol. 9 (3), 1992, pp. 5–8.

Heritage Council of New South Wales. *Annual Report*, 1982.

Hermes, M. 'Developing a Course in Australian Prehistory and Cultural Resource Management for Tertiary Aboriginal Students at Bachelor College', *Australian Archaeology*, vol. 35, 1992, p. 66.

Hiscock, P. 'Technological Change in the Hunter River Valley and its Implications for the Interpretation of Late Holocene Change in Australia', *Archaeology in Oceania*, vol. 21, 1986, pp. 40–50.

Historic Houses Trust of New South Wales. *Hyde Park Barracks Museum Plan*, Historic Houses Trust, New South Wales, Sydney, 1990.

Hodder, I. 'Interpretive Archaeology and its Role', *American Antiquity*, vol. 56 (1), 1991, pp. 7–18.

—— *The Archaeological Process: An Introduction*, Blackwell, Oxford, 1999.

Hoffman, T. L. and Lerner, S. *Arizona Archaeology Week: Promoting the Past to the Public*, Archaeological Assistance Program Technical Brief No. 2, US Department of the Interior, Washington, 1988.

Hope, J. 'Double Bind: Women Archaeologists in the New South Wales National Parks and Wildlife Service', in H. du Cros and L. Smith (eds), *Women in Archaeology: A Feminist Critique*, Research School of Pacific, Asian and Australian Studies, Australian National University, Canberra, 1993, pp. 175–90.

—— 'Pleistocene Archaeological Sites in the Central Murray–Darling Basin,' in M. A. Smith, M. Spriggs and B. Fankauser (eds), *Sahul in Review: Pleistocene Archaeology in Australia, New Guinea and Island Melanesia*, Department of Prehistory, Research School of Pacific Studies, Australian National University, Canberra, 1993, pp. 183–96.

—— 'Aboriginal Burial Conservation in the Murray–Darling Basin', *Historic Environment*, 11 (2 & 3), 1995, pp. 57–60.

Hope, J. and Littleton, J. *Finding out About Aboriginal Burials*, Murray–Darling Basin Aboriginal Heritage Handbooks, Mungo Publications, Sydney, 1995.

Horton, D. *Recovering the Tracks: The Story of Australian Archaeology*, Aboriginal Studies Press, Canberra, 1991.

Hosty, K. and Stuart, I. 'Maritime Archaeology over the Last Twenty Years', *Australian Archaeology*, vol. 39, 1994, pp. 9–19.

Hubert, J. 'A Proper Place for the Dead: A Critical Review of the "Reburial" Issue', in R. Layton (ed.), *Conflict in the Archaeology of Living Traditions*, One World Archaeology Series No. 8, Unwin Hyman, London, 1989, pp. 131–65.

Jack, I. 'Historical Archaeology and the Historian', *Australasian Historical Archaeology*, vol. 11, 1995, pp. 130–8.

Jack, S. 'Divorce or Reconciliation: History and Historical Archaeology', *Australasian Historical Archaeology*, vol. 11, 1995, pp. 124–30.

Johnston, H. 'Pleistocene Shell Middens of the Willandra Lakes', in M. A. Smith, M. Spriggs and B. Fankauser (eds), *Sahul in Review: Pleistocene Archaeology in Australia, New Guinea and Island Melanesia*, Department of Prehistory, Research School of Pacific Studies, Australian National University, Canberra, 1993, pp. 197–203.

Jones, R. 'Submission to the Senate Select Committee on Southwest Tasmania', *Australian Archaeology*, vol. 14, 1982, pp. 96–106.

—— 'Tom Haydon, 1938–1991: Film Interpreter of Australian Archaeology', *Australian Archaeology*, vol. 35, 1992, pp. 51–64.

Jones, R., Ranson, D., Allen, J. and Kiernan, K. 'The Australian National University–Tasmanian National Parks and Wildlife Service Archaeological

Expedition to the Franklin River, 1982', *Australian Archaeology*, vol. 16, 1983, pp. 57–70.

Karskens, G. *The Rocks: The Life in Early Sydney*, Melbourne University Press, Melbourne, 1997.

—— *Inside The Rocks: The Archaeology of a Neighbourhood*, Hale and Iremonger, Alexandria, NSW, 1999.

—— 'Engaging Artefacts: Urban Archaeology, Museums and the Origins of Sydney', *Tasmanian Historical Studies*, forthcoming.

Keel, B. C. 'The Future of Protecting the Past', in S. Smith and J. E. Ehrenhard (eds), *Protecting the Past*, CRC Press, Boston, 1991, pp. 291–6.

Kelly, M. *Anchored in a Small Cove: A History and Archaeology of The Rocks, Sydney*, Sydney Cove Authority, Sydney, 1997.

Kiernan, K., Jones, R. and Ranson, D. 'New Evidence from Fraser Cave for Glacial Age Man in Southwest Tasmania', *Nature*, vol. 301, 1983, pp. 28–32.

Knoop, R. 'Public Awareness and Archaeology: A Task for the Voluntary Sector', *Antiquity*, vol. 67, 1993, pp. 439–45.

Langford, R. F. 'Our Heritage—Your Playground', *Australian Archaeology*, vol. 16, 1983, pp. 1–8.

Lewin, R. 'Human Origins: The Challenge of Java's Skulls', *New Scientist*, 7 May 1994, pp. 36–40.

Lilley, I. 'Australian Archaeologists in the Pacific, 1974–94: A Guide for Non-specialists,' *Australian Archaeology*, vol. 39, 1994, pp. 46–53.

Lloyd, C. *The National Estate: Australia's Heritage*, Cassell, Sydney, 1977.

Lourandos, H. Forces of Change: Aboriginal Technology and Population in South-western Victoria, PhD thesis, University of Sydney, 1980.

Lourandos, H. and Ross, A. 'The Great "Intensification Debate": Its History and Place in Australian Archaeology', *Australian Archaeology*, vol. 39, 1994, pp. 54–62.

Lydon, J. *Many Inventions: The Chinese in The Rocks, 1890–1930*, Monash Publications in History, Melbourne, 1999.

McBryde, I. *Guests of the Governor: Aboriginal Residents of the First Government House, Sydney*, Friends of First Government House, Sydney, 1989.

—— 'Those Truly Outstanding Examples . . . Kakadu in the Context of Australia's World Heritage Properties—A Response', in J. Domicelj, S. Domicelj, M. Raza and O. Snarez (eds), *Australian Heritage Commission Technical Publications No. 1*, Commonwealth of Australia, Canberra, 1990, pp. 15–19.

—— 'The Past as Symbol of Identity', *Antiquity*, vol. 66, 1992, pp. 261–6.

—— 'Dream the Impossible Dream? Shared Heritage, Shared Values or Shared Understanding of Disparate Values?', *Historic Environment*, vol. 11 (2 & 3), 1995, pp. 8–14.

McCarthy, F. 'The Australian Institute of Aboriginal Studies', *Australian Journal of Science 27*, vol. 11, 1965, pp. 305–7.

McDonald, J. and Ross, A. 'Helping the Police with Their Inquiries: Archaeology and Politics at Angophora Reserve Rockshelter, NSW', *Archaeology in Oceania*, vol. 25 (3), 1990, pp. 114–21.

McDonald, J., Rich, E. and Barton, H. 'The Rouse Hill Infrastructure Project (Stage 1) on the Cumberland Plain, Western Sydney. Recent Research and Issues', in

M. Sullivan, S. Brockwell and A. Webb (eds), *Archaeology in the North*, North Australian Research Unit, Australian National University, Darwin, 1994, pp. 259–63.

Mackay, R. and Karskens, G. 'Historical Archaeology in Australia: Historical or Hysterical? Crisis or Creative Awakening?', *Australasian Historical Archaeology*, vol. 17, 1999, pp. 110–15.

McKinlay, J. R. and Jones, K. L. *Archaeological Resource Management in Australia and Oceania*, New Zealand Historic Places Trust, Wellington, 1979.

McQueen, J. *The Franklin: Not Just a River*, Penguin, Sydney, 1983.

Mansell, M. 'The Last Tasmanian', in – Gaby and – Marion (eds), *Racism in Tasmania*, Australian Union of Students, Carlton, Vic., 1978, p. 2.

—— 'Comrades or Trespassers on Aboriginal Land?', in C. Pylons and R. Flanagan (eds), *The Rest of the World is Watching*, Macmillan, Sydney, 1990, pp. 101–6.

Marrie, A. 'Museums and Aborigines: A Case Study in Internal Colonialism', *Australian and Canadian Studies*, vol. 7 (1 & 2), 1989, pp. 63–80.

Meehan, B. 'Aboriginal Skeletal Remains', *Australian Archaeology*, vol. 19, 1984, pp. 122–42.

Meehan, B. and Jones, R. *Archaeology with Ethnography: an Australian Perspective*, Department of Prehistory, Research School of Pacific Studies, Australian National University, Canberra, 1988.

Merrillees, R. S. *Living with Egypt's Past in Australia*, Museum of Victoria, Melbourne, 1990.

Ministry of Planning. *Cemeteries of Victoria: Guidelines for Management, Maintenance and Conservation*, Ministry of Planning, Melbourne, 1992.

Moser, S. Archaeology and its Disciplinary Culture: The Professionalisation of Australian Prehistoric Archaeology, PhD thesis, University of Sydney, 1995.

Muckelroy, K. *Maritime Archaeology*, Cambridge University Press, Cambridge, 1978.

Mulvaney, J. 'The Australian Aborigines, 1606–1929: Opinion and Fieldwork, Parts I & II', *Historical Studies of Australia and New Zealand*, vol. 8, 1958, pp. 131–51, 297–314.

—— 'The Stone Age of Australia', *Prehistoric Society*, vol. 4, 1961, pp. 56–107.

—— *Archaeology Manual No. 4*, Australian Institute of Aboriginal Studies, Canberra, 1968.

—— 'Prehistory from Antipodean Perspectives', *Proceedings of the Prehistoric Society*, vol. 37, 1971, pp. 228–312.

—— 'Two Remarkable Parallel Careers', *Australian Archaeology*, vol. 10, 1980, pp. 96–101.

—— 'Towards a New National Consciousness', *Forum*, vol. 21 (3), 1983, pp. 88–9.

—— *A Good Foundation: Reflections on the Heritage of the First Government House, Sydney*, Australian Government Publishing Service, Canberra, 1985.

—— 'A Question of Values, Museums as Cultural Property', in I. McBryde (ed.), *Who Owns the Past?*, Oxford University Press, Melbourne, 1985, pp. 63–71.

—— 'Preface', in G. Connah, *The Archaeology of Australia's History*, Cambridge University Press, Cambridge, 1988, pp. xiii–iv.

—— 'Reflections on the Future of Past Cultural Landscapes', *Historic Environment*, vol. 7 (2), 1989, p. 2.

—— 'Reflections on the Murray Black Collection', *Australian Natural History*, vol. 23 (1), 1989, pp. 66–73.

—— 'Preface,' in J. Mummery (ed.), *Prehistory and Heritage: The Writings of John Mulvaney*, Occasional Papers in Prehistory No. 17, Department of Prehistory, Research School of Pacific Studies, Australian National University, Canberra, 1990, p. v.

—— 'Past Regained and Future Lost: The Kow Swamp Pleistocene Burials', *Antiquity*, vol. 65, 1991, pp. 12–21.

Mulvaney, J. and Kamminga, J. *Prehistory of Australia*, Allen & Unwin, Sydney, 1999.

Mummery, J. (ed.) *Prehistory and Heritage: The Writings of John Mulvaney*, Occasional Papers in Prehistory No. 17, Department of Prehistory, Research School of Pacific Studies, Australian National University, Canberra, 1990.

Murray, T. 'Relativism, Conservation Philosophy and Historical Archaeology', in M. Pearson and H. Temple (eds), *Historical Archaeology and Conservation Philosophy: Papers of the Historical Archaeology Session, ANZAAS Conference, 1982*, Heritage Council of New South Wales, Sydney, 1983, pp. 1–19.

Murray, T. and White, P. 'Cambridge in the Bush? Archaeology in Australia and New Guinea', *World Archaeology*, vol. 13 (2), 1981, pp. 255–63.

National Trust, New South Wales. *Cemeteries: A Policy Paper*, National Trust of New South Wales, Sydney, 1987.

Nicholas, G. P. 'Indigenous Land Rights, Education and Archaeology in Canada: Postmodern/postcolonial Perspectives by a Non-Canadian White Guy', in I. Lilley (ed.), *Native Title and the Transformation of Archaeology in the Postcolonial World*, Oceania Monograph No. 50, Oceania Publications, Sydney, 2000, pp. 121–37.

Owen, T. 'Potential Errors in the Dating at the Jinmium Site, in Northwestern Australia', *World Archaeological Bulletin*, vol. 9, 1999, pp. 32–7.

Pardoe, C. 'Sharing the Past: Aboriginal Influence on Archaeological Practice, a Case Study from New South Wales', *Aboriginal History*, vol. 14, 1990, pp. 208–22.

—— 'Competing Paradigms and Ancient Human Remains: the State of the Discipline', *Archaeology in Oceania*, vol. 26 (2), 1991, pp. 79–85.

Pearson, M. and Sullivan, S. *Looking After Heritage Places: The Basics of Heritage Planning for Managers, Landowners and Administrators*, Melbourne University Press, Melbourne, 1995.

Phillip, A. (ed. J. J. Auchmuty), *The Voyage of Governor Phillip to Botany Bay*, John Stockdale, London, [1789] 1970.

Proudfoot, H., Bickford, A., Egloff, B. and Stocks, R. *Australia's First Government House*, Allen and Unwin and the Department of Planning, Sydney, 1991.

Pulleine, R. H. 'The Tasmanians and their Stone Culture', *Australasian Association for the Advancement of Science*, vol. 19, 1928, pp. 292–314.

Ranson, D., Allen, J. and Jones, R. 'Australia's Prehistory Uncovered', *Australian Natural History*, vol. 21 (3), 1983, pp. 83–7.

Reynolds, H. *Fate of a Free People*, Penguin, Ringwood, Vic., 1995.

Richardson, L. 'The Acquisition, Storage and Handling of Aboriginal Skeletal Remains in Museums: An Indigenous Perspective', in R. Layton (ed.), *Conflict in the Archaeology of Living Traditions,* One World Archaeology Series No. 8, Unwin Hyman, London, 1989, pp. 185–8.

Robinson, P. 'Selling Our National Heritage: State Tourism', in A. Sheill and A. Stephen (eds), *The Lie of the Land,* National Centre for Australian Studies, Monash University, in association with the Powerhouse Museum, Sydney, 1992, pp. 41–3.

Rosenthal, A. *The Documentary Conscience,* University of California Press, Berkeley, Calif., 1980.

Ross, A. If There Were Water: Prehistoric Settlement Patterning in the Victorian Mallee, PhD thesis, Macquarie University, 1984.

Rouse Hill Infrastructure Consortium. 'Rocks of Ages', *Rouse Hill Infrastructure News,* vol. 1 (2), 1993, p. 4.

—— 'Seeing the Sites', *Rouse Hill Infrastructure News,* vol. 2 (1), 1994, p. 4.

Royal Commission into the Aboriginal Deaths in Custody. *National Report: Overview and Recommendations,* Australian Government Publishing Service, Canberra, 1991.

Ryan, L. *The Aboriginal Tasmanians,* 2nd edn, Allen & Unwin, Sydney, 1996.

Sagazio, C. (ed.). *Cemeteries: Our Heritage,* National Trust of Australia, Victoria, Melbourne, 1992.

Scenery Preservation Board, *Report of the Chairman for the Year 1937–1938,* Lands and Survey Department, Hobart, 1938.

Smith, K. C. 'By Land or by Sea: Archaeology Programs for Youths at the Museum of Florida History', in K. C. Smith and F. P. McManamon (eds), *Archaeology and Education: The Classroom and Beyond,* National Parks Service Archaeological Assistance Study No. 2, US Department of the Interior, Washington, 1991, pp. 13–17.

Smith, L. 'What Is This Thing Called Post-processual Archaeology ... and Is It Relevant for Australian Archaeology?' *Australian Archaeology,* vol. 40, 1995, pp. 28–31.

Spooner, N. A. 'Human Occupation at Jinmium, Northern Australia', *Antiquity,* vol. 72, 1998, pp. 173–8.

Staniforth, M. 'A Future for Australian Maritime Archaeology?', *Australian Archaeology,* vol. 50, 2000, pp. 90–3.

Stockton, E. *The Aboriginal Gift: Spirituality for a Nation,* Millennium Books, Alexandria, NSW, 1995.

Strachan, S. 'Interpreting Our Maritime Heritage: Australian Historic Shipwreck Trails', *Historic Environment,* vol. 11 (4), 1995, pp. 26–35.

Stuart, G. E. 'Conclusion: Working Together to Preserve Our Past', in P. M. Messenger (ed.), *The Ethics of Collecting Cultural Property: Whose Culture? Whose Property?,* University of New Mexico Press, Albuquerque, New Mex., 1989, pp. 243–52.

Sullivan, S. 'The Custodianship of Aboriginal Sites in Southeastern Australia', in I. McBryde (ed.), *Who Owns the Past?,* Oxford University Press, Melbourne, 1985, pp. 139–56.

—— 'Report of the Archaeological Advisory Panel', in H. Temple and S. Sullivan (eds), *First Government House Site, Sydney: Its Significance and Future,* Sydney, 1985, pp. 28–31.

Sullivan, S. and Bowdler, S. *Site Surveys and Significance Assessment in Australia*, Department of Prehistory, Research School of Australian Studies, Australian National University, Canberra, 1984.

Summers, A. *Damned Whores and God's Police*, Penguin, Ringwood, Vic., 1975.

Tacey, D. *Edge of the Sacred: Transformation in Australia*, HarperCollins, Sydney, 1995.

Temple, H. Historical Archaeology and its Role in the Community, MA thesis, University of Sydney, 1988.

Temple, H. and Sullivan, S. (eds). *First Government House Site, Sydney: Its Significance and its Future*, Proceedings of Seminar No. 2, Department of Environment and Planning, Sydney, 1985.

Thomas, D. H. *Archaeology*, Holt, Rinehart & Winston, New York, 1979.

Thomas, I. 'Models and Prima-donnas in Southwest Tasmania', *Australian Archaeology*, vol. 41, 1995, pp. 21–3.

Thompson, P. *Bob Brown and the Franklin River*, Allen & Unwin, Sydney, 1984.

Thorne, A. 'Mungo and Kow Swamp: Morphological Variation in Pleistocene Australians', *Mankind*, vol. 8 (2), 1971, pp. 85–9.

—— Kow Swamp and Lake Mungo: Towards an Osteology of Early Man in Australia, PhD thesis, University of Sydney, 1975.

Thorne, A. and Macumber, P. 'Discoveries of Late Pleistocene Man at Kow Swamp, Australia', *Nature*, vol. 238, 1972, pp. 316–19.

Thorne, A. and Ross, A. *The Skeletal Manual: A Handbook for the Identification of Aboriginal Skeletal Remains*, NSW National Parks and Wildlife Service and Police Aborigines Liaison Unit, Sydney, 1986.

Tickner, R. *Distinctly Australian: The Future for Australia's Cultural Development*, Cultural Policy Statement, Australian Labor Party, Canberra, 1993.

Tilley, C. 'Excavation as Theatre', *Antiquity*, vol. 63, 1989, pp. 275–80.

Trigger, B. *A History of Archaeological Thought*, Cambridge University Press, Cambridge, 1989.

Truscott, M. 'Indigenous Cultural Heritage Protection Programme', *Australian Archaeology*, vol. 39, 1994, pp. 127–8.

Truscott, M. and Smith, L. 'Women's Roles in the Archaeological Workforce', in H. du Cros and L. Smith (eds), *Women in Archaeology: A Feminist Critique*, Research School of Pacific, Asian and Australian Studies, Australian National University, Canberra, 1993, pp. 217–21.

Vinnicombe, P. 'An Aboriginal Site Complex at the Foot of Mount Eliza, which includes the Old Swan Brewery Building', *Historic Environment*, vol. 9 (1 & 2), 1992, pp. 53–62.

Webb, S. G. 'Reburying Australian Skeletons', *Antiquity*, vol. 61, 1987, pp. 292–6.

—— *The Willandra Lakes Hominids*, Department of Prehistory, Research School of Pacific Studies, Australian National University, Canberra, 1989.

Weissensteiner, R. Indiana Jones Fantasy vs Archaeological Reality: Examining the Portrayal of Archaeology in Popular Film, BA (Hons) thesis, Australian National University, Canberra, 1993.

West, A. L. 'Aboriginal Man at Kow Swamp, Northern Victoria: the Problem of Locating the Burial Site of the KS 1 Skeleton', *The Artefact*, vol. 2 (1), 1977, pp. 19–30.

Wettenhall, G. 'The Murray Black Collection Goes Home', *Australian Society*, December 1988–January 1989, pp. 17–19.

White, P. *The Past Is Human*, Penguin, Sydney, 1974.

White, P. and O'Connell, J. *A Prehistory of Australia, New Guinea and Sahul*, Academic Press, Sydney, 1982.

Whitehouse, J. F. 'Future Management Options', in H. Temple and S. Sullivan (eds), *First Government House Site, Sydney: Its Significance and Its Future*, Proceedings of Seminar No. 2, Department of Environment and Planning, Sydney, 1985, pp. 32–8.

Williams, E. *Complex Hunter-Gatherers: A Late Holocene Example from Temperate Australia*, British Archaeological Reports No. 423, Oxford University Press, Oxford, 1988.

Williams, R. *This Is the Science Show*, Australian Broadcasting Corporation, Sydney, 1995.

Willmot, E. 'The Dragon Principle', in I. McBryde (ed.), *Who Owns the Past?* Oxford University Press, Melbourne, 1985, pp. 41–8.

—— *Dilemma of Mind: The Inaugural David Unaipon Lecture*, Kaurna Higher Education Centre, University of South Australia, Underdale, SA, 1991.

Wood, V. K. Angophora Reserve Rockshelter: A Faunal Analysis, BLitt Thesis, Australian National University, Canberra, 1989.

Wylie, A. 'The Complexity of Gender Bias', in H. du Cros and L. Smith (eds), *Women in Archaeology: A Feminist Critique*, Research School of Pacific, Asian and Australian Studies, Australian National University, Canberra, 1993, pp. 53–60.

Xiberras, A. 'Aboriginal Skeletal Remains at VAS: Information for Koori Communities', *Site*, vol. 10, 1991, p. 11.

Xiberras, A. and du Cros, H. 'Aboriginal Involvement in Monitoring and Protecting Cultural Sites within the Wurundjeri's Tribal Boundaries, Melbourne', in J. Birckhead, T. de Lacy and L. Smith (eds), *Aboriginal Involvement in Parks and Protected Areas*, Aboriginal Studies Press, Canberra, 1992, pp. 221–6.

Yellen, J. E. 'Women, Archaeology, and the National Science Foundation: An Analysis of Fiscal Year 1989 Data', in M. Nelson, S. Nelson and A. Wylie (eds), *Equity Issues for Women in Archaeology*, Archaeological Papers No. 5, American Anthropological Association, Washington, 1994, pp. 53–8.

Young, L. 'Museum of Sydney, on the Site of First Government House', Exhibition Review, *Australian Historical Studies*, vol. 26 (105), 1995, pp. 666–7.

Zdenowski, G. 'Civil Liberties', in T. Bonyhady (ed.), *Environmental Protection and Legal Change*, Federation Press, Sydney, 1992, pp. 145–73.

Zimmerman, L. J. 'Made Radical By My Own: An Archaeologist Learns to Accept Reburial', and 'Human Bones as Symbols of Power: Aboriginal American Belief Systems Towards Bones and Grave-Robbing Archaeologists', in R. Layton (ed.), *Conflict in the Archaeology of Living Traditions*, One World Archaeology Series No. 8, Unwin Hyman, London, 1989, pp. 60–7, 211–16.

Index

Compiled by Kerry Biram

Note: Page references in italics are to maps and plates.

DATE DUE
